MW01294240

reformatting politics

reformatting politics

INFORMATION TECHNOLOGY AND GLOBAL CIVIL SOCIETY

edited by

JODI DEAN

JON W. ANDERSON

GEERT LOVINK

Routledge
Taylor & Francis Group
New York   London

Routledge is an imprint of the
Taylor & Francis Group, an informa business

Routledge
Taylor & Francis Group
270 Madison Avenue
New York, NY 10016

Routledge
Taylor & Francis Group
2 Park Square
Milton Park, Abingdon
Oxon OX14 4RN

© 2006 by Taylor and Francis Group, LLC
Routledge is an imprint of Taylor & Francis Group, an Informa business

Printed in the United States of America on acid-free paper
10 9 8 7 6 5 4 3 2 1

International Standard Book Number-10: 0-415-95298-0 (Softcover) 0-415-95297-2 (Hardcover)
International Standard Book Number-13: 978-0-415-95298-9 (Softcover) 978-0-415-95297-2 (Hardcover)
Library of Congress Card Number 2006006848

No part of this book may be reprinted, reproduced, transmitted, or utilized in any form by any electronic, mechanical, or other means, now known or hereafter invented, including photocopying, microfilming, and recording, or in any information storage or retrieval system, without written permission from the publishers.

Trademark Notice: Product or corporate names may be trademarks or registered trademarks, and are used only for identification and explanation without intent to infringe.

Library of Congress Cataloging-in-Publication Data

Reformatting politics : information technology and global civil society / edited by
 Jodi Dean, Jon W. Anderson, Geert Lovink.
     p. cm.
 Includes bibliographical references.
 ISBN 0-415-95297-2 (hardcover : alk. paper) -- ISBN 0-415-95298-0 (pbk. : alk.
 paper)
    1. Information society. 2. Information technology--Political aspects. 3. Political
 participation--Computer network resources. 4. Civil society. I. Dean, Jodi, 1962- II.
 Anderson, Jon W. III. Lovink, Geert.

HM851.R434 2006
322.40285--dc22   2006006848

Visit the Taylor & Francis Web site at
http://www.taylorandfrancis.com

and the Routledge Web site at
http://www.routledge-ny.com

Contents

III. Formats

Foreword

SASKIA SASSEN

Networked communication technologies contribute to the unsettling of existing arrangements. This has been fairly well established. Less noticed is the fact that these technologies themselves evince unstable meanings as they migrate among contexts and get assembled and reassembled into diverse formations. These traits point to the possibility, and likelihood, of additional mutations. Thus, propositions developed in research about these technologies need to be subjected to critical reexamination, and frequently so. Such reexaminations also allow us to detect recurrent patterns and contingent ones. The fact itself of mutating formations may indicate that it might be easier to know more about the technical properties of these technologies than about the interactive domains within which these properties become performative.

The essays in this volume seek to capture these kinds of organizational and discursive shifts in one specific sphere, that of civil society organizations (CSOs). The engagement of CSOs with an increasingly networked transnational space articulated by information and communication technologies (ICTs), illuminates at least two critical conditions (and their mutations) in that articulated space.

One condition is what the editors of this volume refer to as the settings within which these technologies get used by CSOs. Settings are a feature insufficiently addressed in the pertinent research that has tended to focus on (disembedded) technical properties and the discursive practices of users. Prominent among the settings within which CSOs function today are neoliberal corporate contexts, supranational organizations, and normative orders dominated by older legitimacies, such as human rights politics and nation-based citizenship. These essays show us that settings have consequences for outcomes. The fact that these are the settings within which CSOs tend to function introduces a variety of formats (demands for accountability, adjustment to institutional dynamics that precede today's ICTs, and so on) that do not align with the properties of networked communication technologies. Several of the essays herein document in great detail how this misalignment explains the disappointing outcomes for CSOs that have used these technologies in such settings. One prominent example is the United Nations World Summit on the Information Society initiative. In this sense, then, the editors observe that formats derived from the politics of liberal democracies centered in nation-states (representation, nation-based citizenship) do not quite fit networked communications. The latter deborder the political formats of today's nation-state based liberal democracies.

The second condition is the extent to which there is no necessary correspondence between certain technical features, notably openness and distributed outcomes, and equality—or at least tendencies toward equality. In their aggregate, the essays herein tend to show us the limits of the convergence of, on the one hand, technical properties that enable decentralized access and free choice, and, on the other, a variety of outcomes that we might summarize under the notion of equality—equality of voice, of participation, of representation, and so on. Going against the grain of much of the general literature on networked communications is the strong tendency for the combination of open networks and multiple choices to produce power law distributions (given a certain numerical threshold of participants and choices). The editors of this volume themselves do not quite elaborate on the fact that such outcomes are partly the result of (socially shaped) organizational and individual logics rather than an inherent attribute of the technology. But this fact does come through in a variety of the essays, perhaps most clearly in the essay on the winner-takes-all patterns evident today in web log accessing at a time when the numbers of both web logs and visitors to them have grown rapidly. More generally, at least some of the essays point to the presence, albeit not easily legible, of hierarchies precisely in the most open and least organized networks. The meaning of this distributional tendency is clear: network openness does not necessarily produce equality in the resulting distribution.

Different types of domains illuminate these issues differently. I have long found problematic the assumed correspondence between technical properties that are meant to deliver distributed outcomes and notions of democratizing effects. I fully agree with this volume's critical approach. In the late 1980s and early 1990s, when the aura of democratic enhancement attributed to these technologies was at its highest, I was already disturbed in my research findings about how these networked technologies were shaping global finance. It was clear that the use of networked technologies in global finance was not producing a more democratic outcome (such as the distribution of capital where most needed and with the greatest possibility of maximizing development multiplier effects). On the contrary, such use was leading to greater concentration among the most powerful financial actors and sites (global cities). The outcome was thus a clear instance of the power law distribution: even as the new technologies raised the number of participants (investors and financial centers) and the overall volume of the global financial market, the leading participants raised their global share. A focus on global finance was already at that time producing knowledge about networked technologies that went against the dominant interpretations. In that sense, global finance became heuristic for me—probably the kindest comment I can make about finance. In terms of the language in the prior Social Science Research Council (SSRC) volume, *Digital Formations*, finance endogenized a social logic (its utility logic) into the digital network, thereby altering the distributive capacities of the technology. What made this social "distortion" of technical properties particularly significant was that finance even then was a far more intensive, knowing, and effective user of the new technologies than any CSO I was aware of. Further, it made the technologies move in particular directions, setting the innovation agenda, and making visible what the editors of this volume refer to as the migration potential of these technologies. Finance made it clear—already in the 1980s—that these networked technologies had the capacity to assemble, disassemble, and reassemble in novel configurations.

The editors of this volume make a major advance: civil society organizations also develop power law distributions as they scale up. It is not only in finance that the mix of openness and choice produces something akin to a winner-takes-all pattern. In many ways a focus on finance is a simpler heuristic move than a focus on CSOs that are meant to be in the business of democratizing outcomes. Thus, beyond the fact that finance gave us a research finding that problematized the relation between networked technologies and democratizing outcomes at a time of heightened expectations with the new technologies, the research findings presented in this volume are in many ways more radical. The trade-off is that finance made legible the problematic character of strongly held notions of democratizing outcomes at a time when there was little if any critical input.*

Several of the essays in this book show us how the mix of openness and decentralized access itself produces such uneven outcomes even in civil society where, unlike global financial institutions, organizations aim at being democratic. This adds an enormously important dimension to the prior SSRC volume's effort to detect how the social logics of users alter the technically possible outcomes: as those social logics become endogenized in the digital network they "distort" the engineer's design, so to speak. The assemblages constituted through technologies and users/social actors constitute digital formations that do not necessarily conform to the technical designs of the hardware and software involved.

In a major interpretive move, the editors posit that these various patterns signal that networked communities exceed the capacities of notions of democracy centered in nation-based liberal states. In positing a post-democratic governmentality, they are emphasizing the unsuitability of those earlier notions for analyzing the current political condition and the need for new formats of politics in a world of networks. They use the term *postdemocratic*, rather than *pre-* or *antidemocratic*, to capture how ICTs enable "affiliations and engagements" that cannot be housed in traditional democratic notions of representation, accountability, and legitimacy. In their aggregate, the essays in this volume begin to lay bare the reason we need different political formats.

---

* Those were times with few, if any, critical analyses. Among the exceptions was the work by one of the editors of this volume, Geert Lovink, who already was detecting the limits of these technologies in civil society fields to deliver the much touted promise of "enhanced democracy." Today again, Lovink has put out one of the strongest calls for the need to reformat network politics, and declared the existing formats, particularly the Internet, perhaps beyond repair for redistributive politics.

Preface

JODI DEAN, JON W. ANDERSON,
AND GEERT LOVINK

This book originated in discussions among the three of us while affiliated with the Social Science Research Council (SSRC) committee on Information Technology and International Cooperation (ITIC). Like other recent SSRC committees, the ITIC committee aims included incorporating the "revolution" in information technology into thinking about social issues and social theory—in this case, particularly as realized in international or transnational contexts. Two volumes have already emerged from earlier stages of that project: *Bombs and Bandwidth: The Emerging Relationship between Information Technology and Security*, edited by Robert Latham (New York: New Press, 2003) and *Digital Formations: IT and New Architectures in the Global Realm*, edited by Robert Latham and Saskia Sassen (Princeton, N.J.: Princeton University Press, 2005). In turning to civil society organizations, SSRC chose to extend the committee's work into an experiment for engaging this community through the very processes being examined by placing papers it commissioned online (at http://www.ssrc.org/programs/itic/it_civil_society/) to continue the discussion—in effect, to make practice out of social science. Here, we take another direction. This book is not a collection of reports or a product of that committee's meetings; instead, it arises out of conversations there, among the editors, and with others—to all of whom we are indebted for provoking and providing sites for our thinking. The choice of the material is no doubt a subjective one, for which only the editors, bearing in mind their different backgrounds and interests—theoretical, empirical, critical, and political—are responsible.

Contributors to this volume draw from parallel, overlapping, or contributory discussions that we think converge on the topic this book aims to highlight, which is reformatting politics in a networked society. The connection is networked communication, such as exemplified in but not limited to the Internet, whose ramifications for government and commerce have been widely explored, but not so widely nor very deeply in civil society. A special feature of network communications—of network society—is how quickly they transcend national frames and the ontologies of national framing; so, a principal topic here is transnational civil society organization. Each of these concepts is problematic; this book begins with how they are problematic, not least politically, and what those problems inscribe in the politics in network society.

From problems, we proceed to a sample of sites. We refer to these as *sites* rather than as *cases* because there are as yet few full-blown case studies of transnational civil society organizations' use—particularly innovative use—of information technologies comparable to those in governmental and economic sectors that elicit their distinctive politics beyond observations that nongovernmental organizations challenge states in these spheres. We think this is problematic in ways beyond the counterclaims that states still matter, or adapt to, new conditions. The record is inconclusive because the phenomena are emergent, and experience has in many ways outrun established concepts and categories of analysis. Current reality is a mix of visions, partial accounts, incomplete projects, and occasionally acute observations that open an intermediate ground we wish to sample between visionary statements and full-fledged case studies.

A major site is the United Nations World Summit on the Information Society (WSIS), which unfolded as a series of conferences culminating in Geneva (December 2003) and Tunis (November 2005) with multiple policy proposals, research papers, and comments over the preceding two years, and that register some of what is theoretically problematic as experiential crisis. Here we approach this process as part of the reformatting of politics for network society with studies that distill long observation of WSIS as one stop in a continuous process of global policy making around information and communication technologies.

The reformattings we are dealing with here are emergent phenomena, but our point is not to develop a theory of emergence or of transformation. Our point instead is to identify what is problematic in them for thinking about politics and for the politics they entail.

We are grateful to all of the participants in the SSRC's meetings on ITIC and to the organizers, Dr. Robert Latham of the SSRC and Saskia Sassen of the University of Chicago and the London School of Economics, for the stimulation of discussions with them. The SSRC also brought the three of us together for additional discussion that launched this book, which we also pursued during the Incommunicado 05 conference on Information Technology in Development in Amsterdam with support from our individual institutions, as well as online (also supported by our several institutional affiliations). Material support for permission to include Hans Klein's essay "Understanding WSIS" (which originally appeared in the journal *Information Technology and International Development* 1, nos. 3–4 [2004]: 3–14), and portions of Lina Khatib's "Communicating Islamic Fundamentalism as Global Citizenship" (which originally appeared in the *Journal of Communication Inquiry* 27, no. 4 [2003]: 389–409) was provided by the publication fund of the Department of Anthropology of the Catholic University of America.

Introduction: The Postdemocratic Governmentality of Networked Societies

JODI DEAN, JON W. ANDERSON, AND GEERT LOVINK

How are activists and new technologies transforming each other and the global spaces in which they interact? Information and communication technologies (ICTs) are clearly having an impact on contemporary politics, but what kind of impact? Until now, academic research and popular interest have focused on markets and states, dot-coms, and dot-govs. But what about dot-orgs?

Even as information-age enthusiasts have celebrated the new forms of participation that globally networked communications enable, this enthusiasm has tended to focus on the activities of individuals who are empowered to point and click, sign petitions, engage as virtual citizens, and register their opinions on millions of blogs, online forums, listservs, and newsgroups, using a variety of devices. Corresponding to this ideal participant is the similarly individualized consumer, a ready recipient of multiple messages from friends and advertisers at any place and any time. Just as the global participant can join in virtual struggles anywhere she chooses, so can the global consumer make purchases, consume ads, and contribute to the circulating content of communicative capitalism—and again, as communication technologies are ever smaller, ever more personal, at any place and time.[1]

There is something deeply strange about this image of the mobile global consumer-participant. First and foremost, mobility is a privilege of citizenship and economic class. Second, the economic and political activities of this fantastic consumer-participant are virtually indistinguishable. And, third, when we think more closely about these activities, we see that they shift into forms of passivity. The very same activities suggest both engagement and disengagement. Political commitment can be demonstrated with a word, a signature, a click. And this makes it difficult to distinguish it from apathy: "Well, I didn't really have time to do anything, so I just signed the petition, forwarded the link, posted the news on my blog."

In our view, to focus on individual activities in a space of flows occludes important changes in political and civic activity brought about by new media of networked communication. Such a focus moves from the state and the economy directly to the individual, overlooking a wide spectrum of intermediating groups and institutions. Thus, it fails to ask the right questions about political changes because it ignores the dot-orgs, the organized groups acting in a terrain in between that of state and economy, the terrain of civil society. *Reformatting Politics* addresses this omission. We highlight the ways that civil society organizations (CSOs) are using information and communication technologies to challenge previous configurations of power and influence and produce new ones.

At the most general level, the research into CSOs and ICTs presents what we understand as a postdemocratic governmentality. We use the term *postdemocratic* (not *pre-* or *antidemocratic*) to designate the way that ICTs enable affiliations and engagements that simply cannot be conceived within the democratic imaginary. That is, they replace democratic suppositions of representation, accountability, and legitimacy with a different set of values. Our emphasis here is on subsidiarity, "multistakeholderism," expertise, and reputation management, but this list is of course changing and incomplete. We use Michel Foucault's term *governmentality* to designate the interaction of codes of conduct, strategies of power, and forms of knowledge that produce the subjects and objects of networked politics.[2] As Thomas Lemke explains, "The concept of governmentality allows us to call attention to the constitution of new political forms and levels of the state such as the introduction of systems negotiation, mechanisms of self-organization, and empowerment strategies."[3]

In his careful working through of Foucault's late, unpublished lectures, Lemke argues that the utility of the concept of governmentality stems from the way it articulates a kind of political knowledge, a knowledge part of the practice, systematization, and rationalization of a field to be governed (or steered, the Greek word for which is *cyber*).[4] Insofar as governmentality involves knowledge of what one is trying to produce, it has a reflexivity helpful for analyzing networked communications technologies. An additional benefit of the concept stems from the way it emphasizes indirect techniques of leading, directing, and controlling rather than simple oppositions between freedom and coercion. Given that networked politics involves the distribution of responsibility among different levels and across a variety of domains, this third quality of indirection makes the concept of governmentality useful for understanding the field in which CSOs form and operate.[5]

Networked Communications: Don't Believe the Hype

Internet politics demonstrate the features and problems of network society and networked communication. The Internet has a mixed history of technologies migrating from context to context, acquiring and discarding conceptions of its structure and purpose, new allies, and reflexive appreciations of new kinds of political spaces and dimensions of political agency.[6] Insofar as technological migration has enabled political practices beyond those recognized within the frame of actually existing democracy, some have suggested that the Internet is itself producing a new, upgraded democracy.[7]

Internet hype is a good point of entry. In one version, the Internet was said to have been conceived for reliable communication in the event of thermonuclear war, then to have escaped the Cold War and the clutches of the Pentagon into academe, only then to have been co-opted by corporate elites who commanded the technology. It is possible to construct almost the opposite story. The Internet, in the form of inter-networking, was created by engineers for their own work, initially as contractors to a U.S. government defense think tank that already formed a network (which president Dwight D. Eisenhower had earlier labeled the "military-industrial complex" and warned of its postdemocratic lack of accountability and representation) and cobbled together from existing network technologies (packet switching, time sharing and multiuser computing, local and wide-area networking, and the development of a computer science of programming sophisticated and modular enough to fit any hardware or operating system).[8]

Through bases in computer science (itself removed from engineering to arts and science faculties) and the "revolving door" networks that had come to sustain university research, the Internet passed from utility project to academic laboratories. It spread through their networks and supporters beyond any defense interest, migrating to the National Science Foundation via a combination of utility and "national defense" justifications previously used for the U.S. interstate highway system and for government support of language and area studies in the Cold War. From there, under successive administrations ideologically committed to downsizing and outsourcing government services, the Internet was passed to corporations that had built its hard infrastructure (the "backbone") and were created to handle parts of its "soft" infrastructure, such as domain-name administration. Under this regime, features of flexibility, open access, universal carriage, and flattened hierarchy were celebrated and often condensed into the notion that users actually organized it, rather than the other way around in previous telecommunications (both telephony and broadcasting). Such celebration of course overlooks the fact that such users were its builders, a fact registered in the ironic joke that to make it work one had to "assume an engineer."

Internet reflexivity has ranged from utopian hype to voices of moral crisis (from free pornography to unvetted information to just plain noise) that point to a real hybridity of unstable aggregations. It was never completely public or private; it migrated among government, academic, and corporate sectors, not least because it was not a unitary technology but itself an agglomeration of several existing ones, each with its own body of technical experts and their cultures of work, accountability, and legitimacy. For years, important features of Internet governance were partly in the hands of engineers, constructed through ad hoc consultation and often guided through reputation management. Until his death, a single engineer maintained the crucial hierarchical bit, the master address register, from a university laboratory, which was justified on a combination of technical expertise and professional reputation.[9] At his death, this and other functions of adjudication passed to the semiprivate, semipublic Internet Corporation for Assigned Names and Numbers (ICANN). Composed of a small group of experts, ICANN secured U.S. government sanction over the soft infrastructure of the Internet, including admission of new members to governing and owning functions. Attempts at election of replacements foundered over which "stakeholders" to recognize. In other words, the constituency model of democratic politics failed, and management by reputation in a network environment showed, rather than contained, these strains.

Equally hybrid has been another combination of old and new politics that became the WSIS process, named for the World Summit of the Information Society convened under the auspices of the United Nations. Not so uniquely as claimed but certainly dramatically, this "process" bypassed institutional channels and included significant participation by CSOs, ranging from professional standards bodies and development and technology groups to nongovernmental advocacy agencies and academics. The CSOs drew on a variety of legitimacies, from technical expertise to appeals to universal values to post–Cold War European institutionalism (subsidiarity) to American implementations of free-market ideologies. Not only did this wide variety of legitimacies absorb bits and combinations of bits of expertise from engineering and social development, but they also incorporated specific professional practices such as producing position papers, attending conferences, and marketing results. Such practices refracted the features of politics in network society onto the Internet, including its ever growing list of stakeholders. Their agendas ranged from privacy concerns and education to access in rural areas and "capacity building" among a rapidly growing army of professionals, both from the "global South" and the "global North."

These stakes came to focus on governance issues, principally control of top level "domains" (thus who could be attached to the Internet under them) and of information coming into them. For some, WSIS was a next stop in a series of international jamborees (from the 1997 Toronto Global Knowledge Conference to the G8 Digital Opportunity Task Force initiative), glamorizing disciplinary and other visions of global ICTs. For others, it revived "tricontinentalist" hopes for a new information and communication order embodied in universal "communication rights;" and for others a step in transforming the "statist" system of intergovernmental organizations with civil society actors securing places at the decision-making tables of the International Telecommunications Union, or the International Standards Organization, or at ICANN, that would pass it from national (U.S.) to global (UN) auspices. Others saw business opportunity, including the opportunity to push agendas of ICTs for development; others saw a threat of authoritarian governments. Much of this took place through the medium of the Internet and assumed its properties. Position papers were posted and comments invited, recalling the earlier practice of engineers seeking each others' cooperation, but with virtually no limits on participation, around which intense controversy swirled.

Two key features of network society showed up in the WSIS process: its enormous overhead, quite contrary to promises of immediacy, and the failure of CSOs to construct complex organizations. Right-wing think tanks rejected nongovernmental organizations' (NGOs') claims to represent universal values such as human rights, religion, and culture.[10] They rejected as well NGOs' claims to represent technical expertise, particularly alternative and populist expertises. "Civil society" turned out to be an already existing Information and Communication Technologies for Development (ICT4D) NGO network that took the UN Declaration of Human Rights, did a "find: *human*; replace: *communication*" in order to produce a declaration and a movement that could run a campaign. If the "rights" formula worked in other contexts, why not here?

The representation issue in network society turned irresolvable. At one point a 2003 WSIS conference split off a partly separate civil society conference. After another round of position papers and comments, the concluding conference nominally failed to resolve the key issue of removing ICANN to "truly" international auspices. Nevertheless, it reflexively registered success, measuring it in terms of expanded participation, the advance of alternative and multiple legitimacy claims, and the networking among participants that enhanced their reputations as stakeholders. In this way, WSIS encouraged articulation of agendas, positions, stakes, and other forms of symbolic capital in a new politics of communication and information—despite its relative invisibility among the general public.

This brief history of migrating technologies, alliances, and practices affirms the fundamentally performative character of network society and networked communications. Technologies, alliances, and practices are immediate, flexible, migratory, and mutable in ways highly contingent on who "shows up" and "gets it." Network society is intensely reflexive on its own processes, although perhaps less so on their settings. Those settings should have a high interest for thinking about the postdemocratic reformatting of politics in network society, beginning with how it precedes as well as follows the spread of network communications into the world, and where that happens.

Old Formats Don't Work

The hybridity, reflexivity, mobility, and performativity characteristic of networked society and networked community exceed the capacities of previously conceived notions of democracy. Thus, by presenting the findings collected here as indicative of a postdemocratic governmentality, we are emphasizing the unsuitability of the concepts appropriate to the era of the nation-state for analyzing the present one, and the new formats of politics in a world of networks.

A simple imagining of the politics of the nation-state begins with the idea of the people. A state consists of people, whether they are perceived as already present or as a project for the future, the people to be called into being. What makes one people distinct from another people is their nation. Belonging to a nation, in other words, is a characteristic of all people and it differentiates peoples from one another. A state is legitimate when constituted so as to represent the interests of its people (the nation). If the state can somehow embody the collective will of its people it can be assumed to be legitimate. If it does not embody their collective will—if it relies on exclusion or distortion such that it cannot reasonably be assumed to be something to which people would have consented—then this state is not legitimate. In the twenty-first century, even authoritarian states gesture to this image; the only ones that do not are religious states, like the Vatican or, more problematically, Iran or Saudi Arabia.

At any rate, in the late eighteenth century, a dominant strand of Anglo-European thought concluded that the best way for the interests of the people to be represented was through constitutional forms establishing liberal or parliamentary democracies. These versions of democratic governance eschewed direct democracy for more distributed forms of representation. Additionally, they framed specific sites and practices as in need of protection from the people in their collective capacity. These sites and practices tended to be understood as private, as rights against the state (or people), and as the very conditions for being and acting as (one of) the people.

This simple image of the nation-state as the political form of the people is like a line drawing or cartoon. It can't do justice to the nuances of specific faces as they change over time or across spectra that include authoritarian states, patterns of migration and colonization, and the very instabilities within the notion of a nation. Nevertheless, it is recognizable as a kind of animating idea.

Despite the many significant changes that information and communication technologies effect, the simple image of the nation-state continues to format thinking about politics. In the 1980s and '90s, for example, advocates for ICTs in the United States and Europe presented networked communications as tools for democracy, as the way to materialize ideals of the people's informed political participation. It was thus important to build an information superhighway so that people could be more involved in government. The World Wide Web would be a repository of government documents. People could consult them whenever necessary, learning about various important issues and availing themselves more easily of the benefits of governance. The speed of networked communications would enable mass "town halls" as dispersed people could debate key issues in real time. More people would be brought into "the conversation" and their deliberation would benefit them as citizens as well as the process of democracy as a whole. In this way of thinking about networked communications, then, technology was a tool. And, consequently, when the benefits did not materialize the tool was blamed—rather than "real" information, all people could find on the Internet was pornography and conspiracy theory.[11]

The problems involved in thinking about technologies as tools have been well documented, and we won't repeat those arguments here.[12] Rather, we are interested in how that the idea of technology as a tool of democracy forecloses inquiry into the myriad ways that networked communications disrupt the democratic image. First, it presumes the boundaries of the nation-state even as the technologies themselves traverse national borders (a denial of technological migration and informational mobility). Second, it presumes the field of political practices as a field separate from culture and the economy even as networked technologies accelerate, intensify, and hybridize political, cultural, and economic practices to configure and produce new political spaces, fronts, and opportunities (a denial of reflexivity). Third, it presumes the agents of politics—citizens, parties, and governing officials—even as networked technologies produce assemblages of power in often unpredictable ways (a denial of the mutability of assemblages and of contingent effects). Differently put, what are often identified as the destabilizing effects of networked information technologies also destabilize the very presumptions of democratic action.

Given the wide range of theoretical engagement with the transformations brought about by the networked society, one would expect attunement to technological migration, informational mobility, reflexivity, mutable assemblages, and contingent effects to inform thinking about global communications networks. With few exceptions, this has not been the case.[13] Many theorists and activists continue to rely on the old terms. They extend the political topography of the nation-state (in a very particular European form!) to the global arena, construing the space of politics as "global civil society."[14] In so doing, they reduce the mutable assemblages of globally networked issues, scandals, struggles, and interests to the subject forms of organizations, thereby installing suppositions of intentionality, accountability, and predictability at odds with the protean reflexivity of information flow. The political concept of rights, for example, is a powerful ideal, vital to many political struggles. Nevertheless, insofar as rights remain tied to (recognized and enforced by) nation-states, arguments for rights—to communication, to free speech, to information, to access—are appeals made to those who can and will uphold these rights. As such, they efface the ways that networked communications exceed top-down modes of governance. To this extent, such appeals fail to acknowledge the postdemocratic character of networked communications.

Linked to the emphasis on global civil society as the primary political arena has been an increase in the prominence of NGOs. NGOs adopt an international remit and permission, often self-permission, to interact with intergovernmental organizations. These groups do not represent constituencies, although they may mobilize them. They stake legitimacies—indeed, their very existence as players at tables where decisions are made—on mixes of universal values (human rights, religion), technical expertise, ideologies of "multistakeholderism," and reputation management. To an extent, representation per se has no meaning; instead, interactions performatively produce and reproduce a morphing set of expectations for participants.

Within today's postdemocratic governmentality, the sites and subjects of political practice morph and migrate. Such shifts have implications for the notions of legitimacy and accountability through which democratic governance has been justified and assessed. What, for example, is the proper way to think about constituency in network politics? Communication crosses multiple boundaries, linking concerns from divergent sites into larger issues, and enabling issues to migrate from one domain to another. Moreover, if legitimacy cannot be understood in terms of the consent of the governed—if, in other words, mass forms of entertainment, consumption, and dissimulation have broken the presumptive link between popularity and right—then what distinguishes legitimate from illegitimate political practice? Similarly, if nationally inscribed forms of citizenship belie the global consequences of state actions, then the notion of elective representatives somehow accountable to particular constituencies is equally outmoded. In sum, networks are reformatting political practices in ways that surpass and subvert assumptions about representation, accountability, and legitimacy built into presumptions about democratic society.

To explore further some of the components of the postdemocratic governmentality emerging at the intersection of CSOs and ICTs, we turn to four concepts: subsidiarity, multistakeholderism, expertise, and reputation management.

Subsidiarity is the principle that decisions should be taken at the lowest possible level—that is, the level closest to the citizen. A fundamental principle of the European Union (and component of Catholic thought), it was established as a key element of European law in the 1992 Treaty of Maastricht. Superficially about finding the "natural" level at which governing functions can optimally be performed, the discourse around subsidiarity is constructed through claims to technical expertise. Like ideals of human rights, and the discourses of help and aid, the concept of subsidiarity is mobile, adaptable to right as well as left issue framings. When linked to claims for a global civil society and the work of NGOs, moreover, it becomes part of a broader, postdemocratic governmentality that sees itself as supplanting the nation.

Sometimes the argument for supplanting the nation is a functional one: transnational networks and NGOs do what nations fail or neglect to do. Yet it also appears in connection with the devolution and decentralization of subsidiarity in the form of an emphasis on *multistakeholderism*. This unwieldy term has gained traction in the arenas of aid and international development, although it originates in critiques of their national counterpart, the welfare state. In this prior context, it was explicitly set forward to break up what was seen as large constituencies that developed around specific government programs into more individual, isolatable "stakeholders" in a program. It also had an early currency in business settings as a rationale for eroding shareholder rights vis-à-vis management. In its current version, multistakeholderism similarly distances the programs of CSOs from constituency politics. Insofar as multistakeholderism uncouples CSOs from direct accountability to an actual constituency, it provides the necessary link between the abstract, universal values guiding a particular organization and the practical, concrete technical expertise that the organization supplies.

Again, like subsidiarity, the notion of multistakeholderism is available to both the Left and the Right. On one hand, it can hold at bay rightist critiques of leftist CSOs as unelected busybodies. It can be advanced to claim a place at tables where decisions are made and policies formed. On the other, it provides a rightist rationale for sloughing off unwanted public responsibilities by "defunding the Left" (in the words of Newt Gingrich, former Republican Speaker of the U.S. House of Representatives). More important for our argument here, multistakeholderism reflects an otherwise underrecognized reality of global civil society organizations— namely, their detachment from constituency politics and imbrication in a postdemocratic governmentality.

The *expertise* component of postdemocratic governmentality needs to be understood within the more general framework of the idea of a network society, an idea now approaching its second decade. From the heuristic concepts of nodes and links has grown the stronger claim that networks are the social morphology of an "information age" with a material base in networked communications, as exemplified in the Internet. The form of one is the form of the other, and likewise their properties and politics. This may be true in a very specific way, namely, the incorporation of the Internet in the 1990s into the economic regime that Robert Cox refers to as "flexible accumulation."[15] This is the neoliberal regime that celebrates choice, free markets, and the sorts of mobilities that network society and networked communication feature. What counts as expertise, then, is counted within this frame, this set of economic assumptions. At the same time, however, this neoliberal story is not usually the one associated with the Internet.

A popular (and romantic) story of the Internet is one of freedom and empowerment—of outlaw hackers; liberation from meat space; freedom from the constraints of raced and gendered identity; the power to say anything, create anything, connect with anyone—often with a decidedly libertarian cast. That libertarianism is further naturalized through the gloss of technical expertise. Because the story of free information and communicative mobility overlooks the Internet's "hidden" costs, including a long period of public sector development, much lobbying and alliance-building by its developers, and shifting rationales advanced to assemble support, as we discussed above, the actual overhead of the Internet is often underestimated. That is also the case with social and political networks more generally. Much effort goes into creating ties and links, very much in proportion to their content and often duration. This is the problem of unstable assemblages and contingent effects that can disrupt democratic processes of representation, which require a stable object, and accountability, which requires a stable subject, that are elements of democratic (constituency) politics.

Because hidden costs, unstable assemblages, and contingent effects are so easily overlooked, many NGOs and CSOs fail to develop complex structures. Instead, they rely on indirect techniques of leading and directing—techniques that emerge through gaps between well-told local narratives and vague, anxiety-ridden generalizations. One explanation for this mode of self-organization can be found in the CSO's overwhelmingly corporate environment of government agencies, private philanthropies, intergovernmental conferences, and the commercial service economy. Another explanation is financial: finance is the most advanced portion of network society. The money trail leads to patrons with corporately organized middlemen. At this point, however, the story diverges into embracing versus not embracing the features of network society, including its economy and commitment to so-called flexible accumulation.

On the one hand are civil society organizations, typically with progressivist casts, who seek the funding of philanthropies and government agencies. The latter, rooted in industrial-period models that institutionalize intentionality in bureaucracy, take integrated programmatic approaches. They fund projects with goals, and those goals commonly do not include what is called in the trade "capacity building" in the organizational sectors of civil society, including capacities in networked communication to do research and to foster activism. Essentially, what obtains is a contracting model that presumes transactions between established entities, institutions, and service-providers, as well as accountability for those transactions. A sort of accounting practice may set in that—in the testimony of many practitioners—limits the accumulation of experience and development of theory to collections of "best practices." Not all civil society organizations face this regimen, and not all that face it are on the political left; but many do because of left preference for the public sector.

By comparison, on the political Right in the United States, complex networked structures of think tanks, bloggers, multiple levels of donors, and revolving doors between government and private employment have emerged; these are enduring, if not stable, alliances (registering to the Left as "a vast right-wing conspiracy"). Setting aside the possibility that some conspiracy on the right cleverly marginalizes the Left, these different outcomes reflect how the money flows are organized. Liberals are not organized in a fundamentally different way. The fight over hegemony these days is fought out by "mobs" and "swarms" that optimize their links and Real Simple Syndication (RSS) feeds. The difference is one of employing both creative and financial resources. The Right employs a more venture capital model more explicitly dedicated to building up a business; in other words, it funds capacity building. Right-wing activists and their theorists have embraced network organization in a way that those on the Left haven't. They operate in a setting denominated by venture capital, investment, and complex organizations that link differentiated but relatively independent parts through which their personnel circulate. This world is stratified broadly into think tanks that turn core ideas into strategies, lobbying organizations devoted to tactical advancement of particular bundles of issues that consultants refined into modules in policy institutes, all surrounded by publicists and pundits providing flexible rationalization on the spot. They link local, grassroots organizations to national ones, using each to foster more of the other and the circles of reciprocity that circulate people, money, ideas.

More left-leaning NGOs, however, remain in a world of institutions, accountability, and pay for service. Even though they heavily rely on volunteers, their core staff is part of the professional managerial class (including audits by PriceWaterhouseCoopers, KPMG International, and others). Increasingly NGOs are made accountable to the same "social responsibility" and "corporate ethics" rules that they themselves once made up for multinationals. Foundations and agencies fund projects—actually, put them out to contract—and in return require outcomes assessments, where the outcomes are project activities. NGOs in this setting function as service suppliers, not as partners in exchanges or as nodes in a network whose currency is links. They are part of, but don't themselves form, complex organizations. Thus, they can't break out from political economies of accountability through to the level of strategic design. This is not a matter of sharing a common ideology with government agencies and private foundations; they usually do share one in helping and doing good. That forms a community of interest—of rhetorical solidarity but not organizational solidarity—that in institutional terms means isomorphism. Leftist NGOs are bound up in a culture of grants, projects, and accountability—the typical organization of industrial society—while others operate in a world of venture funding—particularly on the Right, which is, above all, about capacity building. Reduced to the individual level, networking is mostly working on the Net, which has its own (high) overheads. The leftist NGO dream is thus of "core funding." By core funding the Left has in mind the unrestricted grants from government agencies and/or foundations that support (i.e., pay the overhead for) the successful intergovernmental organizations that specialize around food, health, and telecommunications. Consequently, political strategies to "defund the Left" by downsizing the state can exacerbate lack of capacity building on the Left while having the opposite effect for the Right.

The neoliberal economic setting in which CSOs and NGOs work helps make sense of their adaptation to an additional aspect of postdemocratic governmentality, the shift away from representation and toward expertise. For CSOs and NGOs this expertise extends from financial knowledge to technological knowledge to knowledge of procedures, rules, and best practices, to knowledge of the language, ideals, and principles guiding government and private funders. Knowing how and speaking for universal values become the basis of their claims to participate. Representation moves in the network society and with networked communication (of any to any, instead of one to many) from identities and groups to agendas, activities, and relationships. Focus shifts to issues, which have more fluidity, as Noortje Marres shows in her contribution to this volume. They can be broken up (modularized) and combined or aggregated with others.

This is both where "alternative" civil society organizations gain purchase, and where the so-called mediatization associated with networked communication arises. Nothing seems so easy as manipulating reality in this realm. Media speeded up, senders and messages multiplied, and the "remix" culture that accompanies more people and more manipulation facilitated through ever easier-to-use (and easily acquired) technology become at some point difficult and then impossible to deconstruct in real time. There is no rational response when experience is first of all of transitoriness. Experiences of diasporas and of creolization come forward from the margins, highlighting less displacement and mixture than the centrality of *reputation management* as a vital component of network society's postdemocratic governmentality. Its accomplished actors focus on reputation over representation. Esther Dyson, one of the 1990s' Internet business gurus and a strong advocate for technological expertise, once explained that a reason to contribute to the Net for free was to gain invitations to talk about it outside it for a fee—in other words, to capitalize reputation. These days, this logic is translated into techniques of how to climb up the Google hierarchy and the so-called A-list of most influential blogs. Reputation is measured in terms of links and clicks, not just in speakers' fees.

By the same token, translocal politics are no longer an exception, or marginal, to the "real thing." They are sites like any other of information mobility; their unstable assemblages are "normal," further underscoring the prominence of reputation management over rights or representation. Even the fact of organization may be denied as spokespersons protest that they speak only for themselves, on the grounds of their technical expertise and the basis of a claim to universal values (a basis available to any other who would choose to speak).

Like the open-ended, intermediate spaces of creoles and diasporas, node-and-link structures are better thought of as performative.[16] There is nothing to represent, yet presentation is problematic for creoles and diasporas. Node-and-link structures rely on a currency of reputation, or what some initial encounters with network society and networked communication rendered as "trust."[17] Indeed, much of the reflexive discourse about network society and networked communication is not about rights so much as about trust, which is earned through competent performance (and feedback). Where trust is earned through competent performance, technique—communication—is the object; the idea is to feel direct connection.

In sum, subsidiarity, multistakeholderism, expertise, and reputation management are all components of the postdemocratic governmentality that emerges through the interconnections of CSOs and networked information and communication technologies. NGOs in civil society exemplify the rise of nonstate actors and their connection to global changes under neoliberalism. States are not displaced. Rather, they are joined—and some of their work is supplemented and extended—by local, translocal, and nonstate actors whose presence reformats the political field. Participation comes to be based not on representation of constituencies, but on the presentation and mediation of ideas. Politics overflows electoral legitimacy as accountability is displaced from constituencies to discursive regimes that include evocations of universal values, appeals to subsidiarity and multistakeholderism, and technical expertise or a new elitism based on system knowledge and reputation management. High levels of uncertainty are mediated neither by self-appointment nor institutionally based expertise, but by reputation systems that emerge at sites of interconnection between networks.

Notes

1. On communicative capitalism, see Jodi Dean, *Publicity's Secret: How Technoculture Capitalizes on Democracy* (Ithaca, NY: Cornell University Press, 2002).
2. Michel Foucault, "Governmentality," in *The Foucault Effect: Studies in Governmentality*, ed. Graham Burchell, Colin Gordon, and Peter Miller (Hemel Hempstead, England: Harvester Wheatsheaf, 1991), 87–104.
3. Thomas Lemke, "Comment on Nancy Fraser: Rereading Foucault in the Shadow of Globalization" *Constellations* 10, no. 2 (2003): 172–79.
4. Thomas Lemke, "Foucault, Governmentality, and Critique," *Rethinking Marxism* 14, no. 3 (2002): 49–64.
5. To this extent, the concept affiliates well with Alexander R. Galloway's emphasis on protocol as "a diagram, a technology, and a management style" and an analysis of networked societies in terms of "management, manipulation, and control." See Galloway, *Protocol: How Control Exists after Decentralization* (Cambridge, MA: MIT Press, 2004), xviii.
6. See Geert Lovink and Soenke Zehle, eds., *Incommunicado 05 Reader* (Amsterdam: Institute of Network Cultures, 2005); available online at <http://www.networkcultures.org/weblog/archives/IncommunicadoReader.pdf>.
7. See the book and related discussion *Extreme Democracy*, edited by Jon Lebkosky and Mitch Radcliffe; available online at <http://www.extremedemocracy.com>.
8. The first professional history of the Internet is Janet Abbate, *Inventing the Internet* (Cambridge, MA: MIT Press, 1999); much the same story is told more journalistically in Katie Hafner and Matthew Lyon, *Where Wizards Stay Up Late: The Origins of the Internet* (New York: Simon and Schuster, 1996). For a chronological account by the engineers who created it, documenting design decisions and extensions of the Internet, the Internet Society provides *A Brief History of the Internet* by Barry M.Leiner et al.; available online at <http://www.isoc.org/internet/history/brief.shtml>.
9. See Milton Mueller, *Ruling the Root: Internet Governance and the Taming of Cyberspace* (Cambridge, MA: MIT Press, 2002), esp. section 2, "The Story of the Root."
10. For example, the conservative American Enterprise Institute partners with the Federalist Society in NGO Watch, which is dedicated to "highlighting issues of transparency and

accountability in the operations of nongovernmental organizations (NGOs) and international organizations (IOs)" through publications and conferences and a website—<http://www.ngowatch.org/>—that provides a list of papers and experts, online resources, journals, and watchdog organizations. Its particular concern is that "nongovernmental organizations are not just accredited observers at international organizations, they are full-fledged decision-makers."

11. Jodi Dean, "Why the Net Is Not the Public Sphere," *Constellations* 8, no. 3 (2001):95-112.

12. See, for example, Mark Poster, "CyberDemocracy: Internet and the Public Sphere," available online at <http://www.hnet.uci.edu/mposter/writings/democ.html>.

13. One of the most significant exceptions, albeit one that does not focus on global information and communications networks, is Michael Hardt and Antonio Negri, *Empire* (Cambridge, MA: Harvard University Press, 2000).

14. See, for example, Helmut K. Anheier, Mary H. Kaldor, and Marlies Glasius, eds., *Global Civil Society 2004/2005* (Thousand Oaks, CA: Sage, 2004); and John Keane, *Global Civil Society?* (Cambridge: Cambridge University Press, 2003). See also Manuel Castells, *The Rise of the Network Society*, vol. 1 of *The Information Age: Economy, Society and Culture* (Malden, MA: Blackwell, 1996), 469.

15. Robert Cox, *The Political Economy of a Plural World* (New York: Routledge, 2003).

16. For an early recognition of network features in creoles and a generalization of the notion to cultural communities, see Lee Drummond, "The Cultural Continuum: A Theory of Intersystems," *Man*, n.s., 15, no. 2 (1980): 352–74. An influential generalization of diasporas as "ethnoscapes" is Arjun Appadurai, "Disjunction and Difference in the Global Cultural Economy," in *Modernity at Large: Cultural Dimensions of Globalization* (Minneapolis: University of Minnesota Press, 1996).

17. A prominent example is Francis Fukuyama's neoliberal paean *Trust: The Social Virtues and the Creation of Prosperity* (Glencoe, IL: Free Press, 1995).

SECTION I
Networks

CHAPTER 1

Net-Work Is Format Work: Issue Networks and the Sites of Civil Society Politics

NOORTJE MARRES

Introduction

During the last decade we have witnessed the proliferation of new information and communication technologies (ICTs) and the exponential growth of civil society organizations (CSOs).[1] The "network" is one of the prime conceptual, practical, and technical sites where these two developments come together. Arguably the most important feature of ICTs—of which the Internet is a fundamental component, both discursively and logistically—is that they facilitate networked forms of organization (of information and people). Non-governmental organizations (NGOs)—which have increased in number and in influence on institutional political processes—especially at the intergovernmental level—are also often characterized in terms of networks.[2] Features that currently distinguish these organizations are their propensity to form partnerships, both among themselves

3

and with (inter-)governmental bodies and, sometimes, for-profit actors, and more radically, their commitment to decentralized and distributed ways of working.

This convergence between ICTs and CSOs finds specific expression in two notions that are frequently evoked to make sense of the practices these organizations engage in and the role of ICTs in facilitating them: the *social network* and the *info-network*. As regards civil society practices, a wide variety of terms is used to load meaning into these networking activities, with "building partnerships" and "awareness raising" on one end of the spectrum, and "making friends" and "sharing knowledge" on the other. This variety can be taken as an indication of the great divergences in style and status among the groups, movements, and organizations that are brought together under the heading of "civil society." But establishing and fostering "contacts" and spreading information are now ubiquitous activities of these entities, regardless of their institutional or rather less "institutional"—status, geographical location, and the issues they work with. Importantly, characterizations of civil society practices in terms of social and info-networking make the importance of ICTs as a facilitator of these practices forcefully clear. As a bottom line, there is e-mail as a technology of social networking (and an incredibly successful one at that), and the simple and straightforward website as an obvious example of info-networking (albeit an arguably less successful one). Considering the ubiquity of these networking activities in the civil society sector, and the obvious merits of ICTs in this respect, it is in some sense ridiculous to question the usefulness of the concepts of the "social network" and the "info-network" to explain why ICTs matter to CSOs. However, it is far from self-evident that the *politics* of civil society can be understood in these terms.

In this chapter, I argue that the notions of the social network and the info-network are of limited use if we are to appreciate the interventions of CSOs in public debates, their roles as critics of governmental institutions, corporations, and other CSOs, and their attempts to force powerful actors to act upon social, economic, environmental, and humanitarian problems. A different concept of the network provides a more fruitful heuristic to account for the political practices of CSOs and the difference that ICTs can make in this respect: the issue network. The social network casts exchanges among actors in terms of *collaboration*, and is therefore ill-suited if we want to acknowledge the *antagonistic relations* in which CSOs are implicated, especially where their politics are concerned. The info-network highlights the *proliferation* of information through networks, and for this reason it is not a very helpful notion if we want to attend to the important work of *articulation*—of issues—that CSOs perform. With regard to the role of ICTs in facilitating the politics of civil society, the problem with the notions of the social network and the info-network is that they tempt us to think of the interconnections between ICTs and CSOs in terms of an *alignment* between the technical sphere, on the one hand, and the sphere of social organization and knowledge formation, on the other. If we are fully to appreciate the role of ICTs in the political practices of CSOs, however, we must also consider how these technologies are and may be *integrated* into these practices, operating upon their substance. The notion of the issue network has definite advantages in this respect.

At the same time, to adopt this concept is to complicate matters. It brings along specific assumptions about the type of politics that CSOs engage in, which are much more demanding than those alluded to above that is, that it is useful for civil society actors to make acquaintances and spread the word. If I can be forgiven for complicating matters in this way, it could be because to account for civil society politics in terms of issue networks is to attempt to take seriously the specificity of networks as sites of politics. It is also an attempt to understand civil society politics as a practice in which substantial and technological considerations are closely intertwined.

The Issue Network as a Site of Civil Society Politics

The concept of the *issue network* is used today to characterize a variety of political practices that add to and intervene in the representative politics characteristic of national democracies and the international system. The term has been taken up to describe the issue politics or "lifestyle politics" pursued by grassroots organizations and individuals in mobilizing around affairs that affect people in their daily lives, from the environment to media ownership and gender issues.[3] The term is equally applied to more professionalized practices of what are then called NGOs, most notably those of advocacy. Here the notion serves to highlight the open-ended alliances formed by NGOs working on common social, environmental, and humanitarian issues, as part of their attempts to put these issues on the agendas of political institutions.[4] Importantly, these contemporary uses of the "issue network" represent in some respects a radical break with the classic definition of the term. Today, the concept is generally considered to be affirmative in that it denotes a form of political organization that is compatible with, or even an instance of, liberal democracy. But when the American political scientist Hugh Heclo coined the term in the 1970s it was to problematize, and indeed criticize, the new politics of issues in which NGOs were engaging.[5] According to Heclo, this form of politics *weakens* democracy. It is important to consider this origin of the notion of the issue network, however briefly, as it reminds us that we are dealing here with an "un-innocent" mode of political intervention.

In his seminal article "The Issue Network and the Executive Establishment," Heclo described a new form of political organization on the rise in Washington, D.C., during the administration of president Jimmy Carter. "Issue-activists" and "issue-experts" were forming "loose alliances" in which they defined political affairs "by sharing information about them."[6] For Heclo, the emergence of issue networks had to be understood in the context of a wider development, which he described as the "broadening of organizational participation in policy-making." Especially problematic about the phenomenon, according to Heclo, was that the "issue people" now got to define political affairs well before governmental officials, politicians, and the general public got involved. This was bound to alienate the broader public—not so much because they were excluded from participation in issue formation, but because the specialist, technical discourses in which issues were being defined did not "speak" to more general and basic concerns of institutional outsiders. For this reason, Heclo argued, the proliferation of issue networks brings with it a democratic deficit.

We should keep this original critique of issue networks in mind as we explore the merits of the notion for an account for the politics of civil society, and the role of ICTs therein. Heclo's initial analysis warns against easy equations between civil society participation in politics and democracy. It tells us that issue formation in networks is likely to entail political interventions, the legitimacy of which is contested. This is so, not only because adverse interests seek to undermine these interventions, but because a shortage of institutional legitimacy is the condition under which those operating beyond the representative political system inevitably work, and because the failure to translate the concerns of affected actors is a real risk that those involved in issue formation must face.[7]

While an affirmative account of civil society politics in terms of issue networking thus entails a repurposing of this term, there are good reasons for such a repurposing. The notion has at least three distinctive merits. As a first, general point, the "issue network" proposes that participants in such a network are connected to one another *by way of* the particular issue with which it is concerned. This proposal has the advantage of dispelling some of the mystery surrounding the question of how CSOs that have arisen and operate in radically different social contexts, may nevertheless develop common projects.[8] As the legal scholar Annelise Riles points out, actors in civil society networks do not necessarily share much in terms of culture or lifestyle.[9] Taking up the concept of the issue network, we can say that, in this context, the issues take on special importance as providing, enabling, or even necessitating, connections among actors. A second, more specific, merit of the "issue network" is that it draws attention to the work of issue formation, and more specifically, that of *formatting* issues, as a crucial dimension of the politics of civil society. (Such format work is of particular interest when considering the role of ICTs in the political practices of CSOs.) Third, the concept invites us to attend to the ways CSOs—especially in as far as their politics is concerned—are implicated in extended configurations of actors and issues that are marked by *antagonism*. I first highlight the latter two features of the issue network, and the ways in which they make up for some of the limitations of notions of the social network and the info-network, before turning to the more specific question of ICTs in their relation to civil society politics.

Two Merits of the "Issue Network"

In the study of advocacy, it is today widely accepted that the network represents an important contemporary site for issue formation by NGOs and social movements. In *Activism beyond Borders*, the international relations researchers Margaret Keck and Kathryn Sikkink rely on the notion of the issue network to account for the politics of transnational NGOs, and in doing so they point at "the framing of issues" as a prime political project pursued by these networks. One of the crucial undertakings of NGO networks, they point out, is to define, translate, and label the issue in question: "Network actors actively seek ways to bring issues to the public agenda by framing them in innovative ways and by seeking hospitable venues."[10] This is an essential component of the political strategy of advocacy networks, they argue, since by choosing new frames, that is, new labels and keywords, and we might add, new formats—an issue may acquire resonance in political circles and public spheres.

To be sure, the issue network also fulfills a function that transcends that of providing a platform for "agenda setting" by CSOs. If it is by virtue of CSOs' shared issues that they acquire a common political project, then the issue network may also be considered a site where civil society, as a political force, comes into being. And, when a network serves as its location, then the practice of framing issues takes on a distinctive form. Issue formation is something that happens in the circulation of information: as reports, press releases, news, articles, slogans, and images circulate in the network, the stakes are defined, addressees for the issue emerge, and its urgency is made apparent. Thus, in this context, issue formation takes on the aspect of a collective, technologically mediated, distributed practice. This points toward a first merit of the concept of the issue network: it highlights a specific political effect that CSOs seek to achieve when sharing information, namely, the political articulation of the issues to which they are committed. In adopting the perspective of the issue network, then, we won't forget the larger political project of civil society: to generate issue definitions with a critical edge, which may cut into institutional processes of opinion-, decision- , and policy-making, so as to open up a space in which action upon issues becomes possible.

The second feature of the issue network important for understanding the politics of civil society is the way it draws attention to the extended political configurations in which CSOs easily become implicated. This aspect of the issue network has not received much emphasis in the work on advocacy discussed above. But in policy studies the issue network is defined as a relatively open network of *antagonistic* actors that configure around a controversial issue. The issue network is here opposed to the policy-network, which is defined as closed, standing in the service of the de-politization of issues, and prone to achieve consensus (and as heavily institutionalized).[11] Defined in these terms, the "issue network" invites us to focus on the broader networks of dissenting actors from the governmental, non-governmental, and for-profit sectors as the sites at which CSOs engage in controversies over specific affairs. To say "issue network" is then to ask: how do CSOs insert themselves, or how are they implicated by others, in formations of opponents and allies (as well as actors between these two extremes) that have configured around a common issue?

This question leads us into tricky territory. The implication of CSOs in extended networks of dot-gov, dot-org, and dot-com is a controversial matter itself. Connections among CSOs and (inter-)governmental organizations, donors, and corporate bodies have been a topic of particularly intense contestation among civil society groups, as they raise troubling questions about the real autonomy of CSOs, the vulnerability of their work to appropriation by governmental and for-profit actors, and their commitment to radical action. The concept of the issue network, however, at the same time aids us in getting a clearer view of contentious relations between civil society and its outside. Defined as an antagonistic configuration, the perspective of the "issue network" allows us to appreciate that actors that come together in such a network may do so precisely because they disagree over the issues in which they are jointly implicated, and the ways in which these are to be addressed. Moreover, as we explore how CSOs are affected by the wider circulation of information, people, and resources in extended issue networks of dot-gov, dot-com, and dot-org, we may come to better appreciate the efforts that some CSOs make to dis-embed their activities from these networks.

The concept of the issue network invites us to focus on the framing of issues as a crucial dimension of civil society politics. It encourages us to explore how CSOs intervene in, or seek to dis-embed their activities from, extended networks of governmental, for-profit, and non-governmental actors. I now consider the advantages of the concept of issue network over "social network" and "info-network" for describing civil society politics in networked terms—before turning to the specific question of the role of ICTs in facilitating it. To the degree that the notions of the social network and the info-network have informed accounts of the ways in which ICTs facilitate civil society practices, the political challenges that CSOs face have not received sufficient attention.

When Social Networking and Info-Networking Are Not Enough

Studies of the relations between ICTs and CSOs often rely on the notions of the social network and the info-network in at least two ways. First, in early work on this subject the notion of the social network was used to establish the connection between the *general* phenomena of civil society and the new ICTs of the 1990s —most notably, the Internet. Thus, the political scientist Craig Warkentin has argued that the relevance of the Internet for global civil society principally derives from the fact that, as a transnationally implemented network technology, it provides a perfect forum for the social networks of global civil society: "the Internet's inherent qualities facilitate the development of global civil society's constitutive network of social relations."[12] Second, the "social network" and the "info-network" are drawn upon to specify the *particular* uses that CSOs currently make of ICTs. In their report, "Appropriating the Internet for Social Change," Mark Surman and Katherine Reilly distinguish the technical network (i.e., networked ICTs), the social network (i.e., coalitions of CSOs), and the intermediate notion of the network as a site of info-sharing, to elucidate such usage.[13] In accordance with the latter two network concepts, they focus on "collaboration" and "publishing" as two important practices in which CSOs take advantage of ICTs.[14] As I mentioned in the introduction, it is in some respects absurd to question the adequacy of these characterizations of civil society practice for the simple reason that they have served as guiding principles in the integration of ICTs into these practices. As long as our thinking about ICTs and CSOs is guided by the notions of the social network and the info-network, however, we risk leaving crucial dimensions of the politics of civil society underconceptualized, and thereby, underexplored. It is here that the issue network has something valuable to add.

A first difficulty with the social network and the info-network is that when they organize descriptions of civil society practices, it becomes hard to account for the formal dimension of these practices in positive terms— and this is precisely a crucial dimension of the politics of CSOs. The principal features that these types of networks are famous for are informality and relative amorphousness. The notion of the social network foregrounds relatively unregulated or underregulated relations: social networks arise in the exchange of information and things among people, in the absence of institutionalized relations among them, or beyond or alongside such relations.[15] As for networks for information sharing, they are classically conceived of as smooth, flat, and formless spaces, as in the work of Manuel Castells on the space of flows.[16] Considering this, it should not surprise us that when formal features of social and info-networks are observed, these are easily interpreted in negative terms. This is especially the case where CSOs are concerned: normative conceptions of civil society tend to mobilize ideals of openness and egalitarianism.[17] When social or info-networks in which CSOs are implicated turn out to have discernable shapes, this is then be taken to mean that they are more centralized, less distributed, more hierarchical, and less inclusive than the ideal of the network as an unbounded, informal, decentralized form of organization promises. The (ideal) features of informality and amorphousness of networks have led the French sociologists Luc Boltanksi and Ève Chiapello to question the viability of the network as a site of democratic politics, which is then conceived of as an intrinsically institutional activity.[18] In line with this argument, the German sociologist Ulrich Beck criticizes social network theories for their lack of concern with the specificity of institutional arrangements.[19] Such critiques of networks and their theorization fail to acknowledge that this feature of informality is what makes the network a fruitful form of organization for civil society politics. The network works as an underinstitutionalized form of organization.

The argument of these sociologists that informal social relations and amorphous networks of info-sharing by themselves cannot account for democratic politics, however, is not so easy to dismiss. At this point, a first advantage of the "issue network" over the "social network" and the "info-network" for an account of the politics of civil society, becomes clear: as this concept points toward the *framing* of issues as a crucial aspect of civil society politics, it draws our attention to the engagements of CSOs with the formalities of politics, without forcing us to deny that such engagements are enabled by informal relations among these actors and their audiences. As CSOs organize as issue networks, and/or insert themselves into broader issue networks of dot-gov, dot-com, and dot-org they can be seen to participate in the formalization of their issues, transforming them into specific claims.

In the spring of 2004, for example, environmental organizations and NGOs monitoring financial institutions organized into a network and put forward the demand that the World Bank phase out its funding of fossil fuel projects by 2008. This claim was taken from a World Bank commissioned report, called the "Extractive Industries Review." In its mobilizations, the network took it up as an effective translation of issues of the environment, poverty, and governance into a concrete demand. Considering such engagement of CSOs with major institutions, we can observe a second difficulty with the concepts of the "social network" and "info-network." As they foreground relations of collegiality or solidarity and sharing, they lead us to focus on the networks that CSOs and their audiences form among themselves. These notions are therefore not very well suited for an account of the broader configurations of dot-gov, dot-com, and dot-org in which CSOs are implicated, especially where their politics are concerned.

Importantly, such extended networks cannot be understood as a combination of the social network and the info-network. This becomes clear when we take seriously the argument made by the American pragmatist philosopher, John Dewey, that it is in the nature of political communities to bring together actors who do not relate socially. (The circumstance, highlighted by Annelise Riles, that CSO networks cannot be expected to be held together by thick social or cultural bonds, receives a general formulation in Dewey's political theory: he observes this to be the case for political communities broadly speaking.)

In his classic work on democracy and technology *The Public and Its Problems*, John Dewey explicitly distinguished the political community from the social community.[20] He proposed that political communities consist of actors that are *indirectly* implicated in a common issue. According to Dewey, political communities bring together actors who do not have much in common as far as their daily lives are concerned, but who are jointly implicated in a problem, which puts their respective forms of life at risk. Political communities in this sense consist of *strangers* according to Dewey.[21] To give a contemporary example, agro-industrialists from Kansas and Dutch vegetarians may not share much in terms of lifestyle or culture, nor is it necessary for them to interact with one another as part of their daily lives. But when pig genes were inserted in American export corn, these actors became caught up in a common issue. The Deweyian approach to politics helps to make it clear why the political task of issue formation involves connections that differ from social and informational ones. When CSOs engage in the articulation of issues, they must work with relations among relative strangers, among whom social bonds are largely absent. Moreover, we should add to Dewey's definition of the political community that an issue must be expected to disclose antagonistic relations among actors: it is precisely to the degree that their interests in the issue exclude one another that a given problem turns into a political affair. Where CSOs engage in issue formation, we must expect them to become implicated in actor configurations in which the definitions of issues are contested. So spreading information about the matter at hand is not enough; issue framings put into circulation by antagonistic actors must be actively countered.

One could say that the Deweyian definition of the political community underestimates the degree to which the articulation of issues requires intensive social and info-networking. For example, before southern African women's organizations can achieve an intervention in the wider issue networks that have configured around women's issues, they must have engaged in issue formation among themselves, invented a language in which to phrase their concerns and commitments, and found the precise formulations that capture them effectively. But while issue formation may thus require collaboration and information exchange, it cannot be reduced to such activities insofar as it constitutes a *political* practice. In its emphasis on friendly relations among actors who share certain affinities, the notion of the social network directs attention toward networks of, precisely, friends and colleagues. As such, it de-emphasizes the ways in which civil society actors, as they engage politically, become antagonistically implicated in stranger networks (or from which, as an alternative political strategy, they actively seek to dis-embed their practices.) The notion of the info-network entails a conception of the spread of information as a matter of the diffusion, propagation, or proliferation of bits and pieces of knowledge. It thereby de-emphasizes the fact that issue formation involves articulation, that is, the active (re-)formatting of issues, and contestation of divergent issue-formattings, that are circulating in the issue network. The concept of the issue network not only makes up for these limitations of the "social network" and the "info-network;" it also directs attention to roles of ICT in civil society politics that remain under-explored as long as the other two network concepts organize accounts.

ICTs as Mediators of Issue Formation

When we use the notions of the social network and the info-network to describe relations between CSOs and ICTs, we are tempted to account for these relations in terms of a fortunate *alignment* between the organizational forms of civil society and those that characterize these technologies. As I mentioned in the introduction, these network concepts direct our attention to morphological similarities between ICTs and CSOs: CSOs share information and form partnerships; ICTs—the Internet, but also telephony and old fashioned mail systems—represent technical networks that provide a forum for such organizational networking. Early accounts of the relations between the Internet and civil society adopted this isomorphic schema. Craig Warkentin has argued that "[b]ecause the Internet's inherent characteristics and transnational reach parallel (or correspond to) those of global civil society, the medium serves as both a logical and an effective tool for establishing and maintaining social connections that can contribute to global civil society."[22]

Recent accounts point to the drawbacks of this approach. Most generally, it leads us to underestimate the extent to which the use of ICTs *transform* civil society practices, and vice versa, since it describes ICTs and CSOs as being already similar—before interferences occurred between them. But of course, the rise to prominence of the Internet may be *responsible* for the fact that CSOs increasingly organize themselves as networks. The effects of this transformation are not unambiguously positive. The energies invested in the formation of partnerships among organizations may go at the expense of loyalties to the particular, rather more grounded, contexts in which these organizations operate. Conversely, the concepts of public debate and dialogue that are so central to discourses about civil society have left their marks in ICTs, providing important justifications for the organization of online spaces as fora for debate.[23] To appreciate such transformations of both civil society practices and ICTs, then, we must approach ICTs as active *mediators* of civil society practices.[24]

The concept of the issue network directs attention to a second aspect of the role of ICTs in civil society practices that risks being left out of the account where morphological similarities between ICT and CSOs are at the center of attention. The latter approach leaves unanswered the question of how ICTs enable or disable the articulation of *the issues* around which CSOs mobilize. The application of a "correspondence model" to the relations between ICTs and CSOs leads to a preoccupation with information exchange and the social relations constituted in the process of this exchange. Accordingly, the *substance* on which civil society politics operates—the affairs that it is concerned with—is here easily lost from view. The perspective of the issue network invites us to approach ICTs as mediators of civil society practices, and more particularly, as mediators of issue formation. The principal question to be asked with regard to ICTs thus becomes: how do these technologies transform civil society practices of the formatting of issues? And more straightforwardly: how do ICTs enable transformations of the issues of civil society politics? How do they constrain their articulation?

With respect to the first question, now that many CSOs rely on the new ICTs to organize advocacy campaigns, they increasingly engage in "issue-splicing." As CSOs working in particular issue areas link up their campaigns with those of CSOs working in other areas, setting up joint campaign web sites, among others, objects of civil society concern, such as ICTs or the environment, come to be framed as hybrid affairs, as also involving issues of governance, women's issues, indigenous rights, and so on. We can wonder whether the pursuit of such a logic of hybridization comes at the expense of more creative practices in which NGOs could develop new issue framings, and an aesthetics that could ensure a place for issues in political discourses. To give an example of the more specific ways in which ICTs disable and enable issue formation by CSOs: when news of missing journalists in Central Asia is posted on a website in PDF format, this is probably bad news for the missing journalists; a PDF that sits somewhere on a server is not likely to contribute to the transformation of this tragedy into a political issue. If, on the other hand, the news release is emailed to NGOs working on media freedom, addressing people personally and inviting posting, this is more likely to contribute to issue formation.[25] As an example in which info-technological practices of issue formation are not dedicated to intervention in extended issue networks, but instead, serve as a means of disengagement from these larger configurations around issues, we can think of collaborative data base building projects, in which only those actors willing to let collectives tinker with their data will participate.

To approach ICTs as enabling and disabling the format work performed by CSOs, in their (dis-)engagement with or from broader issue-networks, is to embrace a particular understanding of the politics that these actors pursue. The task of these organizations, we then say, is to articulate and frame issues in such a way that dominant issue framings circulating in broader issue networks are effectively contested and transformed, thereby opening up a space for intervention that otherwise would have remained closed. Of course, such an understanding of the politics of civil society leaves undiscussed many other practices of CSOs, such as fostering bonds of solidarity among CSOs and their supporters. Nevertheless, an exploration of the ways in which ICTs constrain the format work performed by CSOs has relevance beyond the important but admittedly narrow question of the politics of issue formation in that it approaches ICTs as *substantially integrated* in civil society practices. As opposed to the *alignment* between the aims of civil society and the tools of information and communication, the perspective of the issue network leads us to focus on the *intertwining* of substantive and technological considerations in the networked politics of civil society. Crucially, in the performance of format work, as in the case of the attempt to effectively spread the news of missing journalists in Central Asia, technological and substantial concerns cease to be clearly distinguished. Substantive concerns about the fate of the missing journalists and technical considerations about the information format in which their circumstances are to be rendered public here are intimately related: as I said, when the news of missing journalists in Central Asia goes out in PDF format, this is probably bad news for the missing journalists. If we wish to explore the extent to which ICTs now form a constitutive dimension of civil society practices, and do not just provide a forum for these activities without affecting them, the ways in which these technologies enable and disable format work is thus an important place to start.

Conclusion

The concept of the issue network, I have argued, enriches our understanding of the networked politics of civil society, and the role of ICTs in facilitating it. It invites us to focus on the technological practices of info-politics that civil society groups and organizations engage in, and to approach them as practices of the framing of issues. As CSOs seek to intervene in broader issue networks, or as an alternative strategy, attempt to actively dis-embed their activities from these extended networks, they engage in practices of the formatting and re-formatting of issues. This aspect of civil society politics remains underconceptualized in accounts of the relations between CSOs and ICTs that foreground the social and the info-network as the topos where the two meet. As opposed to the friendly networks of the social and the noncommittal networks of information sharing, the issue network directs our attention to antagonistic configurations of actors from the governmental, non-governmental, and for-profit sectors, and the contestation over issue framings that occurs in them. Here the principal question becomes how CSOs can effectively engage in format work, intervening in issue framings that circulate in the broader issue network with issue-framings of their own, or, alternatively, to dis-embed their framings from these network flows. It is certainly not clear which info-technological applications, exactly, effectively enable such format work. The relation between technical application and political intervention, in the case of issue network politics, often appears to be rather "accidental." For example, in April 2002, a Yahoo discussion lists emerged as a central location on the web for criticism of the World Bank: the websites of several NGOs monitoring international financial institutions singled this list out as a relevant location, by way of hyperlinks.[26] But the absence of a predetermined relation between issue-political practice and technical application may also be taken as an invitation for the issue-politically minded to take an active interest in the possibilities of info-technological format work, and vice versa, for techies to develop an appreciation for issue-specific considerations.

Notes

1. Helmut Anheier, Marlies Glasius, and Mary Kaldor, introduction to *Global Civil Society Yearbook 2001*, ed. Helmut Anheier, Marlies Glasius, and Mary Kaldor (Oxford: Oxford University Press, 2001).

2. Jonathan Bach and David Stark, "Link, Search, Interact: The Co-Evolution of NGOs and Interactive Technology," *Theory, Culture and Society* 21, no. 3 (2004): 101–17.

3. W. Lance Bennett, "Ithiel Sola Pool Lecture: The UnCivic Culture: Communication, Identity, and the Rise of Lifestyle Politics," *PS: Political Science and Politics* 31, no. 4 (1998): 740–61; W. Lance Bennet, "New Media Power: The Internet and Global Activism," in *Contesting Media Power: Alternative Media in a Networked World*, ed. Nick Couldry and James Curran (Lanham, MD: Rowman and Littlefield, 2003) 17–37.

4. Margaret E. Keck and Kathryn Sikkink, *Activists beyond Borders* (Ithaca, NY: Cornell University Press, 1998). The concept of the issue network has also been used to conceptualize a post-institutional politics of problem solving. Thus, in the work of Jean-François Rischard, the issue network represents a form of organization in which actors from the sectors of government, business, and civil society informally work together on major policy problems, thereby circumventing the obstacles that the more "bureaucratic" approaches of international governmental institutions put in the way of solutions. Less provocatively, the issue network is also referred to in proposals for new forms of stakeholder democracy, whereby consultations of relevant parties from business and civil society are to enrich decision-making processes hosted by (inter)governmental organizations, as in the work of David Held. Considering the divergent uses to which the concept of the issue network is being put today, it is clear that political formats are underdetermined by this organizational form. The issue network has been described as a site of, alternatively, contestational, managerial, and consensual politics. In this article, I will focus on the first format. See Jean-Francois Rischard, "Network Solutions for Global Governance," *openDemocracy*, January 16, 2003; available online at <http://www.opendemocracy.net/globalization-institutions_government/article_894.jsp>; David Held, *Global Covenant: The Social Democratic Alternative to the Washington Consensus* (Oxford: Polity, 2004).

5. Hugh Heclo, "The Issue Network and the Executive Establishment," in *The New American Political System*, ed. Anthony King (Washington, DC: American Enterprise Institute for Public Policy Research, 1978) 87–124.

6. Heclo, "The Issue Network," 104.

7. I explore the problem of democratic legitimacy that the organizational form of the issue network brings with it in my doctoral thesis. See Noortje Marres, "Issues in? Publics Out?" chap. 3 in "No Issue, No Public: Democratic Deficits after the Displacement of Politics" (Ph.D. diss., University of Amsterdam, 2005).

8. Keck and Sikkink answer this question by positing that NGOs share basic norms and principles. Such an answer, however, risks importing a universalist notion of a common moral and/or cognitive framework into accounts of civil society practices, a notion hard to sustain empirically. Also, it posits precisely that which requires explanation—namely, how norms and principles come to be widely adopted. Keck and Sikkink, *Activists beyond Borders*, 2.

9. Annelise Riles, *The Network Inside Out* (Ann Arbor: University of Michigan Press, 2001) 57–58.

10. Keck and Sikkink, *Activists beyond Borders*, 17. Keck and Sikkink derive from the issue network the term *advocacy network*, in line with other work in policy studies. The latter term denotes civil society networks, as opposed to networks involving representatives of government and business. I will use the term *issue network* to emphasize that CSOs are likely to be implicated in broader configurations of dot-gov, dot-com, and dot-org, as I explain below.

11. Martin Smith, *Pressure, Power and Policy: State Autonomy and Policy Networks in Britain and the United States* (London: Harvester Wheatsleaf, 1993) 60–67.

12. Craig Warkentin, *Reshaping World Politics, NGOs, the Internet and Global Civil Society* (Lanham, MD: Rowman and Littlefield, 2001) 32.

13. Mark Surman and Katherine Reilly, "Appropriating the Internet for Social Change: Towards the Strategic Use of Networked Technologies by Transitional Civil Society Orga-

nizations," Information Technology and International Cooperation Program, Social Science Research Council, November 2003.

14. Surman and Reilly distinguish two further civil society practices in which ICTs play a crucial role: mobilization and observation. Their report thus invites us to add the "affective network" and the "knowledge network" to the lists of networks in which CSOs and ICTs meet. I do think these network concepts can enrich our understanding of the interrelations between CSOs and ICTs because, among other reasons, they help specify the different uses to which these technologies are put. In this respect, the focus of my account on the social network and the info-network is too limited, and requires expansion. However, the notions of the *affective network* and the *knowledge network*, too, may easily lead us to fail to consider the role that issues play in organizing civil society practices. In issues, affective, political, and epistemological considerations are entangled with ontological concerns: the "being" and "becoming" of actors is at stake in political affairs (human rights, the environment, poverty, gender relations, etc.). The four network types—info-network, social network, affective network, and knowledge network—not only make it difficult to appreciate the entanglement of the epistemological, the social and the political, but also leave out of consideration the ontological dimension.

15. This is the definition of a social network proposed by social network analysists Laura Garton, Caroline Haythornthwaite, and Barry Wellman: "Just as a computer network is a set of machines connected by a set of cables, a social network is a set of people (or organizations or other social entities) connected by a set of social relationships, such as friendship, co-working or information exchange." See Garton, Haythornthwaite, and Wellman, "Studying Online Social Networks,"*Journal of Computer-Mediated Communication* 3, no. 1 (1997); available online at <http://www.ascusc.org/jcmc/vol3/issue1/garton.html>.

16. Manuel Castells, *The Rise of the Network Society*, vol. 1 of *The Information Age: Economy, Society and Culture* (Oxford: Blackwell, 1996).

17. Michael Hardt's characterization of networks of social movements provides a radical example. He describes these networks as horizontal (radically decentralized) and indefinitely expansive, and sharply distinguishes them from centralized, representative forms of organization, which he attributes to political parties. See Hardt, "Porto Alegre: Today's Bandung?" *New Left Review* 14 (2002): 112–118.

18. Luc Boltanksi and Ève Chiapello, *Le nouvel esprit du capitalisme* (Paris: Gallimard, 1999) 160–68.

9. Ulrich Beck, *World Risk Society* (Cambridge: Polity, 1999).

20. John Dewey, *The Public and Its Problems* (1927); reprint (Athens, OH: Swallow Press/Ohio University Press, 1991) 12–36.

21. The notion that publics are made up of relations among strangers has recently been taken up in Michael Warner, *Publics and Counterpublics* (New York: Zone, 2002).

22. Warkentin, *Reshaping World Politics*, 33.

23. Jodi Dean, *Publicity's Secret: How Technoculture Capitalizes on Democracy* (Ithaca, NY: Cornell University Press, 2002).

24. This has recently been proposed by Jonathan Bach and David Stark, who take up a central concept from actor-network theory, that of the co-construction of social and technical entities, for the study of the interrelations between CSOs and ICTs. Arguing for an approach that is sensitive to transformations of both entities, Bach and Stark propose to describe them in terms of a process of co-evolution. While their approach presents a welcome shift away from the isomorphistic approach to ICTs and CSOs, Bach and Stark's account preserves the preoccupation with social and epistemic networks characteristic of earlier work on the subject. See Bach and Stark, "Link, Search, Interact," 101–2.

25. The case of the missing journalists of Central Asia and the ways in which it was (not) built on the web was researched by Richard Rogers during the workshop "Social Life of Issues 6: The Network Effects of Civil Society," organized by the govcom.org Foundation, C3, Budapest, May 2002.

26. "Bank Boycott," discussion list, online at <http://groups.yahoo.com/subscribe/bank-boycott>.

CHAPTER 2

Organized Networks and Nonrepresentative Democracy

NED ROSSITER

The Network Problematic

A specter is haunting this age of informationality—the specter of state sovereignty. As a modern technique of governance based on territorial control, a "monopoly of violence" and the capacity to regulate the flow of goods, services, and people, the sovereign power of the nation-state is not yet ready to secede from the system of internationalism. The compact of alliances among nation-states over matters of trade, security, foreign aid, investment, and so forth, substantiates the ongoing relevance of the state form in shaping the mobile life of people and things. As the Internet gained purchase throughout the 1990s on the everyday experiences of those living within advanced economies in particular, the popular imagination became characterized by the notion of a "borderless" world of "frictionless capitalism." Such a view is the doxa of many: political philosophers, economists, international relations scholars, politicians, chief executive officers, activists, cyberlibertarians, advertising agencies, political spin doctors, and ecologists all have their variation on the theme of a postnational, global world system interlinked by informational flows.

Just as the nation-state appears obsolete for many, so too the term *network* has become perhaps the most pervasive metaphor to describe a range of phenomena, desires, and practices in contemporary information societies. The refrain one hears on networks in recent years goes something like this: fluidity, ephemerality, transitory, innovative, flows, nonlinear, decentralized, value-adding, creative, flexible, open, risk-taking, reflexive, informal, individualized, intense, transformative, and so on. Many of these words are used interchangeably as metaphors, concepts, and descriptions. Increasingly, there is a desperation evident in research on new information and communication technologies (ICTs) that manifests in the form of empirical research. Paradoxically, much of this research consists of methods and epistemological frameworks that render the mobility and abstraction of information in terms of stasis (Rossiter 2003a; 2003b).

Governments have found that the network refrain appeals to their neoliberal sensibilities, which search for new rhetorics to substitute the elimination of state infrastructures with the logic of individualized self-formation within third way style networks of "social capital" (Giddens 1998; Latham 2001, 62–100).[1] Research committees at university and national levels see networks as offering the latest promise of an economic utopia in which research practice synchronically models the dynamic movement of finance capital, yet so often the outcomes of research ventures are based upon the reproduction of preexisting research clusters and the maintenance of their hegemony for institutions and individuals with ambitions of legitimacy within the prevailing doxas (Cooper 2002; Marginson and Considine 2000). Telephone companies and cable television "providers" revel in their capacity to flaunt a communications system that is not so much a network but a heterogenous mass of audiences-consumers-users connected by the content and services of private media oligopolies (Van Dijk 1999, 62–70; Flew 2002, 17–21; Schiller 1999, 37–88). Activists pursue techniques of simultaneous disaggregation and consolidation via online organization in their efforts to mobilize opposition and actions in the form of mutable affinities against the corporatization of everyday life (Juris 2004; Lovink 2003, 194–223; Lovink and Schneider, 2004; Meikle, 2002). The U.S. military-entertainment complex enlists strategies of organized distribution of troops and weaponry on battlefields defined by unpredictability and chaos while maintaining the spectacle of control across the vectors of news media (De Landa 1991; Der Derian 2001; Wark 1994, 1–46). The standing reserve of human misery sweeps up the remains of daily horror.

Theorists and artists of new media are not immune to these prevailing discourses, and reproduce similar network homologies in their valorization of open, decentralized, distributed, egalitarian, and emergent socio-technical forms. In so doing, the discursive and sociotechnical form of networks is attributed an ontological status. The so-called openness, fluidity, and contingency of networks is rendered in essentialist terms that function to elide the complexities and contradictions that comprise the uneven spatiotemporal dimensions and material practices of networks. Similarly, the force of the "constitutive outside" is frequently dismissed by media and cultural theorists in favor of delirious discourses of openness and horizontality. Just as *immanence* has been a key metaphor to describe the logic of informationalization (Rossiter 2004), so can it be used to describe networks. To put it in a nutshell, the technics of networks can be described thus: if you can sketch a diagram of relations in which connections are "external to their terms" (per David Hume and Gilles Deleuze), then you get a picture of a network model.

Whatever the peculiarities the network refrain may take, there is a predominant tendency to overlook the ways in which networks are produced by regimes of power, economies of desire, and the restless rhythms of global capital. How, I wonder, might the antagonisms peculiar to these varied and more often than not incommensurate political situations of informationality be formulated in terms of a political theory of networks? From a theoretical and practical point of view, how might organized networks be defined as new institutional forms of informationalism? Given that institutions throughout history function to organize social relations, what distinguishes the organized network as an institution from its modern counterparts? Obviously there are differences along lines of horizontal versus vertical, distributed versus contained, decentralized versus centralized, bureaucratic reason versus database processing, and so on. But what else is there?

It is not sufficient to identify basic structural differences without also attending to the ways in which network dynamics are conditioned by the combinatory logic of "the political" as it is shaped by materialities of knowledge and modalities of expression. At stake here is a question of epistemology and its conditions of possibility, of how techniques of intelligibility are ordered and acquire variable layers of status and capacities to effect change. To this end, institutional settings function as an enabling force. They provide a framework and set of resources from which emergent idioms of expression can be organized in ways that offer the possibility of sustainability and renewal—something that has not, for instance, been a feature of most tactical media interventions. And for this reason, I maintain that the primary political strategy for networks at the current conjuncture is to engage in the invention of new institutional forms. This essay asserts the need for a strategic turn if the multitudes are to address the problematics of scale and sustainability: *the situation of informational politics.*

The challenge for a politically active networked culture is to make strategic use of new communications media in order to create new institutions of possibility. Such sociotechnical formations will take on the characteristics of organized networks—distributive, nonlinear, situated, and project-based—in order to create self-sustaining media ecologies that are simply not on the map of established political and cultural institutions. As Gary Genosko (2003, 33) asserts, "the real task is to find the institutional means to incarnate new modes of subjectification while simultaneously avoiding the slide into bureaucratic sclerosis." Such a view also augurs well for the life of networks as they subsist within the political logic of informationality that is constituted by the force of the outside.

Networks and the Limits of Liberal Democracy

A network doesn't come out of nowhere. One of the key challenges that networks present is the possibility of new institutional formations that want to make a political, social, and cultural difference within the socio-technical logic of networks. It's not yet clear what shape these institutions will take. To fall back into the crumbling security of traditional, established institutions is not an option. The network logic is increasingly the normative mode of organizing sociotechnical relations in advanced economies, and this impacts upon both the urban and rural poor within those countries as well as those in economically developing countries. So, the traditional institution is hardly a place of escape for those wishing to hide from the logic of networks.

A degree of centralization and hierarchization seems essential for a network to be characterized as organized. Can the network thus be characterized as an "institution," or might it need to acquire additional qualities? Is institutional status even desirable for a network that aspires to intervene in debates on critical Internet research and culture? How does an organized network help us redefine our understanding of what an institution might become? Moreover, what is the political logic peculiar to organized networks? This is the primary question I address in this section, and in order to do so I develop the concept of *nonrepresentative democracy* via a critique of liberal democracy.

Liberal democracy is predicated on an articulation between a constituency of citizens and elected representatives. This articulation has eroded in recent years with the advent of the neoliberal state, which inculcates not so much citizens but consumer-subjects into the corporate-state nexus. The ambivalence that emerges around the composition of political constituencies or subjectivities has been the topic of recent debate associated with Italian political philosophers and activist movements. Paolo Virno (2004) distinguishes between the "multitude" (a plurality) and the "people" (a unity). He sees the former as the basis for a politics that does not involve the transfer or delegation of power (decision making, for example) to the sovereign, which is the model of representative politics through the mechanism of voting at elections. To varying degrees, such a model has functioned as a technique of organizing social and economic relations within the architecture of the state. But to transpose such a model over to ICT-based networks is necessarily weak, since the architectonic arrangement is composed of very different variables, dynamics, forces, spaces, and the like.

To put it bluntly, it is not possible to speak of democracy as a representative, consensus-based politics in the environment of ICT-based networks. In both a practical and theoretical sense, advocates of "e-democracy" are investing in a phantasm with their belief that the central principles of representative democracy (citizenship, participation, equality, transparency, etc.) can be transposed into the realm of networks. For a start, citizenship is a concept and practice coemergent with the state form. Networks are not states. Therefore, in order to think democracy within networks, it is necessary to develop in conceptual and practical ways idioms for non- or postrepresentative politics. Such a task does not abandon the concept or possibility of democracy, but recognizes that democracy is an ongoing project that, in a historical sense, is an idiom that has undergone numerous transformations. In order to develop a concept of nonrepresentative democracy immanent to networks of communication, the work of Chantal Mouffe is, I think, helpful to engage, particularly in terms of her elaboration of "the political" as a field of antagonistic struggles.

Mouffe argues that *agonistic* democracy consists of that which acknowledges the power-legitimation processes of "politics" conditioned by the possibility of "struggle between adversaries" as distinct from the illegitimacy within deliberative or third way rules of democracy that refuse the "struggle between enemies" (2000, 102–3), which is special to *antagonism* and "the violence that is inherent in sociability" (2000, 35). In her recent book *On the Political* (2005), Mouffe both summarizes and develops her thesis on agonistic democracy outlined in *The Democratic Paradox* (2000). In *The Democratic Paradox*, Mouffe presents a compelling (if somewhat repetitive) critique of third way politics and rational consensus models of liberal democracy (per Jürgen Habermas and John Rawls) in terms of the fundamental contradictions within those political idioms: namely, a rhetoric of tolerance and pluralism underpinned by numerous forms and techniques of exclusion inherent within rational consensus models of democracy. Mouffe argues that rational consensus, deliberative models of democracy ultimately fail due to their disengagement with "the political," or field of antagonisms that underpin sociality. With Ernesto Laclau, her call has been for a radical democracy—one that takes antagonism as a condition of possibility for democracy. She argues for an agonistic process whereby a plurality of interests, demands, discourses, practices, and forces procure a space of legitimacy whereby antagonisms are able to be addressed—not for the purpose of transcendence or consensus, but for the purpose of acknowledging that incommensurabilities and dissent are inherent to the politics of sociality.

My critique of Mouffe is based on the limits of her argument when it comes to thinking politics in relation to networks articulated by digital communications media or ICTs. Her model of radical democracy is premised on political institutions of the state as the primary institutional framework for addressing "the political." The network models of sociality made possible by ICTs present new forms of sociotechnical systems, or what I am calling *emergent institutional forms of organized networks*. While I think these networks can be called institutional forms insofar as they have a capacity to organize social relations, they are radically dissimilar to the technics of modern institutional forms such as parliament and auxiliary institutions and departments.

If Mouffe's model of an agonistic democracy is to have any purchase within networked, informational societies, then it is essential to address the ways in which the organization of sociopolitical relations within such a terrain occurs within new institutional forms immanent to the media vectors of communication, and thus sociality. Unless Mouffe's thesis is recast in ways that address the political situation of informational networks in terms of emergent institutions, her advancement of an agonistic democracy whose condition of existence is premised on the persistence of political institutional forms within the space of second nature is one that will remain fixed within an image of nostalgia.[2] In effect, then, a process of translation is required in order to resituate Mouffe's agonistic model of adversaries within the "postinstitutional" terrain of networks. Such work can benefit from considering how Mouffe's notions of "politics" and "the political" operate as constitutive forces within networks.

Networks are predisposed toward a grammar of uncertain potentialities. The traffic in expression across networks comprise the ontic level of communication, which Mouffe (2005, 8–9) and Laclau (2005, 70–71, 87) associate with "politics" as distinct from the ontological dimension of "the political," which "concerns the very way in which society is instituted" (Mouffe 2005, 9). The ensemble of practices, actions, and discourses—or what I am calling *expression*—is a field of competing interests, desires, and demands that undergo processes of translation of "the political." Conflict and dispute are not excluded from expression, as the deliberative model would have it, so much as constitute the very possibility of expression. In a negative sense, the uncertainty of networks arises in part from an incapacity to manage such tensions. At this point the network may self-destruct (see Lovink 2003, 121–26). Mailing lists, for example, are renowned for their inability to deal with the egoistically motivated habits of "trolls" whose primary mission is to exploit the vulnerability of list communities that aspire to principles of openness and tolerance. These are nice virtues, but have proven time and again to be barriers to decision making. The deliberation that typically follows interventions by trolls ends up being the focus of attention and does nothing to advance any political or cultural project of networks. Frequently list members will get bored and unsubscribe. Those lists that do undertake online elections in an effective way—and here, I'm thinking of a mailing list like the Association of Internet Researchers[3]—do not resemble what I would call networks as political technologies and are not the settings for engagements with adversaries as a process of sociopolitical transformation. Representative democracy in online settings results in nothing more than the reproduction of a status quo.

The development of new institutional forms immanent to the media of communication would, I maintain, provide a stabilizing effect for networks insofar as a limit horizon is established that organizes the sociality of networks in ways that go beyond the automated and enculturated protocols and conventions one may associate with mailing lists, for example. A limit horizon operates as a necessary antidote to the dominant assumption (and indeed valorization) of networks as spaces of fluid, ephemeral, fleeting association and exchange (see Lash 2002). Limits, moreover, are established through the operation of the constitutive outside (Rossiter 2004), which is a process of engaging "the political" as a complex of tensions through which exteriorities (other networks, NGOs, universities, intellectual property rights, government policies, exploitation of labor power, geopolitics of information, gender and ethnic differences, etc.) are present within a network of relations as an "affirmation of a difference" (Mouffe 2005, 15).[4]

In the case of organized networks, this affirmation, however, is not as Mouffe would have it, "a precondition for the existence of any identity" (15), since organized networks are not the kind of institutional forms that correspond with "the creation of a 'we'" (15), which is a collective identity found in institutional settings such as the political party or social forms such as "the people." While I acknowledge Laclau's understanding (which Mouffe would share) of collective identities such as "the people" as "the emergence of a unity out of heterogeneity [that] presupposes the establishment of equivalential logics and the production of empty signifiers" (2005, 241)—in other words, a complex of differential relations that coalesce as a unicity ("chain of empty signifiers") in order to stake out a distinction from that which is other—the organized network can never correspond to the logic of "we" or "unity" precisely because it is a sociotechnical form instituted through the logic of immanence and not the logic of the kind of institution embodied in the party-political form of the parliamentary system that Mouffe clings to as the form best able to realize the liberal democratic project as one of democratic pluralism. Mine is not a rejection of liberal democracy per se, but a recognition of its structural, material limits as a representational form and its incompatibility with the technics of communication and the organization of sociality as found in networks.[5] That said, my position does amount to a rejection if liberal democracy cannot undergo a transformation beyond a representational form.

In advocating an adversarial model of agonistic democracy, Mouffe insists that "very important socio-economic and political transformations, with radical implications, are possible within the context of liberal democratic institutions" (2005, 33). In the case of networks we have already gone beyond those settings and modes of social organization. Are we to then abandon any project that seeks to institute networks as political technologies? My argument, of course, is no. The challenge is to imagine and enact a nonrepresentative democracy whose technics of organization are internal to the logic of networks. Such a project calls for the invention of new institutional forms external to the corporate-state apparatus. These new forms are neither purely local, nor are they exclusively global. Rather, they subsist as proliferating sociotechnical forms between micro and macro dimensions of politics and territorial scales, defining their limits according to the contingency of the event.

With organized networks, there is no possibility of representational democracy due to the architectonic properties of immanent forms of sociopolitical organization. Instead, we find the potential for post- or nonrepresentational forms of democracy. And contrary to Laclau's (2004, 27; and 2005, 240, 242) argument against Michael Hardt and Antonio Negri (2000), the logic of immanence does not aim for a "universal *desertion*" or "eclipse" of politics in favor of some kind of postpolitical liberation.[6] The logic of immanence does not negate the role of externalities or "the exterior." Externalities are elements that coalesce as a concrete arrangement whose relations are conditioned by the force of the constitutive outside. This is a process by which the potentiality of immanence is actualized as particular forms and practices (see Deleuze 1988). Laclau (2004, 27) is correct in his critique of Hardt and Negri's claim that with Empire there is "no more outside" or external enemy and thus no space of opposition, but he is mistaken, in my view, to assert that the logic of immanence is unable to account for social antagonisms (Laclau 2005, 245). Since the constitutive outside is integral to the logic of immanence, so too is the potentiality of tensions, struggles, and conflicts as they emerge within the plane of organization or actualization (Rossiter 2004).

Similarly, nonrepresentative democracy does not assume to have eclipsed social antagonisms that underpin the field of "the political." As discussed above, the force of immanence as a population of potentialities is released through the operation of the constitutive outside. This dynamic is comprised of tensions and conflict, and as such can be understood in terms of "the political." Nor is nonrepresentative democracy equivalent to the "post-political" perspectives advocated by theorists such as Ulrich Beck, Anthony Giddens, and Scott Lash.[7] Rather, nonrepresentative systems are conditioned simultaneously by the sociotechnical impossibility of networks to represent and the decline of the civil society–state relation as a complex of representative institutions and procedures engaged in the management of labor-power and organization of social life. While networks may have members and participants, they do not have constituencies as such who are organized around the logic of a body politic. There is no unity or identity such as "the people" or, as Laclau would put it, no heterogeneity articulated as a chain of equivalences, that seeks to have its interests and demands represented by an individual or advocacy body. Individuals may choose to contribute to the expansion and proliferation of the network, they may subsist as potentialities waiting to become unleashed, and indeed they may decide to institute representative mechanisms of governance. But when this happens the network dissembles as a grammar of uncertainty and evacuates the space of "the political."

The concept of the organized network is also distinct from what Mouffe (2005, 95) terms "organized networks of global civil society and business" undertaking the task of realizing a cosmopolitan democracy—a position that Mouffe critiques for its oversight of "the political." Unlike the global civil society networks described by Mouffe, organized networks are not new global institutions but, more modestly and pragmatically, new institutions whose technics are modulated by the spatiotemporal dynamics of the network. As I go on to show in the section that follows, the key model adopted by global civil society movements has been that of "multistakeholderism." This model, I argue, is incompatible with the logic of networks precisely because it is predicated on the logic of representation.

Multistakeholderism and the Architecture of Net Politics

My basic argument is that networks are at a turning point and their capacity to exist depends on developing technics of organization. And it's here that I think there may be opportunities for networks to lever the discursive legitimacy that has arisen for civil society networks at the World Summit on the Information Society (WSIS). This is where specific case studies of networks and how they are operating in a post-WSIS environment at subnational, transregional levels becomes helpful. Those directly involved in project development—frequently, NGOs—have had much experience, but NGOs seem to be coming under increasing pressure as they have moved into a more substantive role as political actors within a neoliberal paradigm that grants legitimacy to those who can function as "external providers." The multistakeholder model doesn't seem to me to be one that enables networks (which I would distinguish from NGOs) to negotiate the complexities of information economies, societies, and the like.

After the closing ceremony of the WSIS, the nagging question that attends all summits remains largely unaddressed: what changes will happen at local, subnational levels? The WSIS process has resulted in two key outcomes for civil society: (1) a hitherto nonexistent discursive legitimacy at the supranational level for civil society values, needs and interests as they relate to the political economy and technics of ICTs; and (2) a cache of resources for dealing with transinstitutional relations made possible by the multistakeholderism experience. The primary post-WSIS challenge will be the extent to which NGOs and civil society movements are able to exploit the newfound discursive legitimacy at local, intraregional levels (Rossiter 2006). At the scalar level, this is a process of renationalizing what at the moment remains a denationalized discourse. Such a problematic is one engaged by indigenous sovereignty movements and human rights practioners and advocates for many years now (Rossiter 2002). In the case of the WSIS the difference is that the political economy of ICTs has expanded the complexity of life understood as communicative relation articulated by media forms.

Since different institutions have different temporal rhythms, the movement of discourse across institutional scales instantiates antagonisms peculiar to "the political." Irrespective of whatever agreements are made in the form of final recommendations, the fact remains that governments are highly unlikely to legislate WSIS policy because their bureaucracies are unable to deal with the complexity of issues that have emerged from the WSIS debates. Perhaps there might have been more concrete outcomes if WSIS debates had somehow restricted the discussion to technical issues alone, but that would require disassociating technical issues from political and economic issues. Furthermore, any national legislation that might eventuate from the WSIS proceedings is faced with the dilemma of policy that has already been made redundant by economies of speed that attend the interrelations between technological innovation and social transformation.

What, then, is to be salvaged from the WSIS for civil society, and what is the relation to net politics? For the most part, multistakeholderism is celebrated as a form of democracy in action. Wolfgang Kleinwächter (2005) captures its spirit:

> The principle of Multistakeholderism is a new and innovative concept for the global diplomacy of the 21st century. While the concept as such is still vague and undefined, non-governmental stakeholders from the private sector and from civil society are becoming step by step an integral part of policy making in the information age. . . . The WSIS process has demonstrated that when the existing legal framework has to be filled with new subject related global policies, a new triangular relationship between governments, private sector and civil society is emerging. These relationships are not hierarchical by nature but will be organized in form of networks around concrete issues. It will depend from the concrete substance of an issue, how the triangular is designed and how relevant trilateral governance mechanism will be organized. (2005)

Absent from Kleinwächter's formalistic celebration of multistakeholderism is the unruliness of "the political." Aligned with the politics of advocacy, Kleinwächter is not able to address the tensions internal to the logic of multistakeholderism as an architecture for relations between international and local NGOs and grassroots organizations.[7] However effective multistakeholderism may be in policy making for an information society, such policy proposals are largely ineffectual unless they can infiltrate the complexity of institutions whose capacities are organized according to incommensurate temporal speeds. Again, this is a problematic of scale and translation.

Yet perhaps the success of multistakeholderism should be measured as an accumulation of resources for negotiating issues among a range of institutional, political, and social actors, as Kleinwächter suggests. Such an ambition is crucially dependent on the capacity of actors to collectively retain institutional memories. Assuming individuals might transcend their institutional codes of secrecy, such a feature long vacated the realm of modern, industrial institutional forms of the state department and corporate firm with the onset of post-Fordism and new forms of flexible organization and mobility, to say nothing of the fragility of networks and their general condition of disorganization.

Multistakeholderism is too closely aligned to the fantasies of deliberative, rational consensus forms of democracy. The emptiness of multistakeholderism as an architecture of change invites new forms of managing the politics of information. An alternative model that is beginning to emerge is that of the organized network—a form whose logic of organization is internal to the dynamics of the media of communication (see also Rossiter 2005). Like the NGO, the organized network is expected to answer to demands of transparency and accountability. Like the Internet, the organized network is mistakenly assumed to adopt a decentralized, horizontal, distributed structure of communication. The organized network is antithetical to both of these presuppositions.

This is not to advocate some kind of return to the archaic form of party politics, as Slavoj Žižek would have it. But it is to suggest that in order for organized networks to undertake planning and development of projects and intervene in prevailing debates, a strategic—rather than tactical—architecture is required. This is where the issue of sustainability transfigures both the discourse of development and the discourse of networks. The politics of information is common to both these realms. Sustainability requires a business model.[7] NGOs have extensive experience at obtaining funding—much more so than networks associated with tactical media activists. The latter, on the other hand, have a high degree of media literacy vis-à-vis the political economy of information, the programming of code, and the performance of critique from within the spectacle of media systems. Collaboration between NGOs and tactical media practitioners could be one of those instances of mutual benefit and scalar enhancement.

While funding possibilities may arise from global relations in the form of donors, business activities, and aid, the social and political force of networks is predominantly local or intraregional. Herein lies a tension of translation internal to networks as they traverse scales for different purposes. And this is where the demands of transparency, accountability, and representation become distinct in the form of externally imposed conditions and internally generated expectations. The management of these dual constituencies brings enormous pressure upon networks and highlights the manner in which "democracy" has multiple meanings determined by the situation of actors. Accommodating these kinds of expectations and demands can absorb huge amounts of energy, time, and structural-technical reconfiguration (online voting, anyone?). Democracy, here, becomes equivalent to destruction.

Mechanisms of accountability and representation conflict with the speed of capital, the flow of information, and can slow the development of projects. Yet they are also sources of trust—the foundation of networks. Can trust, then, be constituted within nonrepresentative sociotechnical systems in alternative ways? Just as "democracy" as a universal principle is rendered dysfunctional when it meets the contingencies of the particular, the question of trust can only be answered on a case by case basis that considers the taxonomy of activities and relations peculiar to any network. But taxonomies are also not enough. Networks cannot be contained, even though they have limits. Similarly, trust cannot be measured, and instead resonates as an indeterminacy within the fluctuating rhythms of network ecologies.

Conclusion

The regimes of value internal to the operation of organized networks, as distinct from networked organizations, are only just beginning to surface. In the case of organized networks, discourses, practices and values are coextensive with the media of communication in the first instance. Networked organizations, by contrast, are a predominantly modern, industrial institutional form. Hence, the role of communications media is secondary to the technics of organization instantiated through the architectonics of bricks and mortar.

In a most reductive sense, the vertical systems of communication within modern institutional forms are the primary reason why so many institutions have had difficulties with the transition into network societies. The TCP/IP (transmission control protocol/Internet protocol) standards for the Internet enable distributed, horizontal forms of communication. This is in contrast to the domain name system (DNS), which functions as the vertical axis of governance for digital technologies using TCP/IP standards. Thus the kind of disputes and tensions that have developed out of the WSIS process, to take one recent example, and debates around Internet governance more broadly (see Rossiter 2006), are substantially different from those found among institutions that operate historically within a modern institutional system.

Put simply, the scene of "the political" in the case of organized networks is coextensive with the media of communication, whereas the boundaries of "the political" do not extend to those modern institutional forms that have been forced to upgrade their networking capacities. Moreover, the gap between these two institutional dynamics is an exemplary instance of what Jean-François Lyotard has called "the *différend*" (1984; 1988), or "phrases of dispute."

In other words, there's a need to think democracy beyond the idiom of representation and consensus—two of the basic principles that have been carried over to the multistakeholder model of managing policy debates among government, business, and civil society stakeholders at the WSIS. NGOs are also are expected to adopt such practices, along with those of accountability and transparency. Again, my view is that such primary components of representative democracy in its state form do not correspond with the dynamics of networks, hence the need for a nonrepresentative idiom of politics. What the particularities of such a model might consist of is going to vary according to situation, needs, forces, processes, interests, demands, and so on of specific networks, but at the same time they are going to be affected by larger macro and structural forces associated with the political economy of ICTs and policies around Internet governance.

One could hypothesize that the ideology of neoliberalism is symptomatic of the problem of institutional forms within a networked, informational paradigm. Neoliberalism is responsive to the problematic of governance in an informatized society that has seen an intensification of abstraction in systems of production and social life. Organized networks emerge within a neoliberal era of governance, yet at the structural level they present the horizon of postneoliberalism, since their technics of communication and organization are beyond the reformist agenda associated with neoliberal governance. As new institutional forms, organized networks create the possibility of new subjectivities that do not correspond with the modern politicoeconomic subjects of either the citizen or the consumer. Similarly, the concept and sociotechnical form of organized networks invites a rethinking of notions of civil society. Issues such as these will only become amplified as the logic of organized networks materializes as a new institutional form.

Notes

1. See Agre (2003) for a brief genealogy of the term *social capital*; see Tronti (1973) for an autonomist deployment of the term.
2. Not even when she is participating with political activists addressing the theme of infopolitics does Mouffe rethink her argument on institutions, as on the occasion of the "Dark Market: Infopolitics, Electronic Media and Democracy in Times of Crisis" conference held at Public Netbase in Vienna in 2002. For full documentation, including Mouffe's (2002) paper "Which Democracy in a Post-Political Age?" see <http://darkmarkets.t0.or.at>.
3. <http://aoir.org>.
4. While there are significant differences, the constitutive outside is an operation similar to what systems theorists and cyberneticists would term "organizational closure" or "noise." See Rossiter (2003a).
5. Those who entertain online systems of voting or "e-democracy" believe they are transposing the central tenets of representative liberal democracy into "virtual" settings. Far from it. Such projects highlight the evacuation of adversaries engaged in a hegemonic process, and instead embody the very failure of representative systems to address the tensions that underscore sociality.
6. Mouffe (2005, 107–15) makes a similar argument to Laclau, claiming the "the constitutive character of antagonism is denied" (107).
7. For a critique of postpolitical theorists, see Mouffe (2005, 35–63). For critiques of Lash's *Critique of Information* (2001), see Hassan (2002), Sandywell (2003) and Rossiter (2004).
8. For a brief outline of some of the tensions peculiar to multistakeholderism as the preferred model of governance at WSIS, see Van der Krogt (2005).

9. I recently outlined some of the alternative funding models that have been proposed in the creative industries in the United Kingdom and the Netherlands. While I'm critical of these models, which include a financing stream heavily dependent on regulating telephone companies and Internet service providers and the expansion of collecting agencies as intermediaries for media productions commissioned under a Creative Commons license, they nonetheless are indicative of a discussion that organized networks can learn from if they are going to have any possibility of scaling up their operations. For a video recording of my talk "Creative Industries, Organized Networks and Open Economies," see <http://libmedia.ln.edu.hk/media3/www/lib/04-05-3/rossiter050524.htm>; an abstract is available at <http://www.ln.edu.hk/ihss/crd/cm200405.htm>.

References

Agre, Phillip E. 2002. "Real-Time Politics: The Internet and the Political Process." *Information Society* 18, no. 5:311–31; also available online at <http://polaris.gseis.ucla.edu/pagre/real-time.html>.

Cooper, Simon. 2002. "Post Intellectuality? Universities and the Knowledge Industry." Pp. 207–32 in *Scholars and Entrepreneurs: the University in Crisis*, ed. Simon Cooper, John Hinkson, and Geoff Sharp. Fitzroy, Melbourne Arena.

De Landa, Manuel. 1991. *War in the Age of Intelligent Machines*. New York: Zone.

Der Derian, James. 2001. *Virtuous War: Mapping the Military-Industrial-Media-Entertainment Network*. Boulder, CO: Westview.

Flew, Terry. 2002. *New Media: An Introduction*. Oxford: Oxford University Press.

Genosko, Gary. 2003. "Félix Guattari: Towards a Transdisciplinary Metamethodology." *Angelaki* 8, no. 1:29–140.

Giddens, Anthony. 1998. *The Third Way: The Renewal of Social Democracy*. Cambridge: Polity.

Hassan, Robert. 2003. "Embrace Your Fate." *Continuum: Journal of Media and Cultural Studies* 17, no. 1:105-09.

Hardt, Michael and Negri, Antonio. 2000. *Empire*. Cambridge, MA: Harvard University Press.

Juris, Jeffrey. 2004. "Digital Age Activism: Anti-Corporate Globalization and the Cultural Politics of Transnational Networking." Ph.D. diss., University of California–Berkeley.

Kleinwächter, Wolfgang. 2005. "Civil Society and Global Diplomacy in the 21st Century: The Case of WSIS or, from Input to Impact?" February, Version 1.0.

Laclau, Ernesto. 2004. "Can Immanence Explain Social Struggles?" Pp. 21–30 in *Empire's New Clothes: Reading Hardt and Negri*, ed. Paul A. Passavant and Jodi Dean. New York and London: Routledge.

———. 2005. *On Populist Reason*. London: Verso.

Lash, Scott. 2002. *Critique of Information*. London: Sage.

Latham, Mark. 2001. *What did you Learn Today? Creating an Education Revolution*, Crows Nest, NSW.: Allen and Unwin.

Latour, Bruno. 1993. *We Have Never Been Modern*, trans. Catherine Porter. Cambridge, MA: Harvard University Press.

Lovink, Geert. 2002. *Dark Fiber: Tracking Critical Internet Culture*, Cambridge, MA: MIT Press.

———. 2003. *My First Recession: Critical Internet Culture in Transition*, Rotterdam: V2_/NAi.

Lovink, Geert, and Florian Schneider. 2004, 29 February. "Notes on the State of Networking," posting to nettime mailing list, http://www.nettime.org. See also *Make Worlds* no. 4, online at <http://www.makeworlds.org>.

Lyotard, Jean-François. 1984. "The *Différend*, the Referent, and the Proper Name," trans. Georges van den Abbeele. *Diacritics* 14, no. 3:4–14.

———. 1988. *The Différend: Phrases in Dispute*, trans. Georges van den Abbeele. Minneapolis: University of Minnesota Press.

Marginson, Simon, and Mark Considine. 2000. *The Enterprise University: Power, Governance and Reinvention in Australia*. Cambridge: Cambridge University Press.

Meikle, Graham. 2002. *Future Active: Media Activism and the Internet*. Sydney: Pluto.

Mouffe, Chantal. 2000. *The Democratic Paradox*. London: Verso.

———. 2002. "Which Democracy in a Post-Political Age?" Paper presented at Dark Markets: Infopolitics, Electronic Media and Democracy in Times of Crisis, international conference by Public Netbase/t0, Muesumsplatz, Vienna, 3–4 October; available online at <http://darkmarkets.t0.or.at/materials/abstract_mouffe.htm>.

———. 2005. *On the Political* London: Routledge.

Rossiter, Ned. 2002. "Modalities of Indigenous Sovereignty, Transformations of the Nation-State, and Intellectual Property Regimes." Borderlands E-Journal: New Spaces in the Humanities 1, no. 2; available online at <http://www.borderlandsejournal.adelaide.edu.au/issues/vol1no2. html>.

———. 2003a. "Processual Media Theory." *symploke* 11, nos. 1–2:104–31.

———. 2003b. "Report: Creative Labour and the Role of Intellectual Property." *Fibreculture Journal* 1; available online at <http://journal.fibreculture.org/issue1/issue1_rossiter. html>.

———. 2004. "Creative Industries, Comparative Media Theory, and the Limits of Critique from Within." *Topia: A Canadian Journal of Cultural Studies* 11:21–48.

———. 2005. "Virtuosity, Processual Democracy and Organized Networks." *Cultural Studies Review* 11, no. 2:110–28.

———. 2006. "The World Summit on the Information Society and Organized Networks as New Civil Society Movements. Pp. 97–116 in *Beyond the WSIS: Towards A Sustainable Agenda for the Future Information Society*, ed. Jan Servaes and Nico Carpentier. Bristol, England: Intellect.

Sandywell, Barry. 2003. "Metacritique of Information: On Scott Lash's *Critique of Information*." *Theory, Culture & Society* 20, no. 1:109–22.

Schiller, Dan. 1999. *Digital Capitalism: Networking the Global Market System*. Cambridge, MA: MIT Press.

Tronti, Mario. 1977. "Social Capital." *Telos* 17:98–121.

Van der Krogt, Stijn. 2005, 27 May. "On Multi-stakeholderism" [sent by Geert Lovink]. Posting to incommunicado mailing list at <http://incommunicado.info/mailinglist>.

Van Dijk, Jan. 1999. *The Network Society: Social Aspects of New Media*, trans. Leontine Spoorenberg. London: Sage.

Virno, Paolo. 2004. *A Grammar of the Multitude*, trans. James Cascaito, Isabella Bertoletti and Andrea Casson, with foreword by Sylvère Lotringer. New York: Semiotext(e).

Wark, McKenzie. 1994. *Virtual Geography: Living With Global Media Events*. Bloomington: Indiana University Press.

CHAPTER 3

Power Laws, Weblogs, and Inequality

CLAY SHIRKEY

A persistent theme among people writing about the social aspects of weblogging is to note (and usually lament) the rise of an A-list, a small set of webloggers who account for a majority of the traffic in the weblog world.[1] This complaint follows a common pattern we've seen with multiuser domains, bulletin board systems, and online communities like Echo and the WELL. A new social system starts, and seems delightfully free of the elitism and cliquishness of the existing systems. Then, as the new system grows, problems of scale set in. Not everyone can participate in every conversation. Not everyone gets to be heard. Some core group seems more connected than the rest of us, and so on.

Prior to recent theoretical work on social networks, the usual explanations invoked individual behaviors: some members of the community had sold out, the spirit of the early days was being diluted by the newcomers, and so on. We now know that these explanations are wrong, or at least beside the point. What matters is this: diversity plus freedom of choice creates inequality, and the greater the diversity, the more extreme the inequality.

In large systems where many people are free to choose between many options, a small subset of the whole will get a disproportionate amount of traffic (or attention, or income) even if no members of the system actively work toward such an outcome. This has nothing to do with moral weakness, selling out, or any other psychological explanation. The very act of choosing, spread widely enough and freely enough, creates a power law distribution.

A Predictable Imbalance

Power law distributions, the shape that has spawned a number of catch-phrases like the "80/20 rule" and the "winner-take-all society," are finally being understood clearly enough to be useful. For much of the last century, investigators have been finding power law distributions in human systems. The economist Vilfredo Pareto has observed that wealth follows a "predict-able imbalance," with 20 percent of the population holding 80 percent of the wealth.[2] The linguist George Zipf has observed that word frequency falls in a power law pattern, with a small number of high frequency words (*I, of, the*), a moderate number of common words (*book, cat, cup*), and a huge number of low frequency words (*peripatetic, hypognathous*).[3] Jacob Nielsen observed power law distributions in website page views, and so on.[4]

We are all so used to bell curve distributions that power law distributions can seem odd. The shape of Figure 3.1, several hundred weblogs ranked by number of inbound links, is roughly a power law distribution. Of the 433 listed weblogs, the top two sites accounted for fully 5 percent of the inbound links between them. (They were InstaPundit.com and AndrewSullivan.com, unsurprisingly.) The top dozen sites (less than 3 percent of the total) accounted for 20 percent of the inbound links, and the top fifty weblogs (not quite 12 percent) accounted for 50 percent of such links.

The inbound link data is just an example: power law distributions are ubiquitous. Yahoo Groups mailing lists ranked by subscribers is a power law distribution (see Fig. 3.2). LiveJournal users ranked by friends is also a power law distribution (see Fig. 3.3). Jason Kottke has graphed the power law distribution of Technorati link data.[5] If you run a web site with more than a couple dozen pages, pick any time period where the traffic amounted to at least one thousand page views and you will find that both the page views themselves and the traffic from the referring sites will fol-low power laws.

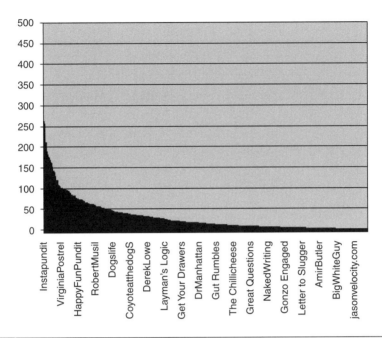

Figure 3.1 Weblogs (433) arranged in rank order by number of inbound links. The data is drawn from N. Z. Bear's 2002 work on the blogosphere ecosystem. A more current version of this project can be found at <http://www.myelin. co.nz/ecosystem/.>.

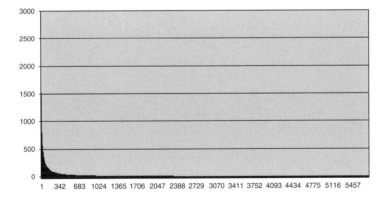

Figure 3.2 All mailing lists in the Yahoo Groups Television category, ranked by number of subscribers. Data from September 2002.

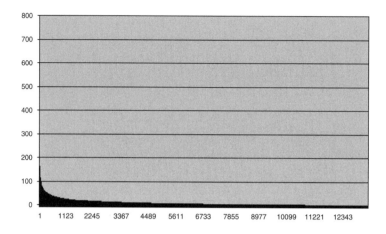

Figure 3.3 LiveJournal users ranked by number of friends listed. Data from March 2002.

Rank Hath Its Privileges

The basic shape is simple—in any system sorted by rank, the value for the "Nth" position will be 1/N. For whatever is being ranked—income, links, traffic—the value of second place will be half that of first place, and tenth place will be one-tenth of first place. (There are other, more complex formulas that make the slope more or less extreme, but they all relate to this Nth = 1/N effect.) We've seen this shape in many systems. What've we've been lacking, until recently, is a theory to go with these observed patterns.

Now, thanks to a series of breakthroughs in network theory by researchers like Albert-Laszlo Barabasi, Bernardo Huberman, and Duncan Watts, among others—breakthroughs described in their books *Linked*, *The Laws of the Web*, and *Six Degrees*—we know that power law distributions tend to arise in social systems where many people express their preferences among many options.[6] We also know that as the number of options rise, the curve becomes more extreme. This is a counterintuitive finding—most of us would expect a rising number of choices to flatten the curve, but in fact, increasing the size of the system increases the gap between the number one spot and the median spot.

A second counterintuitive aspect of power laws is that most elements in a power law system are below average, because the curve is so heavily weighted toward the top performers. In Figure 3.1, the average number of inbound links (cumulative links divided by the number of weblogs) is thirty-one. The first weblog below thirty-one links is 142nd on the list, meaning two-thirds of the listed weblogs have a below average number of inbound links. We are so used to the evenness of the bell curve, where the median position has the average value, that the idea of two-thirds of a population being below average sounds strange. (The actual median, 217th of 433, has only fifteen inbound links.)

Freedom of Choice Makes Stars Inevitable

To see how freedom of choice could create such unequal distributions, consider a hypothetical population of a thousand people, each picking their ten favorite weblogs. One way to model such a system is simply to assume that each person has an equal chance of liking each weblog. This distribution would be basically flat—most weblogs will have the same number of people listing it as a favorite. A few weblogs will be more popular than average and a few less popular, of course, but that will be statistical noise. The bulk of the weblogs will be of average popularity, and the highs and lows will not be too far different from this average. In this model, neither the quality of the writing nor other people's choices has any effect; there are no shared tastes, no preferred genres, no effects from marketing or recommendations from friends.

But people's choices do affect one another. If we assume that any weblog chosen by one user is more likely, by even a fractional amount, to be chosen by another user, the system changes dramatically. Alice, the first user, chooses her weblogs unaffected by anyone else, but Bob has a slightly higher chance of liking Alice's weblogs than the others. When Bob is done, any weblog that both he and Alice like has a higher chance of being picked by Carmen, and so on, with a small number of weblogs becoming increasingly likely to be chosen in the future because they were chosen in the past.

Think of this positive feedback as a preference premium. The system assumes that later users come into an environment shaped by earlier users; the 1,001st user will not be selecting weblogs at random, but will rather be affected, even if unconsciously, by the preference premiums built up in the system previously.

Note that this model is mute as to why one weblog might be preferred over another. Perhaps some writing is simply better than average (a preference for quality); perhaps people want the recommendations of others (a preference for marketing); perhaps there is value in reading the same weblogs as your friends (a preference for "solidarity goods," things best enjoyed by a group). It could be all three, or some other effect entirely, and it could be different for different readers and different writers. What matters is that any tendency toward shared opinion in diverse and free systems, however small and for whatever reason, can create power law distributions.

Because it arises naturally, changing this distribution would mean forcing hundreds of thousands of webloggers to link to certain weblogs and to delink others, which would require both global oversight and the application of considerable leverage. Reversing the star system would mean destroying the village in order to save it.

Inequality and Fairness

Given the ubiquity of power law distributions, asking whether there is inequality in the weblog world (or indeed almost any social system) is the wrong question, since the answer will always be yes. The question to ask is, "Is the inequality fair?" Four things suggest that the current inequality in the weblog world is mostly fair. The first, of course, is the freedom in the weblog world in general. It costs nothing to launch a weblog, and there is no vetting process, so the threshold for having a weblog is only infinitesimally larger than the threshold for getting online in the first place. The second is that weblogging is a daily activity. As beloved as Josh Marshall (TalkingPointsMemo.com) or Mark Pilgrim (DiveIntoMark.org) are, they would disappear if they stopped writing, or even cut back significantly. Weblogs are not a good place to rest on one's laurels. Third, the stars exist not because of some cliquish preference for one another, but because of the preference of hundreds of others pointing to them. Their popularity is a result of the kind of distributed approval that it would be hard to fake. Finally, there is no real A-list, because there is no discontinuity. Though explanations of power laws (including the ones here) often focus on numbers like "12 percent of weblogs account for 50 percent of the links," these are arbitrary markers. The largest step function in a power law is between the number one and number two positions, by definition. There is no A-list that is qualitatively different from their nearest neighbors, so any line separating more and less trafficked weblogs is arbitrary.

However, though the inequality is mostly fair now, the system is still young. Once a power law distribution exists, it can take on a certain amount of homeostasis, the tendency of a system to retain its form even against external pressures. Is the weblog world such a system? Are there people who are as talented or deserving as the current stars, but who are not getting anything like the traffic? Doubtless. Will this problem get worse in the future? Yes.

The Median Cannot Hold

Though there are more new webloggers and more new readers every day, most of the new readers are adding to the traffic of the top few weblogs, while most new weblogs are getting below-average traffic, a gap that will grow as the weblog world does. It's not impossible to launch a good new weblog and become widely read, but it's harder than it was last year, and it will be harder still next year. At some point (probably one we've already passed), weblog technology will be seen as a platform for so many forms of publishing, filtering, aggregation, and syndication that weblogging will stop referring to any particularly coherent activity. The terms *weblog* and *blog* will fall into the middle distance, as *home page* and *portal* have—words that used to mean some concrete thing but were stretched by use past the point of meaning. This will happen when head and tail of the power law distribution become so different that we can't think of J. Random Blogger and Glenn Reynolds of Instapundit.com as doing the same thing.

At the head will be webloggers who join the mainstream media (a term meaning "media we've gotten used to.") The transformation here is a simple one from blogger as host and participant in a conversation to blogger as a kind of star attraction in her own right. As her audience grows large, more people link to and read her work than she can possibly read or link to. She won't be able to respond to everyone who wants her attention, that is, who sends her e-mail or comments on her site. The result of these pressures is that she becomes a broadcast outlet, distributing material without participating in most of the conversations about it.

Meanwhile, the long tail of weblogs with few readers will become conversational. In a world where most webloggers get below-average traffic, audience size can't be the only metric for success. LiveJournal had this figured out years ago, by assuming that people would be writing for their friends rather than some impersonal audience. Publishing an essay and having five random people read it is a recipe for disappointment, but publishing an account of your Saturday night and having your five closest friends read it feels like a conversation, especially if they follow up with their own accounts. LiveJournal has an edge on most other weblogging platforms because it can keep far better track of friend and group relationships, but the rise of general weblog tools like Trackback may enable this conversational mode for most weblogs.

In between weblogs-as-mainstream-media and weblogs-as-dinner-conversation will be Blogging Classic, weblogs published by one or a few people, for a moderately-sized audience, with whom the authors have a relatively engaged relationship. Because of the continuing growth of the weblog world, more weblogs in the future will follow this pattern than today. However, these weblogs will be in the minority for both traffic (dwarfed by the mainstream media weblogs) and overall number of weblogs (outnumbered by the conversational weblogs.)

Inequality occurs in large and unconstrained social systems for the same reasons stop-and-go traffic occurs on busy roads, not because it is anyone's goal, but because it is a reliable property that emerges from the normal functioning of the system. The relatively egalitarian distribution of readers in the early years had nothing to do with the nature of weblogs or webloggers. There just weren't enough weblogs to have really unequal distributions. Now there are.

Notes

1. For noting, see <http://www.fawny.org/decon-blog.html>. For lamenting, see <http:// onepotmeal.com/blog/archives/001178.html>.
2. For more on George Zipf and Zipf's Law, see <http://linkage.rockefeller.edu/wli/zipf/>.
3. Jakob Nielsen, "Zipf Curves and Website Popularity," available online at <http://www. useit.com/alertbox/zipf.html>.
4. Jason Kottke, "Weblogs and Power Laws," available online at <http://www.kottke.org/03/ 02/030209weblogs_and_.html>.
5. Albert Laszlo-Barabasi, *Linked* (New York: Plume, 2003); Bernardo A. Huberman, *The Laws of the Web* (Cambridge, MA: MIT Press, 2003); and Duncan J. Watts, *Six Degrees* (New York: W. W. Norton, 2003).

CHAPTER **4**

Openness and Its Discontents

JAMIE KING

The Idea of Openness

Since the founding of the Free Software Foundation in 1985 by Richard Stallman and the Open Source Initiative in 1998 by Eric Raymond, the idea of openness has enjoyed considerable celebrity. Simply understood, open source software is that which is published along with its source code, allowing developers to collaborate, improve upon each other's work, and use the code in their own projects. The cachet of this open model of development has been greatly increased by the high-profile success of GNU-Linux, a piece of Free-Libre and Open Source Software (FLOSS).

Taken together with the distributed composition offered by, for example, the Wiki architecture,[1] and the potential of peer-to-peer networks like Bittorrent and Gnutella,[2] a more nuanced and loose idea of openness has suggested itself as a possible model for other kinds of organization. Felix Stalder of Openflows identifies its key elements as "communal management and open access to the informational resources for production, openness to contributions from a diverse range of users/producers, flat hierarchies, and a fluid organisational structure."[3] This idea of openness is now frequently deployed not only with reference to composing software communities but also to political and cultural groupings. Thus, FLOSS's "self-evident" realization of a "voluntary global community empowered and explicitly authorised to reverse-engineer, learn from, improve and use-validate its own tools and products," seems to indicate that "it has to be taken seriously as a potential source of organising for other realms of human endeavour."[4] Openness appears to be "paradigmatic." Software publisher and guru Tim O'Reilly's presentation at the Reboot conference in 2003, "The Open Source Paradigm Shift," placed FLOSS at the vanguard of a social phenomenon whose time, he said, "had come." Its methods of ad hoc, distributed collaboration constitute a "new paradigm" at a level consistent with the advent of the printing press and movable type.[5]

Such accounts of the sociopolitical pertinence of the FLOSS model are increasingly common, though of fluctuating coherence. A recent essay by activist Florian Schneider and writer Geert Lovink, for example, exhibits the premature desire to collapse FLOSS-style open organization into a series of other political phenomena: "freedom of movement and freedom of communication . . . the everyday struggles of millions of people crossing borders as well as pirating brands, producing generics, writing open source code or using p2p-software."[6] More soberly, Douglas Rushkoff has argued recently in a report for the Demos think tank that "the emergence of the interactive mediaspace may offer a new model for cooperation." He writes,

> The values engendered by our fledgling networked culture may . . . prove quite applicable to the broader challenges of our time and help a world struggling with the impact of globalism, the lure of fundamentalism and the clash of conflicting value systems. . . . One model for the open-ended and participatory process through which legislation might occur in a networked democracy can be found in the open source software movement.[7]

Rushkoff does not try to draw direct parallels between FLOSS and other forms of activity in the manner of Schneider and Lovink, but argues equally problematically that the model used in open source software composing communities could be usefully applied to democratic political organization. A growing willingness to engage with "the underlying code of the democratic process," he contends, "could eventually manifest in a widespread call for revisions to our legal, economic and political structures."[8]

Clearly, the idea of openness has appeal across rather different constituencies—here we have both the reformist liberals and the radicals claiming openness as their ally. Indeed, as information and communication technologies (ICT) theorist Biella Coleman suggests, "the widespread adoption and use of the idea of openness and its profound political impact" is contingent on its peculiarly transpolitical appeal. "FLOSS," she writes, *resists*

> political delineation into the traditional political categories of left, right or center . . . [but] has been embraced by a wide range of people. . . . This has enabled FLOSS to explode from a niche and academic endeavour into a creative sphere of socio-political and technical influence bolstered by the internet.[9]

The broad-church appeal of the idea of openness suggested by FLOSS need not necessarily be a cause for celebration, especially since many of the constituencies making use of it conceive of themselves as fundamentally opposed. Can the idea of openness these divergent constituencies embrace really be the same? And how can it be that they consider it sufficient to their very different aims?

The chief purpose of this chapter is not to answer these questions by examining the "self-evident" truths of open source production. Such examinations are already being carried out in forums like Oekonux and numerous day-to-day empirical studies.[10] Instead, I am interested in the intense political expectation around open organization among diverse elements of the diffuse activist groups that, post-Seattle, have been loosely referred to as the "social movement" or "social movements." I focus on groups within this movement such as People's Global Action, Indymedia, Euraction Hub, and other "nonhierarchized" collectives. I do not have in mind more traditionally structured organizations like the Social Fora, Globalize Resistance, or so-called "Civil Society" non-governmental organizations.

In the social movement thus defined, openness is clearly becoming a constitutive organizing principle, as it connects with the hopes and desires circulating around the idea of the *multitude*, a term whose post-Spinozan renaissance has been secured by Michael Hardt and Antonio Negri's *Empire*. The multitude is a defiantly heterogeneous figure, a collective noun intended to counter the homogenizing violence of terms such as *the people* or *the masses*. For many thinkers in the postautonomist tradition, this multitude is a way of conceiving the revolutionary potential of a new "post-Fordist proletariat" of networked immaterial laborers. In certain circuits within the social movement, pace Schneider and Lovink, FLOSS organization is seen as the technosocial precondition for a newly emerging radical democracy. However tenuous this assemblage may be, it goes some way toward explaining the way in which FLOSS and openness have become quite central rhetorical terms in the struggle to produce an identity for the networked anticapitalist movement. But it is also true that certain characteristics of the idea of openness have genuine organizational influence within the movement. A study of openness in this context is useful in three degrees: first, to the social movement itself, "internally"; second, to "outsiders" wanting to gain a good understanding of "what it is"; and, third, as a critique of those who would seek to represent the movement with, or attempt to manipulate it through, a particular deployment of the idea of openness.

The Revolution Will Be Open Source

It is too easy to make sweeping generalizations about the ways in which the social movement realizes the idea of openness. Instead, we need to look at the ways in which the kind of openness identified in FLOSS may practically correspond to specific moments of organization in the social movement. In the course of my involvement in Anti-G8 Summits, No Border Camps, People's Global Action (PGA) meetings, and other actions, I have noted correspondences in five key areas:

1. Meetings and Discussions. The time and location of physical meetings are published in a variety of places, on- and offline. The meetings themselves are most often open to all comers, sometimes with the exception of "traditional" media. Anyone is allowed to speak, although there is often a convenor or moderator whose role is to keep order and ensure progress. Summaries of discussion are often posted on the Web. The same is true of Internet relay chat (IRC) meetings, which anyone may attend, and for which the "logs" are usually published. Net-based mailing lists, through which much discussion is carried out, are usually through open subscription and, as with physical meetings, those joining are not vetted.

2. Decision Making. Most often, anyone present at a meeting may take part in the decisions made there, although these conditions may occasionally be altered. Currently, the majority of decision making is done using the "consensus" method, in which any person present not agreeing with a decision can either choose to abstain or veto ("block"). A block causes an action or decision to be stopped.

3. Documentation. In general, documents that form organizational materials within the movement are published online, usually using a content management system such as Wiki. In most cases, it is possible for even casual visitors to edit and alter these documents, although it is possible to "roll back" to earlier versions in, for example, the case of defacements.

4. Demonstrations. The majority of demonstrations are organized using the above methods. Not only is their organization "open," but, within a certain range of political persuasions, anyone may attend. Self-policing is not "hard" but "soft."

5. Actions. Even some "actions"—concentrated interventions usually involving smaller numbers—are "open," using the above methods to organize themselves and, if the action is ongoing, even allowing new people to participate.

Thus, some key moments within the social movement share certain characteristics with the FLOSS model of openness. Indeed, the movement deploys many of the same tools as FLOSS communities (i.e., Wiki, IRC, and mailing lists) to organize itself and carry out its projects. But its characteristic uses of openness are not enshrined in any formal document. Rather, they have developed as a way of organizing that is tacitly understood by those involved in the social movement: an idea of openness that, to differing degrees, inflects its organization throughout. Although the principles are not rigidly followed, there is often peer criticism of groups who do not declare their agendas or who act in a closed, partisan fashion, and, generally speaking, any group or project wanting to keep itself closed has an obligation to explain its rationale to other groups.

Some of these attitudes and principles derive from People's Global Action (PGA), an influential "instrument" constituting a visible attempt to organize around networked openness.[11] The organizational philosophy of PGA, which was formed after a movement gathering in South America in August 1997, is based on "decentralization." With "minimal central structures," the PGA "has no membership" or "juridical personality:" "no organization or person represents" it, nor does it "represent any organization or person."

It is a "tool," a "fluid network for communication and co-ordination between diverse social movements who share a loose set of principles or 'hallmarks'. Since February 1998 PGA has evolved as an interconnected and often chaotic web of very diverse groups, with a powerful common thread of struggle and solidarity at the grassroots level. These gatherings have played a vital role in face-to-face communication and exchange of experience, strategies and ideas. . . .[12]

The PGA has attempted to structure itself around a set of "hallmarks" that have been updated at each key meeting. These are currently as follows:

1. A very clear rejection of capitalism, imperialism and feudalism; all trade agreements, institutions and governments that promote destructive globalization.
2. [A rejection of] all forms and systems of domination and discrimination including, but not limited to, patriarchy, racism and religious fundamentalism of all creeds. . . . [An embracing of] the full dignity of all human beings.
3. A confrontational attitude, since we do not think that lobbying can have a major impact in such biased and undemocratic organizations, in which transnational capital is the only real policy-maker.
4. A call to direct action and civil disobedience, support for social movements' struggles, advocating forms of resistance which maximize respect for life and oppressed peoples' rights, as well as the construction of local alternatives to global capitalism.
5. An organizational philosophy based on decentralization and autonomy.[13]

These hallmarks structure participation in the PGA process. In theory, they allow the network to remain "open" while designating the kinds of activities that don't fall within its field. PGA meetings, for example, do not exclude those who don't subscribe to its hallmarks, but neither would discussions explicitly contrary to them be given much attention. Certain kinds of discussion are openly privileged over others on pragmatic grounds.

Structures like PGA and those being experimented with more widely are part of the social movement's general rejection of organizational models based on representation, verticality, and hierarchy. In their stead comes "nonhierarchical decentralization" and "horizontal coordination." "From this movement," writes Massimo de Angelis, emerges "the concept and practice of network horizontality, democracy, of the exercise of power from below."[14] For this "radical political economist" this form of "social cooperation" is "ours." It is "our" horizontality and these are "our" networks, part of a set of modes of coordination of human activity that, notes De Angelis, "go beyond the capitalist market and beyond the state. . . . we are talking about another world. . . . the slogan on T-shirts in Genoa was entirely correct: another world is not only possible. Rather, we are already patiently and with effort building another world—with all its contradictions, limitations and ambiguities—through the form of our networks."[15] In other words, it is the open, networked, horizontal form of the movement that produces its radical potential for social change: the message, yet again, is the medium.

In the case of the self-described "open publishing" project Indymedia, the open submission structure is said to collapse the distinction between media producer and consumer, allowing us to "become the media." The Indymedia newswire, writes the collective, "works on the principle of open publishing, an essential element of the Indymedia project that allows anyone to instantaneously self-publish their work on a globally accessible web site. The Indymedia newswire encourages people to become the media. . . . While Indymedia reserves the right to develop sections of the site that provide edited articles, there is no designated Indymedia editorial collective that edits articles posted to the http://www.Indymedia.org news wire."[16]

Here, the idea of openness presents itself as absolutely inimical to the "dominant multinational global news system," where "news is not free, news is not open." With open publishing,

> the process of creating news is transparent to the readers. They can contribute a story and see it instantly appear in the pool of stories publicly available. Those stories are filtered as little as possible to help the readers find the stories they want. Readers can see editorial decisions being made by others. They can see how to get involved and help make editorial decisions. If they can think of a better way for the software to help shape editorial decisions, they can copy the software because it is free and change it and start their own site. If they want to redistribute the news, they can, preferably on an open publishing site.
>
> The working parts of journalism are exposed. Open publishing assumes the reader is smart and creative and might want to be a writer and an editor and a distributor and even a software programmer [...] Open publishing is free software. It's freedom of information, freedom for creativity.[17]

Accounts such as this and De Angelis's demonstrate my point that openness is functioning as a primary location for expectations for political change. Not only is openness central to the organization of the social movement, but in many cases the organizational quality of openness is presumed to be inherently radical and necessarily productive of positive change wherever it is deployed. We see this, for example, in the work of the group Open Organisations, comprised of Toni Prug, Richard Malter, and Benjamin Geer, who were previously involved with UK Indymedia, and who until recently have been united in their belief in the radically liberatory potentials of openness. For them, openness is simply an as yet insufficiently theorized and elaborated form. Thus, they have been working on what might be characterized as a "strong" or "robust" openness model that recommends a set of working processes or practices intended to foster it. "Open Organisations" are entities that "anyone can join, [that function with] complete transparency and flexible and fair decision making structures, ownership patterns, and exchange mechanisms, that are designed, defined, and refined, by members as part of a continual transformative and learning process."[18]

Cryptohierarchies and Problems with Openness

In effect, by creating "structured processes," Open Organizations try to provide for openness. In doing so, they implicitly recognize that there are inconsistencies between the rhetoric and behavior of contemporary political organizations. But what are these problems, and who, and indeed where, are the discontents of openness? In fact, they may be found everywhere.

In the case of Indymedia's "open publishing" project, for example, openness has been failing under the pressures of scale. Initially, small "cottage-industry" independent media centers (IMCs) were able to manage the open publishing process very well. But, in many IMCs, problems started when the number of site visitors rose past a certain level. Popular IMC sites became targets for interventions by political opponents, often from the Fascist Right, seeking opportunities to disrupt what they regard as an IMC's "countercultural" potential and a platform from which to spread their own rhetoric. Of course, there is nothing to prevent this in the IMC manifesto; but it has impelled the understandable decision to edit out fascist viewpoints and other "noise," using the ad-hoc teams whose function was previously to develop and maintain the IMC's open publishing system. Some IMCs have ultimately been seen to take on a rather traditional, closed, and censorial function that is all too often undeclared and in contradiction with the official IMC "become the media" line. In other words, Indymedia channels are often politically censored by a small group of more-or-less anonymous individuals to quite a high degree.

This emergence of soft-control within organizations emphatically declared open is becoming a common and tacitly acknowledged problem across the social movement. As with Indymedia, practical issues with open development and organization too often give the lie to the enthusiastic promotion of openness as an effective alternative to representation.

After one PGA meeting, the group Sans Titre had this to say:

> Whenever we have been involved in PGA-inspired action, we have been unable to identify decision-making bodies. Moreover, there has

been no collective assessment of the effectiveness of PGA-inspired actions. . . . If the PGA-process includes decision-making and assessment bodies, where are they to be found? How can we take part?[19]

This problem runs through the temporary constitutions and dissolutions of "open" organizations that make up the social movement. The avowed absence of decision-making bodies and points of centralization too easily segues into a concealment of control per se. In fact, in both the FLOSS model and the social movement, the idea that no one group or person controls development and decision making is often quite far from the truth. In both cases it is *formally* true that anyone may alter or intervene in processes according to their needs, views, or projects. *Practically* speaking, however, few people can assume the necessary social position from which to make effective "interventions." Open source software is generally tightly controlled by a small group of people: the Apache Group, for example, very openhandedly controls the development of the Apache Web server, and Linus Torvalds has the final say on Linux Kernel's development.[20] Similarly, in the social movement, decision making often devolves to a surprisingly small number of individuals and groups. Though they never *officially* "speak for" others, much unofficial doctrine nonetheless emanates from them. Within political networks, such groups and individuals can be seen as "supernodes," not only routing more than their "fair share" of traffic, but actively determining the content that traverses them. Such supernodes do not (necessarily) constitute themselves out of a malicious will-to-power: rather, power defaults to them through personal qualities like energy, commitment, charisma, and the ability to synthesize politically important social moments into identifiable ideas and forms.

This soft control by cryptohierarchies is tacit knowledge for many who have had firsthand experience with "open" organizations. Statements such as the following, by a political activist introduced to what he calls "the chaos of open community" at a Washington State forest blockade camp in 1994 and then later the Carters Road Community, are typical:

> [T]he core group, by virtue of being around longer as individuals, and also working together longest as a sub group, formed unintentional elites. These elite groups were covert structures in open consensus based communities which said loudly and clearly that everyone's influence and power was equal. . . . We all joined in with a vigorous explanation that . . . there were no leaders. . . . The conspiracy to hide this fact among ourselves and from ourselves was remarkably successful. It was as though the situation where no leaders existed was known, deep down by everyone, to be impossible, outsiders were able

to say so, but communards were hoping so much that it was not true that they were able to pretend. . . .[21]

To examine how much this "pretence" is the rule within the social movement is beyond the scope of this chapter. But what is clear is that the five characteristics of "openness" described above, when subjected to scrutiny, reveal themselves as extremely compromised. The details, for example, of meetings and discussions are published and circulated, but this information is primarily received by those who are able (and often privileged to be able) to connect to certain (technological/social) networks. Likewise, the language of a "call" or equivalent can determine whether a party will feel comfortable or suitable to respond to it: like PGA's "hallmarks," language and phraseology are points of soft control, but not points that are openly discussed and studied. Furthermore, meetings may be "open to all," but they can quickly become hostile environments for parties who do not or cannot observe the basic consensus tacitly accepted by long-term actors in a particular scene. This peer consensus can so determine the movement's "open" decision-making process as to turn it into a war of attrition, divergent points of view gradually giving themselves up to peer opinion as the "debate" wears on and on. The "block" or "veto" is in fact rarely used because of the peer pressure placed on those who would use it ("Aw, come on, you're not going to block, are you?"—a common enough complaint at movement meetings). In some cases, the apparently neutral "moderator" role can also become bizarrely instrumentalized, giving rise to the sensation that "something has already been decided," and that the meeting is just for performative purposes.

Likewise, documentation of meetings and decisions usually only tells half the story. Points of serious contention are frequently left out on grounds that the parties involved in the disagreement might not want them to be published. This "smoothing over" of serious difference is quite normal. Participants in IRC discussions habitually inflect what they say because of the future publication of the logs, using private channels to discuss key points and only holding "official" discussions and lines in the open. Too often the open channel only hears what it is supposed to hear and important exchanges are not published.

All of this explains why some activist-theorists are beginning to interrogate the experiment with openness as it is taking shape in the social movement. It comes as no surprise that history has put significant resources at their disposal. Jo Freeman's "The Tyranny of Structurelessness" is a key document, originating from the experiences of the 1960s feminist liberation movement, and provides a critique of the "laissez faire" ideal for group structures still relevant today. As Freeman argues, such structures can become "a smoke screen for the strong or the lucky to establish unquestioned hegemony over others. Thus, structurelessness becomes a way of masking power. As long as the structure of the group is informal, the rules of how decisions are made are known only to a few, and awareness of power is limited to those who know the rules."[22]

Freeman's insight is fundamental: the idea of openness does not in itself prevent the formation of the informal structures that I have described here as cryptohierarchies. On the contrary, it is possible that it fosters them to a greater degree than structured organizations. Underneath its rhetoric of openness, the nonhierarchical organization can thus take on the qualities of a "gang." As Jacques Camatte and Gianna Collu realized in 1969, such organizations tend to hide the existence of their informal ruling cliques to appear more attractive to outsiders, feeding on the creative abilities of individual members while suppressing their individual contributions, and producing layers of authority contingent on individuals' intellectual or social dominance. "Even in those groups that want to escape [it]," writes Camatte, the "gang mechanism nevertheless tends to prevail. . . . The inability to question theoretical questions independently leads the individual to take refuge behind the authority of another member who becomes, objectively, a leader, or behind the group entity, which becomes a gang."[23]

Openness: Open to All Constituencies

This initial investigation indicates that the idea of openness promoted on the heels of the Free-Libre and Open Source software movement is not in and of itself an immediately sufficient alternative to bankrupt structures of representation. There are good reasons many activists are discontent with open organization. If we are going to promote open organization within the social movement, we must scrutinize the tacit flows of power that underlie and undercut it. The anecdotal accounts here suggest that once the formal hierarchical membrane of group organization is dismantled—in which, for example software composition or political decision-making might have previously taken place—what remains are *tacit* control structures. In FLOSS, limitations to those who can access and alter source code are formally removed; what then comes to define such access and the software that is produced are underlying determinants: education, social opportunity, and social connections and affiliations. The most open system theoretically imaginable reveals perfectly the predicating inequities of the wider environment in which it is situated. What adherents of openness must tackle first and most critically is the oldest chicken-and-egg problem: a really open organization cannot be realized without a prior radicalization of the sociopolitical field in which it operates.

Notes

1. See "What is Wiki?" at <wiki.org/wiki.cgi?WhatIsWiki>.
2. See <http://www.zeropaid.com≥ for a review of current peer-to-peer and file-sharing services.
3. Felix Stalder, "One-Size-Doesn't-Fit-All: Particulars of the Volunteer Open Source Development Methodology"; available online at <http://openflows.org/article.pl?sid=03/10/25/1722242>.
4. Adam Greenfield, "The Minimal Compact: Preliminary Notes on an 'Open Source' Constitution for Post-National Entities"; available online at <http://www.v.org/displayArticle.php?article_num=339>.
5. Tim O' Reilly, "The Open Source Paradigm Shift," keynote speech at the Reboot 2003 conference; available online at <http://www.reboot.dk/reboot6/video/>.
6. Florian Schneider, "Re: <nettime>Reverse Engineering Freedom." *Nettime*, 14 October 2003; available online at <http://www.mail-archive.com/nettime-l@bbs.thing.net/msg01248.html>. See also Florian Schneider and Geert Lovink, "Reverse Engineering Freedom," *Make Worlds* 3 (2003); available online at <http://www.makeworlds.org/?q=book/view/20>.
7. Douglas Rushkoff, "Open Source Democracy: How Online Communication Is Changing Offline Politics," Demos, 2003; available online at <www.demos.co.uk/opensourcedemocracy_pdf_media_public.aspx>.
8. Ibid.
9. Biella Coleman, "Free and Open Source Software," in *Survival Kit*, part 1, proceedings of RAM4. Available at http://www.olento.fi/ram4/publication/3.php?name=free
10. See <http://www.oekonux.de>.
11. See <http://www.apg.org>.
12. "Sophie," ChiapasLink UK, "We Are Everywhere! People's Global Action Meeting in Cochabamba, Bolivia," posted to A-infos list, 8 December 2001 at <http://www.ainfos.ca/01/dec/ainfos00120.html>.
13. The PGA hallmarks are available at <http://www.nadir.org/nadir/intiativ/agp/free/pga/hallm.htm>.
14. Massimo de Angelis, "From Movement to Society," *Commoner*, August 2001; available online at <http://www.commoner.org.uk/01-3groundzero.htm>.
15. Ibid.
16. The Indymedia collective statement is available at <http://www.indymedia.org/fish.php3?file=www.indymedia.newswire>.
17. Matthew Arnison, "Open Publishing is the Same as Free Software," March 2001; available online at <http://www.cat.org.au/maffew/cat/openpub.html>.
18. This statement was taken from <http://wiki.uniteddiversity.com/open_organisations>.
19. Sans Titre, "Open Letter to the People's Global Action," 9 May 2002; available online at <http://www.pgaconference.org/_postconference_/pp_sanstitre.htm>.
20 See Paula Roone, "Is Linus Killing Linux?" *TechWeb*, January 28, 2001.
21. Chris Lee, "An Article Concerning the Issue of Covert Power Elites in Open Communities," April 12, 2001; available online at <http://cartersrd.org.au/covert_elites.htm>.
22. Jo Freeman, "The Tyranny of Structurelessness," first printed by the Women's Liberation Movement, USA, 1970. Available online at <http://www.anarres.org.au/essays/amtos.htm≥.
23. Jacques Camatte, "On Organization," in *This World We Must Leave and Other Essays* (New York: Autonomedia, 1995), 30.

CHAPTER 5

Anybody Can Be TV: How P2P Home Video Will Challenge the Network News

DRAZEN PANTIC

Recently, U.S. Secretary of Defense Donald Rumsfeld attested to the revolutionary power of the wireless uploading of digital images to the Internet. Testifying in Congress about the sudden widespread appearance of photographs and video images of the abuses at Abu Ghraib prison in Iraq, he did not address this subject as a technological optimist. Rumsfeld is the farthest thing from a dot-com stock analyst circa 1999, or a computer visionary. Rather, he stuck to the brutal reality, explaining that the combination of cheap digital cameras and the Internet had fundamentally changed the dynamics of newsmaking during wartime.

Today, everyone has access to the latest high quality consumer electronic devices. Every cell phone has the ability to capture images, even movies. Once people begin to use these devices to record the significant events in their lives, there is no way to prevent them from slipping cameras into any location. When sensitive material is captured in digital form, it takes on a life of its own. Circulating across the Internet, it becomes a fact in itself. It is impossible for a military organization to control the flow of disbursed, distributed content production in a network environment.

The mainstream media, even if it prefers to ignore troubling facts, is forced to respond. The story of torture at Abu Ghraib prison had been available to journalists for more than three months before the first disturbing photographs surfaced. The media could have reported on it at any time. But with images, it was established as a fact that could not be avoided. Rumsfeld and his colleagues had better prepare themselves, because this is just a taste of the emerging media ecology that is now on the horizon.

First Sightings of the New

Back in 1999, during the dot-com bubble, many of us shared in the delirium of hope that the information technology (IT) sector could solve all our problems. There was a belief that the Internet would quickly surpass television and become the main source of information for most people. Web content producers borrowed the television news channel metaphor to design what were called information portals, or aggregator sites. These were vast websites meant to provide comprehensive knowledge about a particular sector, as well as news associated with it. Internet portals were thus structured to resemble news channels. They took the idea of staff correspondents, and extended it to include a kind of participatory journalism—content provided for free by nonprofessionals that would be vetted in some way by paid staff.

The Internet's distributed nature, and the potential low cost of entry for media makers, struck us as extraordinarily promising. Here is an excerpt from an essay I wrote at the time, which reflected this belief that the Internet was on the verge of radically transforming our media:

> Programming produced by any big transnational TV network (CNN, BBC, etc.) is, from the standpoint of an Internet user, similar to an aggregator site distributing video material. It may also function as a portal providing a variety of material of interest to the viewer. Similarities abound—sections of a transnational TV network correspond to parts of an aggregator site: a program schedule is analogous to a web site index, news programs function as general information about the portal's community, shows represent particular web pages or sections on the portal. Most importantly, both a TV network and a Web portal try to fulfill the basic media mission: to define its own reality and broadcast that reality to potential followers—TV viewers or Internet users.

That is what is similar, strikingly similar. What is dissimilar is the nature of the different media. Classical TV and radio are linear and give an observer just two choices: to participate passively in a broadcast as is, or to switch it off. The Internet is more flexible and offers more choices, at least in the basic premises of the media. It is also interactive, allowing the viewer actively to participate.

TV and radio networks are also much more expensive in terms of distribution and production, and by their nature as one-way media, they are closed systems. A single corporation can dictate production costs of worldwide video or radio coverage. This immediately implies that discourse, basic ideological standpoint, and focus of coverage are fixed and are at the discretion of the producer. Every transnational, national and local radio or TV station covered the drama in Kosovo. This certainly propelled some more or less peaceful solution.

On the other side, few focus on wars, genocide and turmoil in Africa (Rwanda for example). Events take their course far from the eye or interest of the public. The *New York Times* Africa correspondent covers six or seven countries with populations as big as Europe, and with half a dozen wars in progress. The obvious question is whether better coverage or persistent webcasts could stop or minimize human casualties there. Can a camcorder attached to a satellite phone indirectly save thousands of lives?

The portal sites worked fairly well, but they never attracted a large enough base of participants to be financially successful. As it turned out, too few people are informed and skilled enough to regularly contribute relevant, interesting, catchy news content. More important, though, is that at the time neither the news media nor the IT sector were truly ready to support participatory journalism. The news sector was trying to preserve the monopolistic position it had then and still has. It was deeply reluctant to admit the possibility that anyone could be a journalist. Consider, for example, these remarks by Leslie Gelb, a former editor of the *New York Times* and, until recently, president of the Council on Foreign Relations. At a Columbia University conference about the role of journalism in war, referring to the possibilities of participatory journalism, Gelb said, "journalists are not in the business of truth, they are in the business of news."[1] Gelb put it bluntly: for professional journalists, truth is important, but the top priority is to produce material that sells. Sure, it has to be vetted, the truth must be taken into account, but primarily journalism has to result in a salable product. This kind of professionalism leaves little room for outsider, eyewitness accounts as part of a news reader's daily diet.

At the same time, the IT industry was not yet ready to provide the tools and technology necessary for widespread participatory journalism. Even if the equipment was capable of delivering it, the mind-set of the industry resisted making it available. In early 1999, I collaborated on a project with IBM to build a laptop for remote news correspondents. It included video editing, network capabilities, and other appropriate technology. But we struggled with IBM's engineers over the inclusion of Firewire. They insisted that it was impossible to fit a Firewire card in a PCMCIA slot [Personal Computer Memory Card International Association is the organization that developed the standard for small credit card sized devices, including their slots]. As a result, prototype models we outlined could not do the efficient video transfer necessary to be truly useful to remote journalists, let alone war correspondents (the intended recipients of the laptops), and the project collapsed. Then, a few months later, Apple came out with a laptop that included Firewire. The lessons of this experience have been confirmed repeatedly for me and others who see the potential contribution that digital communications could make to civil society: the state of mind of the IT industry is often more limited than what the technology itself is capable of delivering.

Another reason for the meager success of participatory reporting was that broadband proliferation was extremely limited at the time. Even though there was much talk and high hopes about broadband, its penetration to households, even in the United States, was poor. While quite a few people in both media and IT saw the opportunity for convergence between the two sectors, the basis was not yet there for an effective convergence. In this light, it is worth reconsidering the infamous disaster of the America Online and TimeWarner merger. As we now know, once their corporate marriage was complete, the new entity did not know what to do with itself. Nonetheless, this event pointed in the right direction. It was an important development, even if it came too soon, signaling that convergence between the media and the IT industry is the way to go.

We're Not Gonna Take It

Today the biggest problem faced by both mainstream media and the IT sector is a lack of trust on the part of consumers. Consumers no longer accept the passive position that was common in the last century. They want to participate in media production. Understanding this shift has been the secret behind the huge success of Apple. Steve Jobs and his team realize that the company's future depends on supporting this transition of their customer base from passive audience to digital producers. They sell the notion that anybody can be a content maker, wrapped in attractive, translucent plastic. That notion is Apple's ur-product. The consumer no longer gives a blank check to either the broadcast media or the IT industry. We have all experienced the unreliable reporting in mainstream news, most recently during the run up to the invasion of Iraq, and the visceral disrespect of the monopolistic software industry, which charges exorbitant prices for mediocre proprietary products.

On the positive side, however, we have also witnessed two developments, especially in the years after September 11, 2001. We have encountered the vast amount of direct, unmediated information available over the Internet—on weblogs, personal websites, targeted e-newsletters, independent news portals, and other sources. This information, as a whole, is as reliable as any news seen on the cable networks, while often providing an independent perspective missing from corporate media. At the same time, we have also seen how Free and Open Source Software (FOSS) is on the rise in the IT sector, with companies like IBM and Hewlett-Packard providing secure, high-quality computing for corporate clients. With both the media and IT sectors, we see the emergence of participatory methods that have led to viable, practical, widespread uses.

Meanwhile, many IT products have improved significantly in the last few years, with a wide range of high quality consumer electronic devices for content production on the market. These are low cost, solid tools for audio/video production, editing, and the packaging of media into distribution units, such as Motion Picture Experts Group (MPEG) software, which compresses video into a format suitable for distribution over broadband networks like those widely available in U.S. households today. MPEG files not only allow people to exchange video material over cable and digital subscriber line (DSL) networks, but the quality is good enough for professional broadcasting on traditional television. In fact, as a technical standard, MPEG is identical to what is used in cable distribution. While MPEG is a proprietary technology, the open-source community provided an MPEG-4 compatible video codec (or encoder), called Xvid, which is not controlled by any private entity or corporation. Xvid video files can play on any Quicktime or Real Media compatible player. And there are open-source versions of the players as well. The appearance of open-source versions of this technology ensures its availability to all who want to use it—so that indeed anyone can be a television news producer. Additionally, broadband has now reached many homes. More important, wireless is available on a consumer level, and free wireless networks are emerging in many urban areas.

Together, these factors contribute to the emergence of an entirely new, distributed media environment that can no longer be controlled from the top down.

You, Too, Are a News Producer

Not long ago, the production of high-quality video was expensive and tied to proprietary formats (or codeces). Companies like Avid or Pinnacle produced video editing tools only for high-end professionals from the broadcast industry; their products were too expensive for nonprofessionals. The expertise required to use these tools also went beyond the ability of most people. Just learning the basics meant investing much time into acquiring arcane skills. This alienated people from direct participation in the video documentation of events. If you wanted to record and edit a movie, you needed professional connections.

But over the past four years, a number of factors have contributed to making video production capabilities available to millions of people. This shift began with the introduction of the software product Final Cut Pro, the first consumer-grade video editing program that could produce broadcast quality video on a laptop. In parallel, digital video (DV) cameras came down in price. Once they reached approximately seven hundred or so dollars, there was a huge proliferation of DV cameras. Other contributing factors include: the proliferation of open-source software; simple open standards for video production (like MPEG-2 and -4); increased processing power in personal computers and digital cameras; the availability of consumer products that make MPEG video (like Tivo); and the proliferation of broadband Internet access. Open-source tools for all aspects of video production keep getting better, more sophisticated, and easier to use. Some open-source video editing tools allow for real-time rendering of video and video effects—a process that was unimaginable only a few years ago, even at expensive, exclusive production houses. These resources are now within reach of the average middle-class household. Accordingly, we are seeing a new level of mass participation in video making. These independent productions, done outside of any institutional framework, are already being distributed in the form of high quality video-on-demand over the Internet.

How long will it be before our news reports come directly from local sources with their own video production facilities, in real time, over the Net? Who needs a cable network's team of celebrity reporters, with their jingoistic coverage of "Operation Iraqi Freedom," when I have unfiltered access to images and testimony from the war zone?

It is important to note that this proliferation of low cost tools, and their increasing quality, was made possible by the Free and Open Source Software movement and the push for open standards. Commercial software companies would not have made the commitment to open standards had they not been confronted by open-source alternatives that are cheaper and more flexible. The emphasis on open standards came from the open source community. Companies then saw the advantages of the open approach, and began to adopt it. For example, Apple's Quicktime, which is not open source in nature, makes use of open standards to encode video and audio. Apple made this choice because open standards offer more flexibility, while they also help solve problems with the licensing of proprietary intellectual property, since open standards, by their very nature, are free.

For makers of rich media content, open standards are essential. And open-source hackers have done much to extend the availability of high-quality open standards. The most widely used standard for the formatting of audio on the Internet is MP3, which is not open. It is a propriety standard. But the open source community has developed variations of MP3 that are compatible and nonproprietary. One example is OGG Vorbis, which is both open source and open standard. Apple has cleverly included the OGG Vorbis standard in the Quicktime player and its iTunes music device. It is impressive how far Apple has come to embrace open standards. And other companies have moved in this direction, as well. Today's version of Final Cut Pro also largely operates with open standards and open source. What you pay for, essentially, is the graphical user interface (GUI). This is one of many examples of a software product based on open source software and open standards, with a proprietary container. Another example is Apple's DVD Studio Pro. For this software, you literally pay for the GUI. Everything else is of open source and open standards. And Apple does not object if you don't pay for it.

What is still lacking is the aggregation of these rich media tools into a complete, easy-to-use package. A first effort toward this kind of this bundling is the CD "dyne:bolic." This disk is a complete, open-source, Linux-based, laptop video production and distribution suite. It comes with the following software installed: MPEG4IP (live Internet streaming and capturing clips in QuickTime compatible format); FFMPEG (transcoding and streaming in Flash, Windows Media, or Real format); Cinelerra and LiVES (for editing and publishing video clips); FreeJ (VJ live sets); Audacity and ReZound (for editing audio); and Gimp (image manipulation software). Unfortunately, "dyne:bolic" is not as user-friendly as one would like. But it is an important step in the right direction.

Many other tool suites are appearing everyday. But more than anything else, we need education. People have to learn that they can produce video comparable to professional broadcast quality using these inexpensive, open-source tools. Additionally, by working with open-source tools and producing independent and personalized news, many will realize the intrinsic value of free and uncensored information in network society. If information is not free, all other freedoms can easily be taken away.

Live (via Wi-Fi) from Bryant Park

On January 14, 2003, I went to in New York's Bryant Park for the first successful live broadcast uploaded over a public wireless network for transmission over cable television; I was joined by Kenyatta Cheese and Marti Lucas, the latter of Manhattan Neighborhood Network (MNN), a nonprofit public-access channel in New York that is distributed by Time-Warner Cable. We wanted a proof of concept that established basic procedures for the broadcasting of video in real-time to a cable or satellite television network from remote locations. Public wireless nodes provide enough bandwidth to carry IP video streams at a sufficiently high quality. These clips are perfectly acceptable for television transmission. (Although "broadcast-quality" video is loosely defined as 640 x 480 pixels at thirty frames per second, most viewers will accept the look of 320 x 240 video doubled in size. We also decided that a minimum of eight frames per second was "acceptable" for watching short video clips of thirty seconds or less, although fifteen frames per second—the minimum rate at which the human eye sees fluid motion—is preferable. For audio, we chose sixteen-bit stereo sound, encoded at a minimum of 32 kilobits per second using a standards-complaint audio codec [AAC].)

Moreover, we wanted to do this using a laptop, open-source software, a consumer-grade camera, and an easily available broadband Internet connection—preferably WiFi. The motivation for this exercise was to demonstrate that classic television production equipment, requiring hundreds of thousands of dollars and a specialized infrastructure, is becoming a thing of the past. It is now possible to use a laptop-Internet system for on-the-fly transmissions from remote locations for distribution over a television network. The hardware and software we used was deliberately chosen because it is within the skill level of even a moderately technical person.

So on a freezing winter afternoon we went to Bryant Park with two laptops (one as a backup in case of battery failure, because it was so cold outside), two digital video camcorders, and a couple of professional quality microphones. We established a wireless connection through a local, public WiFi network maintained by the nonprofit organization NYC Wireless, and broadcast from that spot to a computer at MNN studios. The video and audio was captured by the camcorder and fed into the laptop, where it was encoded as MPEG-4/AAC streams, then sent out as a unicast stream via the WiFi connection. At MNN they played the stream through a scan converter—which converts the stream on a computer into a video signal—then broadcast it live on the air. Instead of sending the video/audio to a replication server, a client computer with a static IP address received the stream from across the Internet and played the media out to a video switcher and onto the cable channel/satellite broadcast. The show consisted of the three of us interviewing each other about the laptop-WiFi broadcast process: We can do it! It was totally self-referential delirium, which of course is what television is all about. But what is most encouraging about this technology is how it can lead to new forms of distribution that bypass centralized broadcasting entirely, allowing for the creation and distribution of video programming from within a peer-to-peer (P2P) network.

P2P Television and Effective Video Blogging

When participatory production potential meets the network distribution paradigm, it reaches its most profound level. Many people have observed in the early use of peer-to-peer technology, such as Napster, the power that comes from the sharing of digital resources across a distributed network. When so many computers and creative forces are joined in a network, the power and the impact of the network are much larger than the simple sum of individual resources.

This potential attracted the attention of open-source developers, and they went in two different directions. The first was to create decentralized P2P networks in which the main priority is to protect the privacy of participants (such as Gnuttella, Livewire, etc). The other direction was to coalesce P2P networks so they can more effectively distribute popular resources. One of the best examples of this approach is BitTorrent. The biggest problem for any P2P network is the curse of popularity. The more popular a file becomes, the more bandwidth required to provide it: because more people want that file from you, you need more bandwidth to serve all those requests. For this reason, only high-bandwidth operations could engage in massive P2P distribution of files that are suddenly in great demand. BitTorrent was developed to prevent the bottleneck that happens when timely new video clips become popular. This is especially important for original content that exists only at one or two locations on the Internet. If only a few people have a file when it gets attention, the file becomes difficult to access. BitTorrent addresses this problem through the active sharing of network resources: when each new person starts to download a file, her computer automatically becomes a server of the same file, able to supply other requests from within the BitTorrent network. There is no waiting for the file to completely download before the computer can begin serving. So the more popular a file, the more upstream bandwidth it immediately acquires.

This capability is extremely useful for video. Audio files, of course, are smaller. The network distribution of video requires better logic and sharing of bandwidth. BitTorrent treats bandwidth in a way that makes it much easier for individual households to serve video. Typically, home networks use much more bandwidth for downloading than uploading. Most home DSL and cable networks are designed to handle a large amount of downloads, and they assume you will send up very little. BitTorrent, and similarly designed P2P networks, coalesce all of the upstream capacity for the households in the network, creating an aggregate that is not only large, but efficient. Without a protocol like Bit Torrent, it becomes far less practical to serve video files to more than one downloader at a time. But with this capacity, the serving of independently produced video to large audiences from regular broadband household networks can become a popular practice.

Weblogs, or blogs, are another example of how people are shifting from passive media spectators to active media producers. Now that a rich media layer is being added to blogs—with the appearance of video blogs—it seems that a viable alternative to centralized television networks is emerging. For example, consider what might happen through the joining together of video blogs, Real Simple Syndication (RSS), and BitTorrent. This is a very powerful combination. RSS is a mechanism for the indexing of content on blogs. It also enables the automated entry of content from one blog into another. This very basic approach to syndication, which is already being used (in one of several versions) by nearly one million websites, makes it possible for blog content posted on one site to circulate across the Internet in an instant. RSS allows for the proliferation of metadata so blog content can be indexed not only by other blogs, but also by search engines like Google or Yahoo.

Once it becomes a common practice for independent video to be posted on video blogs, RSS will facilitate the widespread distribution of video across the Internet. Unfortunately, we are still far from effective metatagging of time-based media. One still cannot search through a video clip online for the type of content it has, or its position on the file. You may want to find all the clips on the Internet that mention your name, for example, and the moment when your name comes up in the clip. But while you can do this kind of search with text on webpages, it is still impossible with rich media. For the time being, however, the combination of video tools with blogs and RSS is a viable substitute. In other words, synergy between blogs and video on the Net, especially when coupled with efficient distribution mechanisms like BitTorrent and RSS feeds, has the potential to create a paradigm shift on the media side. Blogs provide reputational mechanisms and metadata for video, while video augments blogs with authentic, interesting, and rich content.

More substantially, blogs and television mesh well because they are both so self-referential. Just as most blogging seems to be about blogging, most television is about television. Television is also a huge cut-and-paste engine that reuses the same material over and over—just as blogs do. Text bloggers are most successful when applying the second degree of scrutiny in the ecosystem of news—either by checking the facts, or reading through the manipulative mannerisms of a typical television, or forcing newspapers to bring in voices they would otherwise ignore.[2] Democratization of television programing in the direction of video blogging could do much more: depart from the existing infotainment matrix created by mainstream media and create new formats and new discourse.

The Sense of What Is to Come: From Netroots to Infotainment to Go

As mentioned earlier, the revolution of growth in consumer electronics is continuing, producing more and more powerful and versatile multimedia devices and making them more and more affordable at the same time Broadband is also growing strong and has already become the dominant Internet paradigm. And that is just the initial step in the direction of what is to come: television is about to explode as broadcast and cable are challenged by Internet-delivered television, offering any show from any producer to any viewer anywhere, anytime.

In politics, the 2008 presidential elections will be all about netroots, democratic and participatory energy from the Net that wages politics over the blogosphere and other Internet locations. Candidates will try to talk directly to their potential voters, sending video clips to their cell phones. But, candidates will also have to be able to open their cell phones for the clips of their voters and general public. Audiences have realized their capacity to exert an influence and experienced the joy of disrupting the established (mainstream) power matrix—whether in print, television, film-making or, hopefully, politics. And those eager participants, powered by broadband, wireless, and cameras of all kinds, will not be willing to go back to their living rooms and assume the role of passive couch potatoes again. Ever.

Notes

1. Leslie Gelb, quoted in Ann Grier Cutter, "Journalists: Must They Remain Neutral in Conflict?" *United Nations Chronicle* 36, no. 2 (1999); available online at <http://www.un.org/Pubs/chronicle/1999/issue2/0299p29.htm>.

2. See Jay Rosen, "Bloggers Are Missing in Action as Ketchum Tests the Conscience of PR," available online.

SECTION **II**
Sites

CHAPTER 6

Communicating Islamic Fundamentalism as Global Citizenship*

LINA KHATIB

There is a debate today about the position of the nation in a globalized world that parallels debate over whether the Internet is better seen as an enabling tool for resisting or opposing globalization or as a global force itself. Some argue that the nation and nationalism are becoming obsolete, with connections being made among cultures and individuals across national boundaries, resulting in cosmopolitanism where the individual becomes a citizen of the world (Naussbaum 1994). Others argue that the nation is strengthened in this context, with individuals holding onto their national identity in the face of usurping global forces (Dorris 1994). However, the world today is witnessing the emergence of affiliations that transcend the nation but do not necessarily mean that the nation is under threat. Those new affiliations can be seen as a kind of "new patriotism" that describes the existence of intersecting affiliations—local, global, regional, and religious.

---

* This chapter is adapted from Lina Khatib, "Communicating Islamic Fundamentalism as Global Citizenship," *Journal of Communication Inquiry* 27, 4 (October 2003), pp. 389-409. Copyright 2003 by Sage Publication. Reprinted by permission of Sage Publications, Inc.

A particular case is Islamic fundamentalism, articulated within, and not in opposition to, processes of globalization, defined here as "those processes, operating on a global scale, which cut across national boundaries, integrating and connecting communities and organizations in new space-time combinations, making the world in reality and in experience more interconnected" (Hall 1992, 299). The Internet as a tool, communicating this global citizenship for Islamic fundamentalist movements worldwide (Beck 2000), becomes a means of constituting, representing, and influencing the existence and growth of various Islamic fundamentalist groups in a global context.

In *Identity Blues*, Ien Ang (2000) argues that the focus on identities as constructions diverts attention from the political realities of identities that are expressed as essentialist (like Islamic fundamentalism). She cites Craig Calhoun's argument that this idea is problematic because it "groups together what seem to the researchers relatively 'attractive' movements, vaguely on the left, but leaves out other contemporary movements such as the new religious right and fundamentalism, the resistance of white ethnic communities against people of color, various versions of nationalism, and so forth" (Calhoun 1994, 22, cited in Ang 2000, 3).

Stuart Hall (1992) singles out Islamic fundamentalism as being the result of the "tension between Tradition and Translation" (312), or between "ethnicity" and "global homogenization" (313). Manuel Castells sees the Islamic fundamentalist identity as a resistant one and describes it as an expression of *"the exclusion of the excluders by the excluded"* (1997, 9; emphasis original). He sees it as defensive against dominant institutions/ideologies and places it in a tension between the "Net and the Self," where there is an opposition between "abstract universal instrumentalism" (the global) and "historically rooted, particularistic identities" (the local) (Castells 1997, 3). In contrast to the Net, which "emerges from interconnected developments in new communication technologies . . . the emergence of mediated 'real virtuality'" (Saukko 2000), Castells casts Islamic fundamentalism as local and as resistant to the Net. But while Islamic fundamentalist movements have often been cast as oppositional to global processes, they articulate their identities in a similar manner to the new social movements. Both constitute a new patriotism, the formation of "linkages between . . . delocalized political communications, and revitalized political commitments," and at the same time provide a means for the production of locality for communities in multiple ethnoscapes (Appadurai 1996, 196). In so doing, Islamic fundamentalism transcends nations, but is not necessarily oppositional to the nation. The Islamic fundamentalist identity itself is fluid and is constructed differently in different contexts. Islamic fundamentalism is experienced locally, but at the same time as a global movement.

Defining Islamic Fundamentalism

There has been considerable disagreement over the term *Islamic fundamentalism* that can be traced to the difficulty of aligning contradictory or "dislocated" identities "into one, overarching 'master identity' on which a politics could be securely grounded" (Hall 1992, 280). Islamic fundamentalism does not refer to movements that are religious only, but also to political movements that aim at establishing a "polity of believers" (Hamzeh 1998). Islamic fundamentalists believe in Islamic authenticity, juxtaposed to what is seen as Western hegemony, which in turn is believed to threaten this authenticity. Western hegemony is not confined to Western countries; it also applies to secular people in the Muslim world who are seen as even worse than the "foreign infidels" (Faksh 1997, 9), and as "representing the interests of the . . . formerly . . . colonial powers" (Taheri 1987, 16). Fundamentalist groups seem to agree on the necessity of jihad (holy war) to preserve and expand the Muslim community, but differ in their interpretation and application of jihad. While some see jihad as nonviolent, others, like the Islamic Jihad Organization, view jihad as military. By "fundamentalist," I mean to refer to "a diverse set of competing political opinions held within the Muslim community" (Ehteshami 1997, 179), and to groups that use Islam as a basis to achieve political power. In doing so I will be concentrating on a set of Islamic fundamentalist groups connected (directly or indirectly) through the Internet with al-Qaeda, the group led by Osama bin Laden that has gained notoriety for the September 11, 2001 attacks.

This sort of Islamic fundamentalism recognizes the national nature of conflicts, yet projects them beyond the nation. An example is the Palestinian group Hamas, which targets its activities against Israel and yet engages in rallying support in other countries (like Britain), where it hails the suffering of Palestinians as a global issue rather than a localized one. Islamic fundamentalism's fluid identity has taken different forms according to the historical context, moving from nationalism to challenging nationalism to a mixture of both. The spread of fundamentalism as a "national" form "divorced from territorial states" has prompted Arjun Appadurai to label its projected identities "postnational," to refer to fundamentalism's emergence as an alternative form "for the organization of global traffic in resources, images and ideas" (1996, 169). Islamic fundamentalism is perhaps most visible in the Arab world (although that view is currently being challenged with the increasing exposure of groups in places like Chechnya, Indonesia, and Kenya). The Arab world has gone through stages in which its regional identity has been put forward and withdrawn in several stages. During the rule of Egypt's Gamal Nasser, for example, there was a resurgence of Pan-Arabism, seen as a reaction to colonial (British, French,

Italian) presence in the region, as well as to the formation of the state of Israel in 1948. Advocacy of a national identity (whether local or regional) has been in conflict with the views of many Islamic fundamentalists in the Arab world who argue for an Islamic identity (Al-Ahsan 1992), which has been seen as an example of the failure of the nation-state system to create a truly national identity (whether local or regional). In this sense, Islamic fundamentalism has arisen as a kind of substitute for a failing Arab identity.

Today Islamic fundamentalism can also be looked at as a global force articulating the three sides of globalization: the material (flow of trade, local/global happenings and repercussions), the spatiotemporal (inter-regional "meetings" across time and space), and the cognitive (transformation of power relations beyond the nation) (Held and McGrew 2000). Al-Qaeda is a network of movements operating worldwide with converging yet variable political agendas. The movements are united in their opposition to Western hegemony, yet the ways they implement this antagonism differs in different contexts. While the movements agree in opposing Israel, for example, not all of them engage in anti-Israeli missions (such missions seem to be conducted mainly by the Islamic jihad, and Hamas in Palestine). The movements thus are global in the sense that they function within a disembedded institution—notably, al-Qaeda, which means "base" in Arabic, does not have a recognized physical base—"linking local practices with globalized, social relations" (Giddens 1990, 79).

Castells (1997) has positively characterized the Internet as the material base of a new social morphology. While some observers characterized it hopefully as a medium of possibility, where the individual can go beyond the social self (Hjarvard 2002; Turkle 1996), it also blurs boundaries between the spaces in which those who are connected exist (Freeman 1999). Whether, as Ella Shohat (1999) argues, cyberspace is another space and not a substitute space, existing local and global power relations are extended to this (new) space, instead of displaced from the physical one. After the September 11 attacks, we are becoming more aware of the connections between Islamic fundamentalism and cyberspace, with the unearthing of Islamic fundamentalist cyberactivities, such as al-Qaeda's messages on its website al-Neda (http://www.alneda.com) supporting the attack and calling for an all-out war between Islam and the West (Out-There News 2002). But even before the attacks, this relationship had already been cemented through the use of chat rooms, e-mail, and various websites. Political conflicts have been carried further through practices like hacking and raids on Internet service providers. The Lebanese group Hizbollah's website was hacked in 2001 after Hizbollah captured three Israeli soldiers at the border in South Lebanon (Scheeres 2001). Its

Lebanese service provider, Destination, also had its home page hacked by a group of Israeli teenagers (Weisman 2001). Six days before September 11, FBI and other agents raided InfoCom Corporation in Texas, crashing five hundred websites with Arab or Muslim connections (Whitaker 2001). The events of September 11 catalyzed more "cyberwar" activities. Al-Neda's messages to rally support against the United States prompted its hacking by an American in 2002 (Di Justo 2002). Visitors to the website today are greeted with the slogan "Hacked, Tracked and Now Owned by the USA." However, other militant groups still have a presence on the Internet. The analysis poses the following questions: How is the Internet used by Islamic fundamentalist groups to express conflicting ideologies toward the nation? How is the Internet used to communicate a Pax Islamica in and outside of the Middle East? How is it used to respond to a changing political climate? What kinds of cyberwars are taking place, and among whom?

Communicating Islamic Fundamentalism

The use of the Internet by Islamic fundamentalist groups reflects an outward vision combined with a global target audience while also paying attention to local issues. The Internet has many uses for such groups. It is used to post messages about the groups' mission statements. It is used to relay photographs and audio and video messages and footage about the groups' activities. It is often used to post the latest news related to the groups and their affiliates. It acts as a convenient way for collecting monetary donations. It allows group member and supporters to find out about the groups' latest actions. It also allows them to communicate via e-mail and chat rooms. The Internet is also used by the groups to sell books, tapes, CDs, and other materials. The groups can also use the Internet to respond to current political situations.

The groups' websites differ in their design and ease of use: some are mainly text-based (like Jihaad'ul'Kuffarin, http://www.jihaadulkuffarin.jeeran.com), while others are more sophisticated, resembling multilayered news portals (like Taliban Online, www.muslimthai.com/talibanonline). Some websites are direct affiliates of specific groups, like the Lebanese Hizbollah (ht tp://www.hizbollah.org), the Afghani Taliban, the Pakistani Tanzeem-e-Islami (http://www.tanzeem.org), the Palestinian Hamas (under the name Palestine Information Center, http://www.palestine-info.co.uk), the Chechen al-Mujahidoun (under the name Qoqaz.net, http://www.qoqaz.net, and also Qoqaz.com, http://www.qoqaz.com) and al-Muhajiroun (a Salafi Islamic fundamentalist group connected to the Taliban; http://www.almuhajiroun.com). Other websites are slightly more ambiguous about their affiliations, such as Jihaad'ul'Kuffarin, which is connected to the Islamic Group (Jama'a Islamiyya) led by the Egyptian Sheikh Omar Abd-el-Rahman, and Supporters of Shareeah (http://www.shareeah.com), which is the site of Sheikh Abu Hamza al-Masri and his followers in Britain. Other websites do not display any overt affiliations, such as Jannah (http://www.jannah.org), as-Sahwa (http://www.as-sahwah.com), Beware of Shiaism (http://www.bewareofshiaism.8k.com), and Maktabah Al-Ansar (http://www.maktabah.net); however, they are connected through hyperlinks to other recognized sites like Shareeah.

The groups' websites pay attention to local issues in the countries in which the groups operate, at the same time that they advocate a kind of global ethics that links their aims and goals, such as the establishment of a global Pax Islamica (Paun 2003). This multifocal approach reflects "a shattered repertoire of mini-roles, instead of a nucleus of hypothetical sense of self" (Canclini 1998, quoted in Network EICOS 2003). The websites pay attention to particular issues in particular nation-states. Thus, Tanzeem is mainly concerned with Pakistan; Qoqaz.net and Qoqaz.com with Chechnya; the Taliban with Afghanistan, presenting information about the Taliban, the history of Afghanistan, and a list of Taliban "enemies" (including the United States); and Hizbollah with Lebanon, reporting the latest attacks by Israel on villages in South Lebanon. This localization can be seen in the sites' mission statements, which contain sections highlighting their accomplishments, both military and civilian. Hamas contains a "Glory Record," summarizing a list of the group's anti-Israeli activities both inside and outside Palestine, starting from 1988 and ending in 1994. Hizbollah's website contains video clips of the group's attacks on Israeli targets and photographs of victims of Israeli violence in both Lebanon and Palestine.

At the same time, the Islamic fundamentalist global outlook illustrates an antagonism toward the nation, with sites like Shareeah declaring that one cannot be a "British Muslim" because national affiliation contradicts the concept of *umma* (the totality of all Muslims). The sites seem to recognize the heterogeneity in the articulation of how Islam is understood in light of interweaving political beliefs and practices like nationalism (Eade 2003). Hence, some sites, like as-Sahwah's, contain articles interpreting Islam as antinationalist, such as "A Muslim's Nationality and His Belief" by Sayyid Qutb, whose writings have been a touchstone of contemporary political Islam. The sites also mirror the groups' global scope of operation and cooperation. Articles on Jihaad'ul'Kuffaarin contain the Jamaa Islamiyya's position on various international events, with headlines like "Mujaahideen Attack Russian Army Base in Dagestan [Chechnya]," "Arab Veterans of the Afghan War," and "the Moro Jihaad: Continuous Struggle for Islaamic [*sic*] Independence in Southern Philippines." Taliban Online boasts headlines like "There is Taliban-like Movement in Iraq's Kurdish

Area" and "Anti-Americanism Alive in a Friendly Country" (referring to Kuwait). Shareeah has a "Projects" section, containing items with titles such as "Department of Education Schools for Girls" and "Food Distribution Program" (in Afghanistan). Many links to the body of the sections are inactive, leaving such "projects" ambiguous.

One way in which the sites link together the local and the global is through their language use. The websites use English as their primary language, with Arabic being the second most popular. Websites like Shareeah, Hizbollah, and Taliban Online use both languages. While the use of English can be seen as an example of "hegemonic globalization" (ESCA 2003), it also reflects the groups' "growing mobility across frontiers" (Robins, 2000, 195). Shareeah also has an option in "Bosnian," while Hamas's website, the Palestine Information Center, uses Malawi, Persian, Russian, and Urdu, in addition to Arabic and English. The websites thus aim at an audience beyond the Arab world. They both hint that the members and supporters of the various groups are of several nationalities or live in different countries and form a community. The sites are localized through mixing Arabic terms (*shaheed, umma, zakaah*) within English-language sentences and in their subject matter, as their contents in different languages sometimes differ. While Hizbollah's website seems to offer identical information in Arabic and English, Shareeah's Bosnian option links to another website altogether with more specific information related to Bosnia. This suggests that the groups' primary affiliation remains with the countries in which they are based.

The Communication of a Pax Islamica

The websites reveal the solidarity of vision among the groups as they converge in their agreement on the establishment of a Pax Islamica. This Pax Islamica is communicated through the websites' statements on the necessity of jihad, commercial activities, and interactive sections and hyperlinks. Thus, Jihaad'ul'Kuffaarin contains an article claiming that the notion of jihad refers to *qital* (military fighting), and not linguistic or other forms of jihad. This is mirrored on al-Mujahiroun's website, which in its "Q&A" section affirms that "jihad as divine terrorism is obligatory in Islam." Tanzeem-e-Islami's mission statement declares that the group is replacing Sayyid Abdul A 'al Maududi's Jama'at-e-Islami in Pakistan and continuing its Jihadi mission. Hamas contains biographies (along with photographs) of major Hamas figures, beginning with its founder Sheikh Ahmad Yassin, and clearly describes the group as *jihadi*. Shareeah's mission statement traces its allegiance to Islamic fundamentalist groups in Egypt and to people like the late Hassan Banna and Sayyid Qutb, two of the early founders of the Islamic movement in Egypt who are known for their projihad views. While al-Muhajiroun describes the group as a mere "Islamic movement" with no overt mentioning of politics, the group is affiliated to the Taliban, also known for their agreement on jihad.

The websites allow the groups to engage in a global flow of trade to materially sustain this Pax Islamica (Held and McGrew 2000). The sites engage in limited commercial activities to help sustain their funds. Shareeah offers users a section dedicated to downloading lectures and Koran interpretations for free; but it also sells lectures and *khutbas* (sermons) on cassette tape, video, and CD. Topics covered are global in scope, with titles including "About the Jihad in Bosnia," "Afghanistan, the Return of Islam," and "Intifada, Blessed Hijacking, The Tricks of Shaytan [the devil]." The site also offers books, with titles like "Defence of Muslim Lands by Shaheed [martyr] Abdullah Azzam" (in Chechnya). Some websites also invite the supporters to donate money, either indirectly, as in as-Sahwah's call for Muslims to give *zakat* (*zakaah*), though the site does not explain where the money donated would go. Others blatantly ask for donations, like Indonesian group Laskar Jihad (Jihad Troopers) which had been connected to al-Qaeda. Its website has been noted as stating, "It takes a lot of fund, equipments [*sic*], and facilities for the daily needs of the Laskar and refugees. Consequently this becomes a responsibility of Moslem society as a whole for the glory of Islam and its believers" (Scheeres 2001). Shareeah also has a section that asks for donations to be made by sending checks to its London address.

The Pax Islamica is also supported through the websites' interactive sections. Stuart Hall argues that the Internet has enabled the formation of a global consciousness through its expansion of "the possibilities of sharing conversations across . . . different divides" (Hall 2003). Most fundamentalist websites enable this by providing e-mail addresses through which visitors can contact the webmasters and the groups behind the sites. This is important for maintaining contact among visitors of the websites and the groups. The sites also give the supporters a chance to "meet" through cyberspace. Al-Muhajiroun offers—besides e-mail—members' mobile phone numbers (in the UK), fax numbers, and a London mailing address, while as-Sahwah contains a discussion board where people can post their opinions. The Internet's time-space compression is best demonstrated by Taliban Online, which seems to be the most technologically sophisticated website of those analyzed. It includes a no-registration-required chat room: the user just needs to choose a nickname to join the conversation, and there are no private chat rooms. The site also contains a "Support Us!" section, which has an option for adding Taliban Online as a link to another website of the user's choice, an option with information about the site designed to be downloaded for Internet relay chat, and a "tell a friend via e-mail" option.

Another way in which the Internet helps sustain this Pax Islamica is through websites' hyperlinks that reflect the group's local and global political affiliations as well as ideological expressions. Hizbollah's hyperlinks, for example, are centered on institutions within Lebanon that are connected with the group, but the site itself is hyperlinked from Tanzeem. Taliban Online is hyperlinked to few websites, including al-Muhajiroun and al-Neda, both of which are inactive. Shareeah contains a large number of hyperlinks divided into sections like "News Sites," "Discussion Boards," "Dawa Sites" (for non-Muslims), and "Chat Sites." Most of the hyperlinks mentioned are active, but some are those to websites that do not exist anymore. It also has hyperlinks copied from Jannah, a news portal. Jannah's hyperlinks include sections like Business, Education, and Community, but also links to sites like Tanzeem and Hizb-ut-Tahrir (a site run by a Jihadi political party based in Palestine; http://www.hizb-ut-tahrir.org). The latter two are also hyperlinked to each other. In addition, Tanzeem is hyperlinked to the Algerian FIS (Front islamique de salut; http://www.fisalgeria. org), the Lebanese Al-Moqawama al-Islamiyya (the Islamic Resistance Support Association run by Hizbollah; http://www.moqawama.tv), the international Muslim Brothers (Al-Ikhwan al-Muslimoun; http://www. ummah.net/ikhwan), and the Pakistani branch of the group (http://www. ikhwan.org.pk). The availability of the websites listed here has fluctuated over time. The diagram in Fig. 6.1 illustrates the hyperlinks among the websites discussed.

Hyperlinks that enable the site visitors to find out about other affiliate groups increase their global connections. The hyperlinks' international scope is another way that various Islamic fundamentalist groups maintain and communicate their global presence. The content of the websites thus challenges the notion of Islamic fundamentalism as having an essentially localist nature. In fact, the groups utilize new media effectively, and thus give form to a global network that is in tune with their global outlooks and aims. For example, after the September 11 attacks, Taliban Online claimed that the Taliban did not support the attacks and that Osama bin Laden denied any involvement. After the raid by British police on the Finsbury Park mosque in London in January 2003, where Abu Hamza preaches, his website Shareeah covered the story on its home page, defending the mosque as a mere place of worship and ignoring the terrorist allegations on which the raid was based. The websites' presentation of such alternative news can be seen as a counter to a West-focused flow of information (Network EICOS 2003), an "aspiration to create a space within global culture" (Robins 2000, 200).

The groups also aim at strengthening their position in global politics through the use of interactive sections, particularly opinion polls. Taliban Online's Survey, for example, has posed questions like "Do you believe the Taliban will defeat Army of disbelievers by the Grace of Mighty Allah?" referring to American presence in Afghanistan. The survey claims that 98.8 percent of votes (3,768,982, according to the site) said yes. In this way, the Internet functions as a tool for "speaking" from "positions within the global distribution of power" (Hall 1996, 237). As Hall argues, "Because these positions change and alter, there is always an engagement with politics as a 'war of position'" (237).

Cyberwars

The Internet has also been a theater for the groups' political actions. It has been alleged that the September 11 attacks were coordinated mainly through e-mail (Norton-Taylor 2002). It has also been alleged that some of the groups' Internet chat rooms had been circulating rumors of an assault before the missile attack on an Israeli airliner in Kenya in December 2002 took place (Butcher 2002). The response to this increased exposure of the Internet as a tool in the hands of "terrorists" has varied from posting messages on the groups' websites appealing for information about potential terrorists (as the British MI5 did in October 2001, posting "contact us" messages on Qoqaz.com; see Norton-Taylor 2001), to surveillance and retention of e-mail records (Byrne 2002), to the actual closing down of sites. During the course in which this article has been written, al-Muhajiroun website was hacked (allegedly by the United States) and "repaired." Al-Muhajiroun and al-Neda sites were among the links available on Taliban Online, but the Links section on Taliban Online later stated that it was "under construction." The site had also been linked to another titled Beware of Shiaism, which contains anti-Shiite information in English and Urdu. Figure 1 shows how the groups are at the same time indirectly hyperlinked to Hizbollah, a Shiite group, which reveals the contradiction in their appeal.

The Internet is also used by the groups to respond to attacks outside cyberspace. Shareeah's articles are compiled in an online magazine titled *al-Jihaad*. After the raid on the Finsbury Park mosque, and with rumors that the British government was going to close down the website ("Rant on Website of Hate," *The Sun* 2003), al-Jihaad posted a disclaimer on its first page, stating, "Supporters of Shareeah does not take responsibility for all the content contained in these articles. And neither to claim to agree with all of the content contained in these articles or that it is representative of our views and beliefs." The articles present in *al-Jihaad* are listed under a

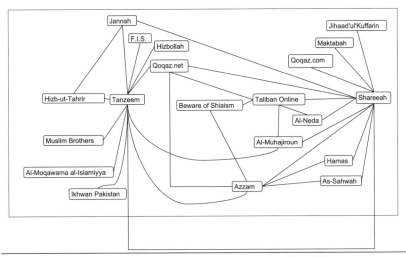

Figure 6.1 Diagram showing hyperlinks between Islamic fundamentalist websites.

"Contributed" section, to imply that their writers are not the people behind the website, and have titles like "Tyrani [sic] in Pakistan," "Anti Israel Reports," and "Stupid Bush." Shareeah was later closed down following the British government's decision to try to expel Abu Hamza from Britain due to his controversial preaching at Finsbury Park.

The fluid nature of the Internet has also been utilized by the groups in order to avoid being forced to disappear from cyberspace through hacking. The website of Azzam Publications (a Chechen site linked to Qoqaz. net) has now been closed down (allegedly by the United States); but just before that it published a posting of fifteen points informing the site users of what to do after the website disappears. The posting urged users to copy material from the website and publish it on their own websites and through discussion boards and e-mail lists. It also advised them to access the site "via proxies or anonymous services, such as http://www.safeweb. com or http://www.anonymizer.com." The posting also encouraged users to utilize the Internet to disseminate information and news about Jihad (Shareeah also encourages visitors to publicize its existence), and informed them that Azzam's products would be available for purchase from the Maktabah Al-Ansar Bookshop.

Indeed, Maktabah's website is selling books, audio and video material, and posters, as well as items like perfume and clothing, while Azzam Publications news postings can now be accessed on as-Sahwah. The case of Azzam illustrates the difficulty of controlling content on the Internet and the range of possibilities available for the groups' existence in cyberspace. The instantaneous nature of the Internet means that the groups can immediately adjust their Web presence according to the political climate. Shareeah's site for example contained a link to al-Neda, which disappeared following the raid on the Finsbury Park mosque. As-Sahwah's "Zakaah Calculator" and the "Click to Give Zakaah" option also disappeared after the raid.

Implications

The Internet has been celebrated as a place of dialogue, perhaps too optimistically as stated by Nathan Gardels:

> As the realm of the global mind grows, it will necessarily encroach on all enclosed spaces—political, national ethnic, linguistic or psychological. Openness and transparency are its bywords; closure of any kind entails the risk of isolation and failure (2000, 2).

David Ronfeldt and John Arquilla (2000) are also prematurely celebratory about the workings of cyberspace when they describe it as a space allowing "peace through knowledge" rather than "peace through strength." They argue for increased freedom of information on the Internet as an essential element toward achieving this peace. Such views neglect other players in the sociopolitical realm, such as Islamic fundamentalists, players that are part of the "global mind" but excluded because of their pathological associations. However, attention is being paid to Islamic fundamentalism as a global player that destabilizes the existing political status quo. Alvin and Heidi Toffler (2000) describe it as a "global gladiator." They point out that such "new forces, now are linked by the Internet, global telecom nets and other advanced technologies . . . and they come accompanied by . . . fund raisers . . . media manipulators and volunteer computer hackers" (2000, 26). The change that forces like Islamic fundamentalism will bring, they argue, is a change in the political representational system, whereby the United Nations will become obsolete as nations are undermined. Thus, the debate seems to center around the idea that Islamic fundamentalism (and Islam in general) is necessarily oppositional to the nation.

Of course, Islamic fundamentalist groups like the Muslim Brotherhood, which has branches in over seventy countries under different names, are advocating a Pax Islamica. For these groups, the Internet provides what Peter Sloterdijk terms a "portable homeland" (2000, 16). Islamic fundamentalism, then, is a force that is "located within and beyond the borders of the nation-state" (Moallem 1999, 324). Benjamin Barber (1992) has argued that Islamic fundamentalism is an example of the fragmentation of the nation into smaller groups in contrast with what he terms "McWorld," or "an emergent, transnational cultural uniformity" (Grosby 1997, 82). This denies Islamic fundamentalism its role in building nations and the existence of Islamic fundamentalist nations like Iran. But the situation is more complex than homogeneity/heterogeneity. I see Islamic fundamentalism as advancing a practice and consciousness better conceived as "global citizenship" with, and not against, tools of globalization. Islamic fundamentalism is not a nativist movement merely "entailing a 'localist' character" (Abaza and Stauth 1990: 218). That is to confound global with other Islamic movements, such as that of the Nation of Islam in the United States, which is a separatist movement aiming at isolating the Muslim community from the "existing social order" (Kepel 1997, 54). Even though the two movements share a "bottom-up Islamization" that offers services to the community to attract common members of society (Kepel 1997, 72), the former actively project a "global citizenship" through positioning on the Internet that combines appeals to universal values and using the technology to link to other groups.

The existence of multiple Islamic fundamentalist groups across the globe adds to the globalism of this network. Some groups are in opposition, such as the Jamaa Islamiyya and the Ahbash in Lebanon; and the groups themselves do not see a need to unite under one name. The existence of several groups is necessary for the protection of the transforming Islamic fundamentalist identity and its survival vis-à-vis opposition by global powers like the United States. The existence of several groups in different countries also serves to cater to the local issues that the groups encounter in the countries in which they exist. Martha Nussbaum's (1994) procosmopolitanism argument for being a "citizen of the world" has generated various responses from thinkers like Barber (1994) and Michael Dorris (1994), who argue that this global citizenship is too demanding and overwhelming, and Charles Beitz (1994) and Immanuel Wallerstein (1994), who say that cosmopolitanism need not reject patriotism, but that the two can be sustained together. This chapter has shown that none of those arguments can be simplistically applied to Islamic fundamentalism. It may have resistant characteristics, but it is not oppositional to global forces. Neither does it fit an opposition of cosmopolitanism to patriotism; instead it articulates a global citizenship that is relational and negotiative within processes of globalization.

References

Abaza, Mona, and Georg Stauth. 1990. "Occidental Reason, Orientalism, Islamic Fundamentalism: A Critique." Pp. 209–30 in *Globalization, Knowledge and Society*, edited by Martin Albrow and Elizabeth King. London: Sage.

Al-Ahsan, Abdullah. 1992. *Ummah or Nation? Identity Crisis in Contemporary Muslim Society.* Leicester, England: Islamic Foundation.

Ang, Ien. 2000. "Identity Blues." Pp. 1–13 in *Without Guarantees: In Honour of Stuart Hall*, edited by Paul Gilroy, Lawrence Grossberg, and Angela McRobbie. London: Verso.

Appadurai, Arjun. 1996. *Modernity at Large: Cultural Dimensions of Globalization.* Minneapolis: University of Minnesota Press.

Barber, Benjamin R. 1992, March. "Jihad vs. McWorld." *Atlantic Monthly*; available online at <http://www.theatlantic.com/politics/foreign/baberf.htm>.

———. 1994. "Constitutional Faith." *Boston Review* 19, no. 5:14–15.

Beck, Ulrich. 2000. "What is Globalization?" Pp. 99–103 in *The Global Transformations Reader: An Introduction to the Globalization Debate*, edited by David Held and Anthony McGrew. Cambridge: Polity.

Beitz, Charles. 1994. "Patriotism for Cosmopolitans." *Boston Review* 19, no. 5:23–24.

Butcher, Mike. "Cyber Hype." Guardian; available online at <http://www.guardian.co.uk/online/story/0,3605,853535,00.html>, 5 December 2002.

Byrne, Ciar.. "Anti-Terrorist Measures 'Threatens web Freedom,." *Guardian*; available online at <http://media.guardian.co.uk/newmedia/story/0,7496,786913,00.html>, 6 September 2002

Castells, Manuel. 1997. *The Power of Identity.* Oxford: Blackwell.

Di Justo, Patrick. "How Al-Qaida Site Was Hijacked." *Wired News*; available online at <http://www.wired.com/news/culture/0,1284,54455-2,00.html>, 10 August 2002.

Dorris, Michael. 1994. "No Place Like Home." *Boston Review* 19, no. 5:18.

Eade, John. 2003. "Local/Global Processes and the Islamisation of Urban Space." School of International Migration and Ethnic Relations, Malmo University; available online at <http://www.imer.mah.se/hemsida_forskning/paper_john_eade.pdf>.

Ehteshami, Anoushiravan. 1997. "Islamic Fundamentalism and Political Islam." Pp. 179–99 in *Issues in World Politics*, edited by Brian White, Richard Little, and Michael Smith. London: Macmillan.

Faksh, Mahmud A. 1997. *Fundamentalism in Egypt, Algeria and Saudi Arabia.* London: Praeger.

Gardels, Nathan. 2000. "Comment: The Global Mind." *New Perspectives Quarterly* 17, no. 1:2–3.

Giddens, Anthony. 1990. *The Consequences of Modernity.* Cambridge: Polity.

Grosby, Steven. 1997. "The Future of Nationality: A Few, Mostly Theoretical Considerations." *International Journal on World Peace* 14, no. 4:81–96.

Hall, Stuart. 1992. "The Question of Cultural Identity." Pp. 273–26 in Stuart Hall, David Held and Tony McGrew, *Modernity and its Futures.* Cambridge: Polity.

———. 1996. "The Meaning of New Times." Pp. 233–37 in *Stuart Hall: Critical Dialogues in Cultural Studies*, edited by David Morley and Kuan-Hsing Chen. London: Routledge.

———. 2003. Interview by Martin Jacques; available online at <http://www.usyd.edu.au/su/social/papers/hall1.html>.

Hamzeh, A. Nizar. 1998. "The Future of Islamic Movements in Lebanon." Pp. 249–73 in *Islamic Fundamentalism: Myths and Realities*, edited by Ahmad S. Moussalli. Reading, England: Ithaca.

Held, David, and Anthony McGrew. 2000. "The Great Globalization Debate: An Introduction." Pp. 1–45 in *The Global Transformations Reader: An Introduction to the Globalization Debate*, edited by David Held and Anthony McGrew. Cambridge: Polity.

Hjarvard, Stig. 2002. "Mediated Encounters: An Essay on the Role of Communication Media in the Creation of Trust in the 'Global Metropolis.'" Pp. 69–84 in *Global Encounters: Media and Cultural Transformation*, edited by Gitte Stald and Thomas Tufte. Luton, England: University of Luton Press.

Kepel, Gilles. 1997. *Allah in the West: Islamic Movements in America and Europe.* Cambridge: Polity.

Moallem, Minoo. 1999. "Transnationalism, Feminism, and Fundamentalism." Pp. 320–48 in *Between Woman and Nation: Nationalisms, Transnational Feminisms, and the State*, edited by Caren Kaplan, Norma Alarcon, and Minoo Moallem. Durham, NC: Duke University Press.

Nussbaum, Martha. 1994. "Patriotism and Cosmopolitanism." *Boston Review* 19, no. 5:3.

Network EICOS. 2003. "Cultural Identity: Development and Sustainability"; available online at <http://www.eicos.psycho.ufrj.br/ingles/ingl%20_ident_cultural/identidadecultural.htm>.

Norton-Taylor, Richard. "MI5 Posts Terror Appeal on Arab Websites." *Guardian*; available online at <http://media.guardian.co.uk/attack/story/0,1301,581273,00.html>, 26 October 2001.

OutThere News. 2002. "Al-Qaeda a Year after 9/11: Triumphant, Frustrated and Watching Wall Street"; available online at <http://www.megastories.com/attack/alqaeda/analysis020906.shtml>.

Paun, Nicolae. 2003. "Interculturalism, Globalization and Cultural Identity"; available online at <http://www.ecsanet.org/dialogue/contributions/Paun.doc>.

"Rant on Website of Hate." *The Sun.*, 22 January 2003.

Robins, Kevin. 2000. "Encountering Globalization." Pp. 195–201 in *The Global Transformations Reader: An Introduction to the Globalization Debate*, edited by David Held and Anthony McGrew. Cambridge: Polity.

Ronfeldt, David, and John Arquilla. 2000. "From Cyberspace to the Noosphere: Emergence of the Global Mind." *New Perspectives Quarterly* 17, no. 1:18–25.

Saukko, Paula. 2000. "The Interconnected Self: Problems and Possibilities in an Emergent Ideal." Unpublished manuscript.

Scheeres, Julia. "Blacklisted Groups Visible on Web." *Wired News*; available online at <http://www.wired.com/news/politics/0,1283,47616-2,00.html>, 19 October 2001.

Shohat, Ella. 1999. "By the Bitstream of Babylon: Cyberfrontiers and Diasporic Vistas." Pp. 213–32 in *Home, Exile, Homeland: Film, Media, and the Politics of Place*, edited by Hamid Naficy. New York: Routledge.

Sloterdijk, Peter. 2000. "From Agrarian Patriotism to the Global Self." *New Perspectives Quarterly* 17, no. 1: 15–18.

Taheri, Amir. 1987. *Holy Terror: The Inside Story of Islamic Terrorism*. London: Sphere.

Toffler, Alvin, and Heidi Toffler. 2000. "Global Gladiators Challenge the Power of Nations." *New Perspectives Quarterly* 17, no. 1:26–27.

Turkle, Sherry. 1996. *Life on the Screen: Identity in the Age of the Internet*. London: Weidenfeld and Nicholson.

Wallerstein, Immanuel. 1994. "Neither Patriotism nor Cosmopolitanism." *Boston Review* 19, no. 5:15–16.

Weisman, Robyn. "Teen Hackers Crash Hizbollah ISP." *NewsFactor Network*; available online at <http://www.newsfactor.com/perl/story/6880.html>, 22 January 2001.

Whitaker, Brian. "US Pulls the Plug on Muslim Websites." *Guardian*; available online at <http://www.guardian.co.uk/elsewhere/journalist/story/0,7792,549590,00.html>, 10 September 2001.

CHAPTER 7

Lost in Transition? The Internet and *Reformasi* in Indonesia

MERLYNA LIM

Introduction

The advent of the Internet as a global communications technology has opened historically unprecedented opportunities for the flow and cross-fertilization of ideas within and across territorial boundaries, bringing promises of empowering people by giving civil society greater voice vis-à-vis the state, political elites, and private economic interests. From this optimistic view, the Internet advances freedom and democracy by opening the public sphere to their voice and cyberparticipation in political affairs. Examples of widespread political reform in East and Southeast Asia that are found to be greatly facilitated by Internet-based flows of information provide evidence for this view. An extreme case of this democracy-Internet connection is South Korea, which along with its fundamental political reforms at the end of the twentieth century began to identify its civil society as being composed of "Netizens"—Internet citizens (Cho 2002).

Contrary views are manifold. Some see the Internet as a threat to democracy through its potential to create Orwellian modes of state surveillance over individual and group behavior. In a somewhat related manner, others take the view that to the extent that it can be said to exist, civil society itself is controlled by elites through manipulation of sociocultural processes of identify formation. Graham (2000), for example, shows how telecommunications are customized to the needs of powerful users and their spaces, casting the Internet as a technology that widens gaps between the powerful and the powerless. Still others document "communes of resistance" rising from civil society to appropriate cybertechnology and its informational flows for organizing violent responses to perceived injustice under global capitalist hegemony (Castells 1997). Still others point to the ways in which capitalism as a process of global accumulation is killing the Internet itself through invasions of unsolicited commercial messages and unrelenting attempts to commodify all cyberflows of information.

The debate over the Internet as a revolutionary facilitator of democracy or as a growing menace to civil society and democracy has no resolution in the abstract. Insights into these issues can only be drawn from historical experiences rooted in specific local contexts. Flows of information, images, and symbolic representations over the Internet are invariably mediated through local constellations of power, including both political/class structures and cultural practices, in ways that transform electronic signals into potent social meanings that can only then become part of contestations to reshape the political landscape. The discussion that follows looks at this localization process and its outcomes, focusing on the civic space dimension of the Internet as it interplays with the rise of civil society in Indonesia during two historical episodes: first, the May 1998 Indonesian students movement (*reformasi*[1]) and, second, the emergence of the Jihad Troopers in the early post-Suharto era. Leading into the first episode in the mid 1990s, nongovernment Internet providers began to create a new kind of civic space—a cybercivic space—that soon allowed Indonesian people to collectively mobilize for political reform. Yet, as the second case illustrates, the Internet also allows for other less civil elements of society to rise to destabilize both civil society and the nation-state.

Civil Society, Civic Spaces, and Identity

In much of the world, localizing the Internet in tandem with political reform has had three interwoven dynamics: the rise of civil society, the creation of civic spaces—both physical and cyberspaces—for the political engagement of civil society, and social mobilization around the formation of collective identity. Although the concept of civil society has been developed from the earlier writings of John Locke (1690) and G. W. F. Hegel (1967), the use here emphasizes Alexis de Tocqueville's (1969) idea of voluntary association and Antonio Gramsci's (1971) separation of civil society from both the state and economy (market) in the public realm. As argued by Friedmann (1998), the key to the existence of civil society is its degree of autonomy from state and corporate economy.

In this sense, the idea of "voluntary" association is taken in the narrow understanding of not being overtly controlled by the state or economy. It does not mean that manipulation of identity or pressures to join certain forms of association are not prevalent. Indeed, whether the tendency is toward hegemony under certain religious or cultural identities or, in the opposite direction, the fragmentation of society into myriad opposing forms of association, the constant turmoil of association within civil society is its hallmark. However, to attribute this voluntary process to an involuntary function of class structure is reductionist and certainly does not fit the case of Indonesia where, for example, neither a large urban middle class nor a proletarianized labor force predominates or subsumes socioeconomic divisions and where capitalist relations are as yet not as fully developed as in the West. In the Indonesian case, at least, association within civil society cannot be solely seen as the manifestation of hegemony under a single economic class. In an archipelago composed of more than thirteen thousand islands and extant precapitalist societies linked with a capitalist world system, shifting modes of association are imbedded in religious, cultural, racial, and class differences that are highly complex. As the discussion below shows, the dissolution of an authoritarian regime thus unleashes this complexity and results in significantly diverse forms of contestations within civil society that take the form of attempts to capture a weakened state apparatus.

Over the past several decades, the rise of civil society has become a singularly prominent political phenomenon as people around the world, including in Indonesia, have joined in movements to gain autonomy from oppressive states through democratic reforms (Douglass and Friedmann 1998). Although globalization plays a key role in the broader political economy of the rise of civil society through, for example, access to information beyond the nation-state, the struggles in the rise of civil society are highly differentiated through varied historical processes of development of localized sociopolitical institutions.

Despite such positive trends, however, authoritarian regimes continue to successfully resist civil society movements in many parts of the world. Equally daunting is the appearance of sectarian organizations from within civil society that seek to dominate or even eliminate nonbelievers or perceived outsiders. In addition, the erosion of both the state and civil society organizations through the expanding influence on the political, economic, and social life of nondemocratic institutions such as the World Trade Organization that make decisions on global-local relations in favor of a global corporate agenda.

Whatever the outcome, the rise of civil society is interdependent with a second but often neglected facet of localization—namely, the creation of civic spaces. The term *civic space* is used here instead of *public space* to clarify the need for spaces in which civil society can engage in its daily practices. When seen from a political perspective, the availability of civic spaces is a basic requirement for democratic practices to flourish in any society (Douglass, Ho, and Ooi 2002). Following from the insights of Michel Foucault (1979) and Henri Lefebvre (1991), instead of simply a pre-existing given or a backdrop for social action, the production of space—particularly civic space—is an active dimension of social life and change. In this context, the Internet can be seen as a potential civic space in which civil society can flourish independently from the state and the corporate economy and can also engage in political action.

Society-technology-space relations revolve around a third dynamic, that of identity formation. Creating identities is a universal human experience and fundamental source of meaning and social power. Collective identity formation—identities shared among individuals—is a primary driving force in contemporary world history (Castells 1997). They are the sources of resistance to globalization and the rise of network society, which in the current era is manifested by the spread of information technologies, in particular the Internet. According to Manuel Castells (1997, 8), collective identities take three principal forms:

1. *Legitimizing identities* are created by dominant institutions of society—notably, political regimes in control of the state apparatus and their followers—to extend and rationalize their rule.
2. *Resistance identities* are generated by those who are being devalued and/or stigmatized by the logic of domination.
3. *Project identities* go beyond resistance to attempt to actively redefine positions in society and, by so doing, transform relations of power in the prevailing social structure.

Resistance identities play a critical role in fostering the rise of civil society against oppressive states and the hegemonic tendencies of global corporate capitalism. These identities become the moral fabric uniting people into communities of "collective resistance against otherwise unbearable oppression" (Castells 1997, 9). They can also further develop into projects that seek to change the course of history by using collective identities as a power base, for example, to overthrow existing regimes or create alternative communes at the margins of society and territorial spaces.

Although often arising from resistance identities against the state, the sustenance of civil society ultimately requires the regulatory powers of the state. In this sense, resistance or project identities must transform into legitimizing identities of a new status quo that can bring together the "apparatuses" that are deeply rooted among people and prolong the routines of state–civil society relations. As the Indonesian case will show, the Internet played a crucial role in creating resistance identities that galvanized civil society to overthrow the New Order Government of President Suharto. In the aftermath, however, continued resistance has created identity projects that are not necessarily leading to a new period of national legitimization, but are instead threatening the vitality of civil society and the state.

Suharto's Panopticon: State Control and Surveillance

Suharto, whose reign of power as New Order president of the Republic of Indonesia lasted from 1966 to 1998, built a "panopticon" of constant surveillance over national territorial space.[2] In constructing a national system of surveillance, the Suharto regime magnified its control through fear of its capacity to identify anyone complicit with antigovernment actions, and it did so in a manner that was greater than its actual capacity physically to enforce its rule. This fear of government was accomplished and sustained through written, verbal, and hidden rules to control all physical spaces as well as the spaces of the human mind. Wherever people went, whatever they thought, they felt that they were under the eye of the state. Although many public parks, civic centers, plazas, and city squares were created during Suharto's New Order government, they were all beleaguered by the purpose of creating spaces for activities symbolically in support of his regime. Uses of these spaces were restricted to state approved functions. By staging events in these spaces to extol the New Order government as a source of Indonesian identity and progress, potential civic spaces were used instead to manipulate people and control the people.

Suharto's success in creating these identities was manifested in the general unawareness among people that they were being controlled or manipulated. For more than three decades people believed that the plazas, squares and parks were places for only having national ceremonies (e.g., a flag ceremony on Monday morning) or for doing regimented national physical exercise (*senam kesegaran jasmani*) on Friday morning and mass jogging on Sunday morning. Those engaged in the exercise programs would wear the same athletic clothing—not unlike prisoners in an exercise yard—as symbolic evidence of loyalty to the nation and ruling regime, while the government created the image that it really took care of its people by providing such spaces. Participating in weekly state-sponsored athletic events was a way for people to thank the state for delivering economic progress and its generosity.

The "Authorized Party"

For more than thirty years the government was able to legitimate itself through such identity promotion in public spaces. There was no space that was "civic" in the sense of being available to civil society at arm's length from the state. Instead, all activities happening in all kind of spaces—private as well as public—in Indonesia were required to be known and permitted by the state. To hold social occasions, religious meetings, sport events, and cultural and art events, let alone political debates, required getting a stamped letter stating that the activity is permitted by the "authorized party." The terminology of *pihak yang berwajib* (the "authorized party") used by the government did not specifically identify who this party or person was. Like the invisible guard at the panopticon, this party could be in any space and time, thus making people engage in self-censorship and self-discipline with the knowledge that the "ghost of Suharto" or "the authorized party" just might be observing their actions.

A particularly ominous form of the use of the term *authorized party* was the posting in every neighborhood, street, and alley of small signboards with the phrase, "All guests who stay more than 24 hours should be reported [to the authorized party]" (*Tamu 1x24 jam wajib lapor*; see Fg. 1). This plain signboard is much more powerful that it appears to be. Much simpler and cheaper than the surveillance cameras mounted by many Western governments, this signboard successfully controlled people without giving any overt feeling of being controlled. Although people might not have actually reported their guests—especially since it was not clear to whom they should be reported—they accepted the idea that government had the right to ask them to do so and that it was the right thing to do. They were also encouraged by such signage to feel suspicious of "strangers" in their neighborhood.

Far above these small neighborhood signs soared an even more powerful eye of the New Order panopticon. It was the "Palapa" satellite (see Fg. 2),[3] images of which were used from elementary school upward (mainly on 1977 and 1984 curricula), to symbolize the unification of Indonesia under the all-seeing communications satellite. When Suharto pushed the button to launch this satellite in July 1976, he declared that day as the day

Figure 7.1 "All guests who stay more than 24 hours should be reported."

of national unity and made an explicit parallel between the satellite and himself as the unifier of the 13,677 islands by Palapa.

Followed by the *Televisi Masuk Desa* (government controlled national television entering the villages) program, Palapa was much more than just technological prestige. It was a provocative symbol of national identity and cultural integration that allowed the government to more emphatically reach and mark the perimeters of national cultural space, to link the boundaries of the far-flung archipelago to the center, and to enable Indonesians throughout the nation to more effectively "imagine their community" (Kitley 1994, 104). By filling the minds of people with the image of unification, the state actually had been "panopticonizing" society by identifying the image of a satellite having surveillance capabilities with nationhood and national identity.

Another key element of the panopticon apparatus of the New Order that is still applied today is the *Rukun Tetangga* (RT) system. In this system, which was taken directly from the Japanese method of organizing neighbors to spy on each other introduced in Indonesia during the Japanese

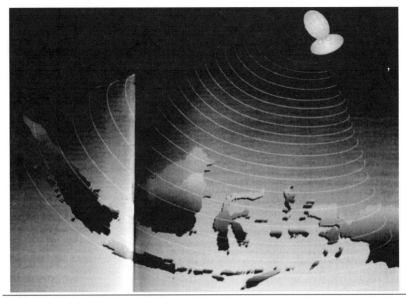

Figure 7.2 Palapa satellite image over Indonesia.

occupation in World War II, the state puts a *Ketua RT* (leader) for every neighborhood block, a *Ketua RW* (*Rukun Warga*) for several RT, a *Lurah* (chair of the village) for several RW, and so on, up to the top level. Within this system, no one can say where the state stops because it is composed of layers of organizations that are not officially state functions but nonetheless reports to the state, right down to the neighborhood block level.

Like the guards watching the prisoners in Jeremy Bentham's panopticon, through its "authorized parties," *Tamu 1x24 jam wajib lapor* signboards, and the image of unification under Palapa and the RT system, Suharto's New Order regime could effectively control society's spaces and, in so doing, provided no real civic spaces at all. This led to a suffocation of civil society, which was furthered by direct action against potential sources of mobilized dissent.

Containing Islam and Universities

In authoritarian states there are generally only two major sources of social movements for political reform that can be sustained. One is religion, especially the dominant religions of a nation that the state does not dare try to destroy; the other is the university, where disaffected intellectuals gather and radicals find sanctuary (Douglass, Ho, and Ooi 2002). Concerning religion, as with his predecessor, President Sukarno, President Suharto viewed Islam as a principal source of identity projects that could effectively challenge his rule, and much of the political effort of the New Order was aimed at containing Islam and capturing its identity for state purposes. Following the practices of Sukarno, Suharto kept the existence of the Ministry of Religious Affairs mainly to control Islam, to create an allegedly "modern, tolerant, and apolitical" Indonesian Islam, by publishing Islamic *da'wah* (educational and legal literature acceptable to the state), governing the development of Islamic discourse produced by Muslim subjects and institutions, and establishing the so-called legal Islamic institutions, all of which were based on the state Pancasila ideology of unity with diversity (not Islam's *shari'a*). The Ministry of Religious Affairs also published an official translation and commentary on the Koran and watched over non-official ones. Another form of marginalization was to force Muslim parties to be united under one party, Partai Persatuan Pembangunan, which for decades gave support only to the rule of Suharto.

In addition to religious quarters, universities, especially the main national public universities such as the University of Indonesia (UI) and the Institute of Technology Bandung (ITB), had been the major sources of political movements in Indonesia since Dutch colonial days. To preemptively quash such activities, Suharto's regime began strategically to diminish the political involvement of students to gather for political mobilization by not only filling university leadership positions with his personnel, but also by redesigning the organization of spaces through campus renovation projects. By locating faculties in UI far apart from each other, so it was almost impossible to walk from one faculty to other, his intentions succeeded as the energy to engage crowds of student and faculty members in multidisciplinary gatherings was effectively dissipated. At the ITB the old student centers, where all student activists used to gather to talk, were torn down. Meanwhile, by consenting to allow periodic police and military sweeps of protestors on campus in both universities via the Bakorstranasda (Regional National Strategic Coordination Board), the state claimed the right to control university campus spaces at will. The disappearance of civic spaces on campus had the direct impact of diminishing the political engagement of universities in national politics.

In sum, through its control of potential civic spaces, the state orchestrated the production and manipulation of images, symbols, and ideas. Nominal civic spaces were captured and transformed into a state theater of choreographed identity formation. Through its propaganda, the state tried to build and sustain what Castells calls a "legitimizing identity" needed by Suharto to remain in power over a vast archipelago of great diversity and always-potential opposition to the regime's hegemonic designs.

The Advent of the Internet

For more than three decades, the Suharto regime enjoyed nearly absolute control over physical spaces, media spaces, and information/communications spaces. The coming of the Internet was highly instrumental in ending this era (Hill and Sen 2000; Lim 2003a, 2003c; Marcus 1998). Initially, at the time the Internet started to develop in Indonesia in the mid-1990s, the state started trying to control the technology, as it had with older media. However, attempts to control failed as the Indonesian economy plummeted with the coming of the Asian financial crisis in 1997–98. In this critical period, corporate attempts to dominate the Internet business also failed. With some help from international funding organizations, civil society groups—especially those from universities and educational institutions—started to build the Internet infrastructure on campuses and from there successfully captured the development of the Internet in Indonesia (Lim 2000b). One outstanding example was the Computer Network Research Group (CNRG) at the ITB, which bypassed the state-owned telecommunications company's domination and successfully hooked into the global Internet by accessing the Internet through a Japanese satellite (Lim 2003b: 237–38).[4] The Internet in Indonesia started in education and research institutions as early as 1993, and had became much more popular after 1996 with the availability of Internet cafés (*warnet*) throughout the archipelago (Lim 2000c).

The Internet itself represents a revolutionary change in the space-time relations of communications. The technologies of cyberspace use space-time relations in a way that severely reduces the effects of borders and defies simple linearity in communications pathways (Derrida 1974). In seeming to annihilate space with time, cybertechnology allows communications through the Internet to appear instantaneously upon demand at multiple points in an ever shifting network of connectivity. In contrast to the printed word or even television and radio, the Internet radically expands the reach of communications and, in so doing, allows for the appearance of vast, previously unimaginable cyberterrains in which ordinary people can engage in exchanges of ideas and construct shared identities.

The Internet's revolutionary technology also allows an unusually high potential for users to bypass, finesse, and otherwise resist attempts by the state to control its uses. The potential for massive increases in abundance of information, points of connectivity, and the spatial scope of communications reaching far beyond the nation-state adds to the difficulty any government or regulatory body faces in monitoring and controlling Internet content. Such limitations on state surveillance and censorship imbedded in the technology create the opportunity for spaces that give substantial autonomy to people not only to share information but to also form collective associations, to create identities of resistance, and to create identity projects seeking fundamental political change. In other words, the technology allows for the creation of what can be termed "cybercivic" spaces that facilitate the rise of civil society in places such as Indonesia.

Yet despite this potential imbedded in the technology, cyberspace is less "virtual" or open to the world than it appears to be. First, it requires physical technology to capture its signals; such technology is not ubiquitous; on a global scale it is, in fact, still rare. It also involves other physical infrastructure, ranging from satellites to telephone or cable networks and Internet cafés to shelter hardware and provide space for real-world users. In addition, all system elements must be managed by real people at real geographical sites. On a global scale, networks of "wired" cities that are centers of local control, management and access to the Internet are the spatial template of cyberspace and, by extension, cybercivic space. In this new geography of the world system, each node is still dependent upon the local production of space.

More specifically, the actualization of cyberspace as a new form of civic space is contingent upon the changing ways in which the localization of global cybernetworks occurs. In Indonesia, the warnet—a small commercial establishment equipped with several computers hooked to the Internet—provides a clear example of how civil society has been able to develop cybercivic spaces within the context of an authoritarian political regime. Since its birth in the mid-1990s, the warnet system has provided the major entry for Indonesians, especially those of the younger generation, into cyberspace. Without the warnet, the Internet would have remained beyond the economic and physical reach of most of the people who now use it. Currently, approximately 60 percent of Internet users in Indonesia access it from the warnet.

Accessing the Internet from warnet (the term may be either singular or plural in construction), unlike connecting from home, office, or public library, is a direct form of social engagement (Lim 2003c). The students and youngsters who sit in front of the computers in the warnet do much more than just surf the Web; they also interact with each other within the physical space of the warnet. While some choose to sit in a partitioned space for privacy, many others who want to enjoy accessing the Internet together with friends create within the warnet a group lounge with several computers (Lim 2003c). For these users, physical space matters as much as cyberspace. Cyberspace reaches into the physical space of the warnet, with the users coexisting in both.

Since its birth, the warnet has been characterized as a "free space." It was born independently, without the intervention of the state or corporations. While who actually founded the warnet remains vague, it started to be very popular in 1996. At that moment the young staff (Onno Purbo and friends), recent graduates, and students of the ITB, through the CNRG—which was actually not formally within the structure of ITB—worked together to build a company, Pointer, whose main task was to build as many warnet as possible in Bandung and Jakarta. They also popularized the concept of warnet by giving free seminars throughout the country (Lim 2003b).

Like all good civic spaces, the warnet provides privacy from both state intrusion and consumer identities while offering a place for meeting others and exchanging ideas and information flowing into cyberspace that connects with other warnet, potentially linking thousands of existing social communities and organizations with each other. Many communities are created virtually but then become face-to-face communities or even legal institutions. This interplay between the virtual and real physical space of the Internet sometimes extends beyond the realm of chatting and e-mailing for friendship. As cybercivic spaces they can transform electronic messages into political action, as was the case in the late 1990s in Indonesia.

The Internet and the Rise of Civil Society in Indonesia

As the most pervasive provider of access to Internet in Indonesia, the warnet gained greater prominence in the late 1990s during the economic and political crisis that undermined both the state's and the corporate economy's ability to maintain their power over access to the Internet. The late 1997 crisis sweeping through Pacific Asia hit Indonesia politically and economically, causing the collapse of both the New Order regime and the nation's export economy. Many state-linked corporate Internet service providers that emerged in 1996 simply collapsed in 1997 due to the combined political and economic crisis, resulting in the failure of the state and its corporate cronies to monopolize the Indonesian Internet. At the same time, the state entered into an identity crisis as people lost the trust they previously had in the New Order. During this crisis, warnet grew in numbers in Indonesia, especially on Java, and rapidly emerged as network points for political activation of civil society via cyberspace.

The major contribution of the Internet to Indonesian society during the crisis is that it provided spaces for people to commingle without overt control of the state and, by extension, the vast business world linked to it. During the 1996–98 period just before and during the peak of the crisis, cyberspace became the principal space through which people could discuss and criticize Suharto's New Order. Among some Internet applications, mailing lists were the most effective tool for political discussion and disseminating political information. Websites were also used to disseminate information; however, since Internet connection at that point was still slow (due to low bandwidth), e-mail-based applications like mailing lists were more accessible. Among some important mailing lists were the first and the most famous Indonesian political list, Apakabar (How do you do? or, What's up?).[5] In the mid-1990s it became a space for political discussions for a wide range of views. For Indonesians, as stated by one of Indonesia's Netizens,[6] Apakabar was a list that accepted opposed opinions (against Suharto's regime); here was "the place for Indonesian activists to freely spill out all kinds of complaints, grumbles or even angriness about the government." Some other mailing lists created by Indonesian students abroad, such as Janus (Indonesians@janus.berkeley.edu), ParokiNet (paroki@uiuc.edu), and IsNet (islam@isnet.org), and several other student mailing lists created in North America, Europe and Australia, also contributed in providing space for political discussions.

Through the Internet, people could gain and share information that previously was controlled by the state and its infamous Ministry of Information—especially forbidden information about such scandals as the massive wealth of Suharto's family and his role in the attempt to take over the government in the "G30S affair" of 1965—as well as left-wing materials. The banned, small, prolabor student party, the Democratic People's Party (PRD in Indonesian), launched their website freely on the Internet without fear of being cracked down by the government.[7] The deeply censored articles of a leftist author Pramoedya Ananta Toer were published on the Internet.[8] Meanwhile, George Aditjondro, a Suharto critic who sought political asylum in Australia, freely posted his report on the corruption of Suharto's family and political cronies in many Indonesian mailing lists.

For the first time, the Indonesian people finally had their own civic spaces, and the warnet became a favorite spot to explore cyberspace. Unfettered access to information and freedom to talk about many things—from politics to sex—gave a color of excitement to warnet all over Indonesia. Among various political information made available, information about the Suharto family's corrupt practices quickly became the most popular. When people wanted to find a scapegoat, the offenses of the Suharto family were seen as a perfect candidate as the cause of crisis.

Because of the long absence of non-government information-gathering in Indonesia, the ability of the Internet to connect the global and local (Indonesia) was crucial. The Internet not only connected Indonesians at home with Indonesians abroad; it also linked Indonesian society to broader global sources of information and to social movements (e.g., in China and Korea) that could inspire Indonesians to organize their own movements. The connectivity among Indonesian students and among universities inside and outside Indonesia was exceptionally vital to the rise of civil society in Indonesia. All of these triggered the emergence of collective identities of resistance to effectively challenge the legitimacy of the New Order regime.

The *Reformasi*: From Cyberspace to the Physical Space

The Internet was crucial, but it was not the sole source of support for political reform (*reformasi*) in Indonesia (Lim 2003a). Megawati Sukarnoputri, the opposition leader, and her party *PDI Perjuangan* (Democratic People of Indonesia in Struggle), campaigned in cyberspace by launching a website,[9] but she also had to go into the streets to hold campaigns all over Indonesia to gain support. The PRD still had to hold road shows at universities to obtain votes from students in addition to its intensive online campaigns through Apakabar and other mailing lists.

Activists still had to make Internet based information available to a wider range of society by transforming it into readable printed media. The journey of one piece of information is described in Figure 3, which shows that in order reach the masses, electronic information from the Internet needed to be transformed into printed flyers and information sheets that were given away or sold by newspaper sellers in the streets. For example, an article about Suharto's wealth from Apakabar was the most popular information available in cyberspace. A student surfing the Internet from a warnet and reading this information would print out the information and fax a copy to a friend, take another to his family, and give additional copies to a news vendor. The friend and family members might also disseminate the information in a similar way, multiplying it exponentially throughout

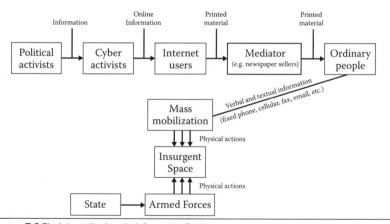

Figure 7.3 The Internet's place in Information Paths.

major cities in Indonesia. At the same time, the news vendor might make more copies and sell them on the street. In Bandung, a one-page summary of Suharto's wealth was sold for just 1,000 rupiah (approximately ten U.S. cents), the hourly wage of an unskilled worker at that time. The news vendor might also sell it to his colleagues, who would also sell it, rapidly disseminating the information to a vast audience.

Empowered by new information and a new sense of collective opposition, people turned from resistance to a more proactive project of finding the right means and moment to confront the state and bring down Suharto and his New Order. Using different means of communication not overtly controlled by government—telephone, fax, cellular phone, and, particularly, e-mail—students and others mobilized people to move to the streets and to occupy parks, plazas, and the frontage of governmental buildings. The peak moment came in May 1998 when thousands of demonstrators representing manifold civil society groups gathered at and occupied the parliament building in Jakarta, demanding that Suharto "abdicate his throne." Other spaces that never had a civic function before were turned into spaces of insurgency; among these were the traffic circle at the Hotel Indonesia and the National Monument.

This story shows that the Internet has been vital to political reform in Indonesia. The flow of Internet information helped to galvanize the energies of civil society to confront the state and help create "insurgent spaces" (Douglass, Ho, and Ooi 2002). Cyberspace, indeed, needs physical civic space to mobilize people. From cyberspace to the warnet and streets of Indonesian cities, the overthrow of Suharto succeeded not in virtual space but through actual political activities in appropriated civic spaces.

Jihad in Cyberspace

Just as it can support civil society to accomplish a historical political revolution, the Internet can also assist another side of the contemporary network society—communal resistance, which opposes not just the state but other segments of civil society that do not follow its doctrines. A project identity can be constructed not on the basis of a multicultural civil society but as continuation of communal resistance to a secular society and state (Castells 1997, 11). *Communal resistance* here refers to groups of people who defend their space or places against perceived antagonistic hegemonic forces. In what Castells calls the "informational" age of today, such communes often "claim historic memory and/or affirm the permanence of their value against the dissolution of history in timeless time and the celebration of the ephemeral in the culture of real virtuality" (Castells 1997, 358).

Religious identities are among the strongest and most important sources of constructing identity (Castells 1997, 12). For Muslims in Indonesia, connectivity to the global network also means connectivity to global Islam. Islamic societies in Egypt, Iran, and other countries become closer and more real through the information and graphic representations available in cyberspace, and the rise of Islamic fundamentalism in the Middle East makes a very significant impression on Muslims in Indonesia. Global Islamic fundamentalism began to flourish as Indonesia entered a period of political and economical uncertainty, presenting a ripe situation for Islamic fundamentalism. Interregional conflict and separatist movements in several places in Indonesia provided more space for fundamentalism to establish itself and grow, which reinforced the process of disintegration of political structures in Indonesia. As noted above, Islam had been marginalized for decades. The fall of Suharto provided an unprecedented opportunity for Muslim communities to rise up and step in the political field.

The Jihad Troopers

The jihad movement is one of the strongest and the most radical forms of Islamic fundamentalism. A group led by Ja'far Umar Thalib, a veteran of the Soviet-Afghanistan war who met Osama bin Laden in Pakistan in 1987, was among the most prominent factions of the jihad movement in Indonesia. Called the *Laskar Jihad* (LJ), or Jihad Troopers, in a relatively short period of time it became one of the strongest Islamic communities in Indonesia. The initial organization, FKAWJ,[10] was founded in 1999 and introduced the LJ—the Muslim fighters for Holy War—to the world in April 2000 when its members, along with other groups of Muslims, held a rally in Jakarta calling for a jihad in the Mollucan Islands, where large Christian communities lived. Around 5,000 young people, some armed with swords and daggers and dressed in white robes and turbans, congregated at a sports stadium to mark the Islamic New Year (BBC News 2000). The leader told the crowds that ten thousand youths were ready to fight in a jihad against Christians in the Moluccas. In the following months, two or three thousand LJ members traveled to the Moluccas to fight alongside local Muslims locked in a cycle of communal violence of burning and killing with the region's Christian population.

While being ultraconservative in its ideology, LJ was ultramodern in its use of technology. The group launched the Laskar Jihad Online (LJO) in June 2000,[11] which has since became the major vehicle to maintain and develop the group's presence. Well-designed and regularly updated (supported by some information technology experts), the LJO showed how a website of a fundamentalist group could be professionally well maintained.

This was not just a religious fundamentalist group; this was Laskar Jihad computer-savvy youth using Internet skills for recruitment and funding.

The first version of LJO was bilingual (Indonesian and English),[12] while the later version, launched on May 13, 2002, was only in Indonesian. In both versions, a daily updated news page is always inserted with citations from the Koran. The website provided information about LJ and its leader, and the argument behind this movement. It offered all information—including news from the battlefield in the Moluccas—in textual, visual, and audio forms. Mutilated bodies said to be Muslims massacred by Christians, burned or damaged mosques, and graffiti on walls containing messages that insult Islam were graphically shown in support of the textual argument that is full of heated rhetoric of resistance to Christianity, Judaism, and globalization à la America (one pictorial was titled "Die America"). The webpages not only justified the movement, but the information provided also tried hard to convince Muslims about the truth of jihad and to raise the emotions of readers through images and sounds. Real Audio files were included. Most contained the speeches of LJ and other radical leaders that tried to boost the spirit of fighting for holy war.

Beyond the website, this group had, as of October 2001, 1,419 members on its mailing list, whose intent was to keep the "troopers" updated with its latest news.[13] What the LJ did was to marry communal resistances based on religiosity with the postmodern weapon of information technology. This was exemplified by the LJ webmaster—a medical student by day, cyberspace holy warrior by night—who wrote as a mission statement for its cybernetwork that LJ's intention was "to show the software site of Jihad, a holy war" (Ebiz Asia 2001).

As a social movement, LJ does not stop in cyberspace. More advanced than the student movements, which traditionally spread their information by photocopying and faxing, the printed information from LJ is published professionally. LJ had print media—a biweekly bulletin, a monthly *Salafy* tabloid, and the *Moluccas Daily*—all sold through more than sixty agencies throughout Indonesia and by thousands of volunteers who stood at traffic lights to disseminate these publications while passing a bucket to ask for donations. The news from LJO was also spread to many Islamic communities, especially to some *madrasas* (Islamic boarding schools) that were funded by Jafar Umar, the leader of the LJ. The printed versions of LJO news were placed on schools' announcement boards, where crowds of pupils would read them during their breaks. Reading and talking about this kind of news collectively helped raise certain feelings in these young people's hearts. Some of them then would see the leader of the LJ as a hero, thus making them want to join him in holy war. These madrasas were clearly major sources of the LJ's candidate warriors.

The LJ also received support from the more traditional media. Some newspapers showed obvious sympathy toward it, while some others tried to be neutral. The contents of many newspapers were actually drawn from LJO, even though most journalists did not mention the source. Not only was LJO the major source of information for these journalists, but also information about the LJ that was passed to readers was based on the LJ's perspective.

By holding rallies all over the country, the LJ group had successfully drawn thousands of students and young people to join its team and become troopers. They also had thousands of youth who collected donations at traffic lights. They were professionally trained to be fighters; they had real weapons and fought real battles; and they successfully gained power and even tacit legitimization from some segments of the state and society. This legitimization was readily shown in its first National Congress, held in May 2002. This congress was opened by Indonesia's vice president, Hamzah Haz, and included some public figures as speakers. The Laskar Jihad story is a success story of how creating resistance identities makes use of cybercivic space to turn embark on a project and, finally, to form a community of resistance against the broader civil society of Indonesia. While the members of the LJ were still in a minority, the LJ had gained much support. Many who reconstructed their defensive identities around the LJ's communal principles wanted to believe in the group and felt sympathy toward its movement.

The LJ disbanded in October 2002, a few days after the Bali bombing, and LJO has since closed down. However, pioneered by the LJ, many projihad movement groups follow in its path. The true believers in this kind of group are small in number—perhaps not even 1 percent of the total population of Indonesia (240 million)—but as a community of resistance that relies mainly on violence, it is an Achilles heel in the process of democratization in Indonesia. Castells suggests that these kinds of communal resistance emerge as negations of civil societies and can lead to the end of nation-states (1997, 66–67).

Conclusions: the New Politics of *Reformasi*

The lessons from Indonesia about the Internet and political change can be summarized under two points. First, the Internet is a powerful technology that can be instrumental in changing equations of power between a regime and the populace at large. This does not mean that the Internet somehow mechanically accomplishes such change. It is, of course, societies' uses of the Internet that does so. The particular difficulties the state confronts in regulating its uses allow a potential for wider societal uses and social mobilization for political reform. The capacity of the Suharto regime to close off other forms of media stands in contrast to its inability to significantly inhibit the spread of Internet access through privately owned Internet warnet that sprung up in major settlements and brought into Indonesia for the first time substantial information deeply critical of his regime.

A second insight from the Indonesia case is about the Internet and identity politics, specifically the political activism that was unleashed leading up to and following the collapse of the New Order government after more than three decades of authoritarian rule. A weakened state provided openings for elements of civil society not only to oppose the state but also to oppose each other. In the case of Indonesia, the Internet became a vehicle for strengthening certain identity coalitions, some of which were not averse to using violence to achieve their own hegemonic designs. The case of the Jihad Troopers illustrates the potential of the technology of the Internet to promote destructive uses of civil society energies, partly through the interplay of global and more local organizations allied with jihad sentiments, an interplay made readily possible by the Internet. While the Jihad Troopers were certainly not the only fractions of society to emerge and use the Internet as a key technology in their political pursuits, they were indicative of a shift in identity politics from prodemocratic movement against an authoritarian state to ethnoreligious movements against other religions, other ethnicities, and the secular state.

The hope of many has been that Indonesia would pass intact through a transition from authoritarianism to democracy. At one level, this can be said to be the case. The government is now elected by the people, and the successive governments after Suharto have upheld the "unity with diversity" ideology of the state and its secular basis. Not too far below the surface, however, is a continuing legitimization crisis that makes prospects less sanguine. Indonesia continues to experience volatile discontents from many sources. Its government is still rated as one of the most corrupt in Asia (Transparency International 2004), and its economy is marked by high levels of unemployment, deep poverty, and capital flight to China and other Asian countries. In a situation lacking the full confidence of the people, and with militant oppositional forces having significant presence in society, the Internet is now playing a more complex role in highly fragmented identity formation, manipulation, and political mobilization.

With the state unable to be a vehicle for social, political and economic justice, and security, the populace tends to rally around leaders who offer provocative symbols and easy political solutions, such as a regression back into the mythological history of jihad, now—perhaps to be paralleled or replaced by other religiocultural reconstructions of history in the future. In such a situation, cybercivic spaces become spaces for resistance identities to be more divisive, with the Internet magnifying discontents without readily assisting in a democratically peaceful social resolution. The question for further analysis is whether Indonesia has entered into a prolonged period of a severely weakened state and fragmented society that risks perpetual instability, or whether the *reformasi* of its system of governance will lead to a stable government under the rule of law. As in two episodes recounted here, the Internet is likely to play a significant role in this process as a technology that is eminently suited to the rapid dissemination of identity-laden information, symbolic meanings, and other information passing as truth to those ready to receive it.

This shows that the interplay between the technology of the Internet and society, whether directed toward secular democracy or religious orthodoxy, neither derives from nor results in linear pathways of sociopolitical change. It is instead marked by breaking points and disjunctures that have no necessary outcomes or future destinations. The fluidity and flexibility of the Internet applications have become the natural raw material from which more important things are built—coalitions, campaigns, networks, and mobilization. They, in turn, create new forms of organizing society and ways of working together that are changing the terrain of civil society and giving glimpses into an uncharted future. The Indonesian story shows that while the Internet can empower civil society, this does not always necessarily lead to democratization. The two cases demonstrate how the openness of the Internet interrelates with the ultimate instability, political indecisiveness, and fractured nature of civil society. The inherently democratic nature of the Internet can assist the civil society to burst into being; yet setting the foundations for democracy on the terrain of civil society is as yet only one of many possibilities.

Notes

1. The term *reformasi* can be translated to "reform" in English. In Indonesian context, *reformasi* is mostly used in reference to the big event that happened on 21 May 1998 when Suharto, the president of Indonesia who had been in power for thirty-two years, finally stepped down after the wave of student protests emerged in major cities in Indonesia, mainly in Bandung, Jakarta, and Yogyakarta. While there are many different analyses about the role of students in the ousting of Suharto, it is inarguable that on the street level of politics it was mainly students who played the main role.

2. Foucault (1979) applies the panopticon as a metaphor for the oppression of the individual by the state in modern society. Foucault observes that control no longer requires physical domination over the body, but could be achieved through isolation and constant possibility of surveillance. He writes that in modern society our spaces are organized "like so many cages, so many theatres, in which each actor is alone, perfectly individualized and constantly visible" (200).

3. Palapa, a name signifying national unity, was chosen by Suharto in July 1975. This name symbolizes the fulfillment of a vow for unity first expressed by Gajah Mada, a revered national hero of the fourteenth century who served as a prime minister of the Majapahit

Kingdom. He had vowed not to partake of Palapa, a national delicacy, until the goal of national unity was achieved.

4. By utilizing Japan's concern about the digital divide, CNRG/ITB appealed to and connected with Japan Corporation Satellite and WIDE Japan, whom then put ITB in the Asian Internet Initiative Project and enabled ITB to create a mass base for the Internet in Indonesia (Lim 2003b, 238).

5. This mailing list was created and moderated by a U.S. citizen, John A. MacDougall. The real name of the mailing list was actually Indonesia-L (Indonesia-L@indopubs.com), but people called it Apakabar, referring to the e-mail address of the moderator (apakabar@clark.net).

6. See <http://dhani.singcat.com/refleksi/2003_06_01_archive.php>.

7. See <http://www.xs4all.nl/~peace>.

8. See <http://www.geocities.com/Broadway/Orchestra/9632/index4.html>.

9. See <http://www.megaforpresident.org/>.

10. FKAJW stands for Forum Komunikasi Ahlus Sunnah Jamaah Wal Jamaah. For background information on the FKAJW and its leader, Ja'far Umar Thalib, see Aditjondro (2000, 2002); BBC News (2002); Harsono (2002); Laskar Jihad Online (2000a, 2000b); and Noorhaidi (2001).

11. See <http://www.laskarjihad.or.id>.

12. See <http://www.laskarjihad.or.id/old.htm>.

13. The mailing list of this group, laskarjihad@yahoogroups.com, which was founded on 17 May 2000 and halted on 4 October 2001, was not meant to be a space for dialogues. It was only a one-directional newsletter that provided news from the battlefield (the Moluccas) and discredited the Christian side of the confrontation.

REFERENCES

Aditjondro, G. J. 2000. "Notes on Jihad Forces in Maluku"; available online at <http://www. angelfire.com/rock/ hotburrito/laskar/ aditjondro500.html>.

———. 2002. "Al-Qaeda, atau Permainan Tentara? Kepentingan Militer di Balik 'Konflik Antar Agama' di Poso, Sulawesi Tengah"; available online at <http://www.geocities.com/ kariu67/gja110402.htm>.

BBC News. 2000. "Muslim Threaten Jihad in Indonesia"; available online at <http://news.bbc. co. uk/1/hi/world/asia-pacific/703749.stm>.

BBC News. 2002. "Who Are the Laskar Jihad?" available online at < http://news.bbc.co.uk/1/hi/ world/asia-pacific/770263.stm>.

Castells, Manuel. 1997. *The Power of Identity*. Vol. 2 of *The Information Age: Economy, Society, and Culture*. Oxford: Blackwell.

Cho, M. R. (2002) "Civic Spaces in Urban Korea: The Spatial Enrichment of Civil Society." *International Development Planning Review* 24, no. 4:419–32.

Derrida, Jacques. 1974. *Of Grammatolog*. Translated by Gayatri Chakravorty Spivak. Baltimore: John Hopkins University Press.

Douglass, M., and J. Friedmann. 1998. *Cities for Citizens: Planning and the Rise of Civil Society in a Global Age*. London: John Wiley.

Douglass, M., K. C. Ho, and G. L. Ooi. 2002. "Civic Space, Globalisation Pacific Asia Cities." *International Development and Planning Review* 24, no. 4:345–61.

EBIZ Asia. 2001. "Life in Days after September 11 Terrorist Strikes," transcript of interviews aired on October 6.

Foucault, Michel. 1979. *Discipline and Punish: The Birth of the Prison*. Translated by Alan Sheridan. New York: Vintage.

Friedmann, J. 1998. "The New Political Economy of Planning: The Rise of Civil Society." Pp. 19–38 in *Cities for Citizens: Planning and the Rise of Civil Society in a Global Age*, ed. M. Douglass and J. Friedmann. London: John Wiley.

Graham, S. 2000. "Constructing Premium Network Spaces: Reflections on Infrastructure Network and Contemporary Urban Development." *International Journal of Urban and Regional Research* 24:183–200.

Gramsci, Antonio. 1971. *Selections from the Prison Notebooks*. Edited and translated by Quintin Hoare and Geoffrey Nowell. London: Lawrence and Wishart.

Harsono, A. 2002. "Profile: Jafar Umar Thalib." *BBC News*; available online at <http://news.bbc.co.uk/1 /hi/world/asia-pacific/1975345.stm>.

Hegel, G. W. F. 1967. *Hegel's Philosophy of Right*. Translated by T. M. Knox. New York: Oxford University Press.

Hill, D., and K. Sen. 2000. *Media, Culture and Politics in Indonesia*. Oxford: Oxford University Press.

Kitley, P. 1994. "Fine Tuning Control: Commercial Television in Indonesia." *Continuum: The Australian Journal of Media and Culture* 8:103–23.

Laskar Jihad Online. 2000a. "Jihad Troopers (Laskar Jihad)"; available online at <http://www.laskarjihad.or.id/english/article/ljtroopers.htm>.

———. 2000b. "Riwayat Hidup Al Ustadz Ja'far Umar Thalib"; available online at <http://www.laskarjihad.or.id/about/cvjafar.htm>.

Lefebvre, Henri. 1991. *The Production of Space*. Translated by Donald Nicholson-Smith. London: Basil Blackwell.

Lim, M. 2003a. "From Real to Virtual (and Back Again): Civil Society, Public Sphere, and Internet in Indonesia" Pp. 113–28 in *Asia.Com: Asia Encounters The Internet*, ed. K. C. Ho, R. Kluver, and C. C. Yang. New York: Routledge.

———. 2003b. "From War-net to Net-War: The Internet and Resistance Identities in Indonesia." *International Information and Library Review* 35, nos. 2–4:233–48.

———. 2003c. "The Internet, Social Network and Reform in Indonesia." Pp. 273–88 in *Contesting Media Power: Alternative Media in a Networked World*, ed. N. Couldry and J. Curran. Lanham, MD: Rowman and Littlefield.

Locke, John. 1690 [1980]. *John Locke's Second Treatise of Government*, ed. C. B. McPherson. Indianapolis: Hackett.

Marcus, D. 1998. "Indonesia Revolt was Net Driven." *Boston Globe*, 23 May.

Noorhaidi, H. 2001. "Islamic Radicalism and the Crisis of the Nation-State." *ISIM Newsletter*; available online at <http://www.isim.nl/newsletter/7/regional/1.html>.

Tocqueville, Alexis de. 1969. *Democracy in America*. Edited by J. P. Mayer. Garden City, NY: Doubleday.

Transparency International. 2004. *Report on the Transparency International Global Corruption Barometer 2004*. Berlin: Transparency International.

CHAPTER 8

Exploring the Potential for More Strategic Civil Society Use of Mobile Phones

OKOTH FRED MUDHAI

Introduction: "Emergent" Technology?

While appropriation of information technologies—the process, rather than the outcome, of using technology strategically, politically, and creatively—is a pressing issue for civil society in the information age, most nongovernmental or civil society organizations (CSOs) have not moved much beyond e-mail and basic websites. Other information and communication technologies tend to be beyond the horizon; in particular, few CSOs have taken advantage of the full strategic value mobile or cell phones offer, especially for mobilization. So far, the mobile phone has taken a backseat in information and communication technologies (ICT) discourse currently dominated by the Internet.[1]

Just as ICTs in general cannot be studied in isolation from the rhythms of daily life (Anderson and Tracey 2002; Mudhai 2003), it makes little sense to try to understand the acquisition and use of mobile phones, personal computers, or the Internet in isolation from one another (Anderson and Tracey 2002, 141; Silverstone and Haddon 1996). In this context I provide some examples and possible directions for focusing on the mobile phone as a vital and significant partner of the more standard networked technologies of the World Wide Web and e-mail.

"Extraordinarily Slender Literature"—Making Sense of the Mobile Revolution

There is a large literature on the scientific-technical aspects of mobile phones, some on economic and cultural features, but little on the technology's sociopolitical impact except in discussion of network technologies. The authors of one of the largest anthologies on mobile communication technologies (MCTs) regret that the literature on mobiles is "extraordinarily slender" (Katz and Aakhus 2002, 317). In the bid to make sense of MCTs, authors have used various perspectives—including postmodernist, feminist, world-systems, developmental, and ethnomethodological—to explore the impact of mobile and other forms of personal communication technologies. Partly relying on industry press releases from Nokia and Orange, George Myerson (2001) linked the communication visions of Martin Heidegger and Jürgen Habermas to the twenty-first-century hype around a "mobilized" world. Similarly, and apparently independently, the IT journalist Howard Rheingold (2002) argues that the 1980s personal computer wave and the 1990s Internet revolution would be overtaken by a twenty-first-century mobile explosion with fast, sophisticated, always-connected smart MCTs (cell phones, personal data assistants, pagers, and portable Internet devices). Writing of the "Mothers and Mobile Phone Mobs: Renegotiating Civil Society," Catharin Dalpino (2000, 52–72) makes hardly more than passing mention of the cell phone. The dearth in empirical enquiry on the mobilizing potential of MCTs, especially in political realms, is striking.

This neglect may reflect complexities of conceptualizing MCTs in theories about ICTs. Theoretical hesitation derives partly from the mobile's relation to an older, more routine and mundane technology and partly from its current state, said to be a process of "convergence." As G.N. Cooper and colleagues have put it,

> In comparison with other technologies, the mobile has a somewhat equivocal status, and is difficult to conceptualize. It seems to belong to the category of 'new media', but much of that literature is not pertinent, for the mobile, resembling in part its ancestor the fixed-line phone, seems relatively transparent, at least at an intuitive phenom-

enological level: speaking on the phone appears so natural that the mediating technology is often forgotten (Cooper et al. 2002, 288).[2]

James Elihu Katz and Mark Aakhus (2002) argue that functional and structuration theories of appropriation fail to deal with some core aspects of the ways that people use mobile and other forms of personal communications and make meaning from them and their use.[3] In particular, they point out that the former is instrumental and goal-oriented at the expense of the symbolic while the latter emphasizes process at the expense of the values that animate it. They propose a perspective that sees mobile phones as both utilitarian and symbolic and highlights how personal technology can be used creatively to empower some individuals, often at the expense of others (Katz and Aakhus 2002, 315).

We see in the emergence of mobile communication, in a wide variety of nations, how the mobile phone initiates new questions about appropriate contact and renews contests over communication competence when new means for communicating require a new practical mastery of everyday activity (Katz and Aakhus 2002, 308).

The search for some method, theory, concept, or a set of them all, needs more attention in the study of the use of MCTs in general and mobile or cellular phones in particular. One place to look is how patterns of individual personal use compares with strategic group use by CSOs.

New "Mass" Medium—Ubiquity Equals Utility?

That mobile phone use far exceeds landline and Internet use in developing countries is one of the more commonly cited phenomena in discussions of ICTs, even though these references hardly go beyond a passing mention. Perhaps the most phenomenal cellular phone growth rate has been in African countries, mainly because they are late or initially slow adopters and because governments have been more forthcoming in liberalizing cellular markets than loosening decades-old strangleholds on the fixed networks.[4] Recent statistics indicate 65 percent of all African phone subscribers are on the cellular networks, and mobile phones outnumber fixed lines in more than thirty of the continent's fifty-four nations.[5] Only Guinea-Bissau had not embraced mobile phone services by mid-2003 (Budde 2003a). Uganda opened to mobiles in Africa, and in mid-1999 the number of mobile subscribers passed the number of fixed line users, now making up more than four-fifths of total phone users (White 2003). Recent dramatic examples include that of Morocco, one of the fastest growing mobile phone markets in the world, from 400,000 subscribers in 1996 to 6.4 million in March 2003. In sharp contrast, Morocco's fixed network declined (Budde 2003b).

Another is that of Nigeria, which recorded the highest annual mobile phone growth rate in the world in 2002, at 369 percent, having added 1.3 million subscribers (Budde 2003b). The demand has been so high in Africa's most populous nation that operators suspended new subscriptions in order to expand network capacity in early 2003. Cell phones cannot yet rival the radio as the mass medium of Africa, but rural penetration makes them more reachable than the Internet.

Mobile coverage is moving beyond the big towns and is often reaching populations ahead of telephone landlines, electricity mains, and drinkable water, even in collapsed states like the Democratic Republic of Congo, Liberia, and Somalia (White 2003). Industry forecasters predict the number of mobile users across Africa will double over the next five years to at least 89 million, from about 47 million in 2003 (White 2003). Around the world, there were nearly 1.5 billion mobile phone users in 2005, from 900 million only three years earlier (see Gebauer 2002; Slawsby et al. 2005). In 2001, predictions for 2003–2005 anticipated more Internet-connected phones than Internet-connected personal computers ("Internet Untethered," *The Economist* 2001), making the mobile phone the predominant means of Internet access (Gebauer 2002). No doubt, statistics conceal the stark disparities within countries (urban versus rural), regions (for instance southern and northern Africa versus the rest of the continent), and globally (the north versus the south). The International Telecommunications Union concede that although Africa has the highest proportion of mobile users among all telephone subscribers, and mobile telephony has grown faster in the continent than in any other region of the world over the past decade, hitting an average 78 percent a year by 2003, the penetration rate in Africa is still far lower than any other region (White 2003). Whereas in America 45 percent of the population are mobile phone users, and Western Europe boasts 75 percent penetration (Gebauer 2002), "owning a mobile phone remains a luxury afforded by less than 5% of Africa's 820 million people" (Dubbe 2003a).

The issue that CSOs need to address is how to utilize the mobile phone features in a deliberate and strategic manner for specific purposes. Text-messaging (SMS) could be easily seen alongside the World Wide Web and e-mail. Even before considering more advanced second-generation technology, such as the Wireless Access Protocol (WAP) and General Packet Radio Service (GPRS) that offer multimedia web-browsing and picture-messaging, and the third generation variant that promises to make the mobile phones the "killer app," the basic second-generation technology offers SMS as a simple, cost-effective application. The earlier move from analog to digital global system for mobile (GSM) communications already offered enough features—better speech quality, confidentiality, built-in security numbers, and international roaming—for the mobile phone to become a "killer app." Indeed, for makers such as Nokia, Africa offers a market for less fancy models (White 2003). When the infrastructure of these advanced MCTs diffuse widely enough to be reasonably affordable, the mobile phone will still remain in contention with other ICTs. For the moment, SMS remains the most appropriate application and cheaper handsets the most practical option that can be easily appropriated by CSOs for their activities especially in developing countries.

More Strategic Mobile Phone Use—Enhancing the Audibility of Southern Voices?

This does not mean that Africa and other developing countries completely lack the more sophisticated cellular technology even in rural areas. A recent BBC report indicates that WAP, launched around 2000 in the West where it failed to take off as had been expected, is of significant value to African villagers. In Senegal, where 70 percent of the population lives in rural areas and very few would normally access market information, Manobi, a joint venture between Senegalese and French entrepreneurs, sends teams to gather information about the prices of foods and goods in the markets in and around the capital, Dakar, and uploads prices to a central database using mobile phones that dial in to the server via WAP (BBC 2002). This greatly improves price transparency and guards against exploitation of illiterate and semiliterate farmers by middlemen. Prices are kept low, and farmers pay for the service as part of a deal between Manobi and the national telephone company. Kenya's Maasai community also network on market intelligence, albeit less formally, in selling their cattle.[6] This model can be applied in political "markets" as well.

In Zambia's elections of 2001 and Kenya's elections of 2002, non-governmental organizations (NGOs), some with official mobile phone policy, used their field observers to monitor elections and gather and then relay information instantly to NGO head offices in the capital cities, where the data and analyses were disseminated to media houses for immediate broadcast by recently licensed private FM radio stations (Mudhai 2005, 93, 239). Unlike previous elections in Kenya, the greater transparency made it difficult for incumbents to rig the vote by altering figures. Alongside use of the Internet and offline CSO agitation and political deal-making by the erstwhile divided opposition, this facilitated the defeat of Kenya's ruling party, which had regularly rigged elections to stay in power for nearly three decades. Cell phones were also crucial to CSOs in the preelection struggles in both countries. For example, in 1996 two NGO leaders arrested for criticizing flawed elections won their freedom after sneaking cell phones into a police cell and ringing sympathizers to put pressure on the regime of Frederick Chiluba. As I have noted elsewehere, "This is just one example of how (we use) cellular phones as a tool of defense, and a tool of advocacy—challenging our government on bad governance and excessive use of force . . . [we] were able to communicate effectively, immediately and promptly" (Mudhai 2005, 244–45).

Another telling potential of the mobile phone for social change in Africa could be gleaned from Nigeria, where residents of the eastern part of the country texted each other to mobilize for a December 1, 2003 symbolic work boycott to protest the poor state of roads (This Day 2003). Ten weeks earlier the National Association of Telecommunications Subscribers (NATCOM) had been joined by the Consumer Rights Project and the National Association of GSM Subscribers of Nigeria in coordinating a daylong mobile phone "switch-off" to protest high charges amidst poor services. "Let's force GSM tariffs down. Join a mass protest: switch off ur fone on sept 19 '03. They'll lose millions. It worked in US and Argentina. Spread Dis txt," read an SMS "virus" that spread the "9/19" protest message (Obadare 2004, 16). Pointing out that Western media ignored this incident, Obadare argues that "mobile phones in the Nigerian context presage the emergence of a new social *space* of politics and agitation" (2004, 4; emphasis in the original). In this context, the "9/19" protest tool has since been deployed in antigovernment protests calling for not only better roads, but also free expression: "For the advocacy targeted at individuals and interest groups, the FOI (Freedom of Information) Coalition proposes to undertake . . . a coordinated mobile phone text messaging campaign targeted at members of the National Assembly" ("Stakeholders Map Out Strategy" 2004).

The increasing mobile phone presence, for instance through "the umbrella people" of Nigeria,[7] led the *Financial Times* to assert that Africa's cell phone boom is "sweeping up all levels of society" and that "no other technology, not even the Internet, has changed lives and work in Africa as much as the mobile phone has" (White 2003). Two years earlier, in a report titled "Africa's Cell Phone Boom: The New Technology Is Causing a Revolution on the Old Continent," *Newsweek* described how "Africans are unleashing the power of the mobile phone. . . ." (Ashurst 2001; Mudhai 2003).

Just as the Internet economy in Malaysia spilled over to politics, the cell phone boom driving Africa's economies is expanding space for political activism.[8] In mid-2004, a growing constituency of Africa mobile phone users was mobilized to send text messages petitioning reluctant African governments to ratify the African Union's Protocol on the Rights of Women in Africa (Mudhai 2005, 99–101). "The facility enables those with poor or non-existent internet access to sign the online petition and takes advantage of the fact that there are about eight times more mobile phone users compared to email users in Africa," said Firoze Manji, director of Fahamu, a human rights organisation that developed the technique.[9] A coalition of human rights groups, spearheaded by women's rights organizations Equality Now and FEMNET (African Women's Development and Communication Network), together with the Oxford Committee for Famine Relief (Oxfam), CREDO (the Centre for Research Education and Development) for Freedom of Expression and Associated Rights, and the Oxford-based Fahamu, developed the campaign strategy. "The use of such mass-based technology is going to be critical in getting people's voices heard in the 2005 G8 meetings to be chaired by Britain's Tony Blair," said Irungu Houghton, Oxfam's Pan Africa Policy Advisor (Mudhai 2005, 100, and n. 14). The Canada-based International Development Research Centre supported this initiative, its research coordinator Sandy Campbell said, because "'Fahamu's strategy with SMS marries advocacy with the technology people actually have, not the technology we hope they have'" (Mudhai 2005, 101, and n. 14). This is a classic case of global technology being applied to alleviate local problems.

It is not just in Africa that the mobile phone is being used for social change as the fax was by Chinese dissidents to coordinate the 1989 Tiananmen Square demonstrations or the Internet by Indonesia's anti-Suharto demonstrators in 1998. One can argue that Africa catalyzed cell phone activism that later caught on in Europe and America. In mid-2005, the Irish rock group U2, led by lead singer Bono (Paul David Hewson), mobilized tens of thousands of concert attendees to text petition antipoverty/AIDS messages to a specified number. These messages, also coordinated in fifteen African countries by the Global Call to Action against Poverty coalition, would be presented to world leaders at the G8 Summit in Scotland.[10] Amnesty International regularly used SMS to lobby for international political causes. The People for the American Way lobby built a "mass immediate response" system that deployed a database of SMS users to SMS-attack right-wing legislators who opposed popular legislation. Though skeptical about the effectiveness of these tactics, Rushkoff (2005) argues that they are suited to the postmodern noncommitted politically apathetic youthful generation. On the other hand, I think there is far greater allegiance to social change among "texters" in the less developed world, first manifested in southeast Asia before African users embraced the cell phone as a political instrument.

The Philippines is distinguished for mobile phone activism. Text messaging played a key role in the January 2001 downfall of President Joseph Estrada. Minutes after the collapse of the Senate's impeachment proceedings against him for plunder charges, hundreds of thousands of Filipinos passed around a text message to gather at a religious shrine, forcing Estrada to step down after four days of intense rallying at the shrine (Rheingold 2002; Tan 2002). More recently, an environmental watchdog NGO called BK (Bantay Kalikasan, in Tagalog) held a campaign in mid-2002 to force the government to implement the country's Clean Air Act of 1999.[11] Their Smoke Belchers campaign enlisted cell phone users to report to BK any vehicle they saw emitting black smoke (Tan 2002). At the end of each week, BK compiled a list of vehicles with five or more complaints and sent it to the Land Transportation Office, the licensing arm of the Department of Transportation and Communications. The office would then summon offending vehicle owners for an exhaust test. Those that failed were required to have their engines cleaned up, and those that didn't comply lost their licenses (Tan 2002). With thirteen million Filipino cell phone users by mid-2003, mostly youths over eighteen, sending out an average of twenty-five million text messages a day—as many as in the entire European Union (Tan 2002)—it is not too hyperbolic to link the success of such campaigns to the mobile phone.

Earlier examples from other parts of the developing world include Bangkok, where in 1992 members of the Thai professional classes, dubbed "mobile phone mobs," coordinated antimilitary demonstrations with student leaders and with one another using cellular phones (Dalpino 2000, 70). More recently, in the October 2003 "Gas War" in Bolivia,[12] cell phone coordination enabled ordinary people from different parts of the country to lay a weeklong siege on La Paz—the biggest such protest in the capital in about three hundred years (Plath 2003). Women went on hunger strikes in churches, coordinated through the mobile communications network (Plath 2003). In South America's poorest country, not many Bolivians have direct access to mobile phones, so theirs were nowhere near the so-called smart mobs phenomena. Instead, "The groups were well organized with cell phones used to co-ordinate between leadership of existing organizations and networks" (Plath 2003). This third-party or two-step flow tactic routes around limited access and underscores the value of more strategic use. Bolivian community radio outlets like Pios Doce (whose transmitter in Oruro was bombed) provide yet another indicator of how such technologies as the mobile phone amplify best when combined with more established forms of communications and organic social networking.

Some critics have contended that the invasion of poor villages by ICT tools like the mobile phone is an imperialist and capitalist scheme by Westerners, especially Americans, to influence the developing world. Akhter (2001, 4–5) argues that the famous Bangladeshi Grameen mobile phone project is a conduit for undesirable "easy access" to poor people by multinational corporations and their products. While these anxieties are understandable, it is difficult to frame the rapid expansion of ICTs wholly as such a strategy—especially when users fully embrace the technology and even gain from it. Hermida (2003) provides testimonies of previously impoverished Grameen village "phone women" proudly praising the transformation in their lives as a result of the Village Phone (VP) project.[13] Although, for sustainability, the VP project is based on commercial funding, its network can be easily appropriated for sociopolitical use. Judging from the Malaysian Internet expansion experience, one may expect that the Bangladeshi VP services, including electronic funds transfer, Internet access, market information, and cell broadcasts (of disasters, etc), are adaptable to ICT versions of mobilization and observation by civil society organizers and activists in times of sociopolitical crises. All it would take is some kind of strategy from CSOs.

These examples reinforce the observation that most existing CSO uses of MCTs tend to be local and national due to the nature of cell phone systems and infrastructure. Transnational potentials have mainly been attributed to ICTs in general or to the Internet in particular by Heidi Ulrich's respecification (2002, 176, 197) of John Arquilla and David Ronfeldt's (1997) "NGO swarm" as a "large number of diverse NGOs focusing on an issue through the use of the Internet." Indeed, an increase in the number of individuals involved in transnational activism around trade-related multilateral meetings—from fifty thousand demonstrators at the 1999 Seattle Third Ministerial Meeting of the WTO, to one hundred thousand at the 2001 Prague annual meeting of the World Bank and the IMF to two hundred thousand at the Genoa G8 Summit in 2001—has been credited to ICT use, albeit in very general terms (Ulrich 2002, 175). Howard Rheingold has reported (2002) that Seattle demonstrators relied on cell phones to coordinate action and evade barricades. So there is need for research inquiries to find out what specific ICT applications are used for what sort of activities by transnational CSOs, and which are most effective for different organizations with different substantive and geographic agendas.

This leads to information disparities among northern and southern CSOs and their repercussions on activism that is labeled *global*. The fact that up to 90 percent of transnational CSOs accredited to major international meetings are based in industrial countries calls for a more critical examination of the dynamics of their agitating for issues that mainly affect developing countries, whose real voices are least represented in their midst. Beier (2003) gives the example of the International Campaign to Ban Landmines (ICBL), headquartered in the United States, whose founding members are all based in northern countries,[14] none of which is mine-affected. The location of these NGOs is understandably based on practical global inequalities, especially "accessible air travel and, more importantly, access to the Internet" (Beier 2003, 804). While these now-essential requisites for activism were credited for enabling ICBL to push states to accede to the 1997 Ottawa Convention banning anti-personnel landmines,[15] Beier notes that "[i]t is primarily in the developing South that these requisites of effective civil society mobilization are not as readily available to majority populations, meaning people living in many of the world's most mine-affected areas are effectively disenfranchised from equal participation in transnational networks of mine action" (2003, 804).

More than the disprivileging of their voices emerges through "structural inequalities that limit access to audible speaking positions" (Beier 2003, 805). A stated preference, in late 2000, that job applicants to ICBL e-mail their applications underscores, ironically, "the effective inaudibility of some voices (notably from many of the world's most mine-affected areas) in the realm of mine action" (Beier 2003, 795–96). Despite his imagery, Beier focuses on the Internet, noting that the "majority of those living in rural mine-affected areas are much less likely to have email access thus their marginal voices can hardly be heard. There are important senses in which they cannot 'hear' either, residing as they do beyond the pale of the Internet-based outreach efforts of the (mine action) campaign (Beier 2003, 804)."

Beier further argues that the "exclusion" of the majority of populations from many of the world's most mine-affected areas from transnational networks due to limited e-mail and Internet access poses a serious challenge not only to mine action "rhetoric" and ensuing ethical practices, but also to the global civil society notion. Although Beier does not clearly distinguish individual and NGO access in the south, the point is worth some attention. A common problem that local NGO partners of transnational CSOs face is gaining regular reliable Internet access to them, without which the local partners miss crucial updates. Strategic mobile phone use, for sending text messages in addition to personal computer e-mails and website updates, is one way transnational CSOs can enable communication with southern partners. NGOs in developing countries that have limited Internet access are likely to be able to access SMS more easily, given the ubiquity of mobile phones compared to landline phones, which are the primary access to the Internet via personal computers in the developed world. Although Cooper and colleagues argue that mobiles render location insignificant, allowing undifferentiated access to the worldwide network of satellite-enabled communication (2002, 288), it is important that transnational CSOs seriously consider the geographical constraints of building true consensus on their campaign issues. Use of

SMS by transnational CSOs in geographically disadvantaged areas would strengthen collaboration with local counterparts.

Concluding Remarks—Toward a Global Appropriation of the Mobile Phone

Among CSO responses—at the 2003 World Summit on Information Society PrepCom3—to Senegalese president Abdoulaye Wade's Digital Solidarity Fund proposal were pleas that the fund should envisage tools beyond the Internet. The mobile phone is clearly one such tool, and Rheingold (2002) envisions text messages in particular as one of the fundamentally new ways that people are engaging in group and collective action. The focus, especially with regard to the developing world, should not be on technological leapfrogging or the buzzwords *2G* and *3G* (second and third Generations of GMS), *MMS* (multimedia messaging service), or *M-commerce* (mobile commerce), but on basic phones offering basic services, especially text SMS.[16] The taking into account of the endurance of deep structural inequalities should be a driving force for more strategic mobile phone use.

Mobile phones need to be used strategically within the wider framework of other related ICTs, as well. Besides the Internet, the private FM radio remains a vital tool—especially for local and national NGO activism—for the developing world. The digital 2G and 3G cellular networks themselves are part of the radio spectrum that includes public access mobile radio, fixed wireless access, and public data and mobile satellite services. These are state controlled resources, and as CSOs embark on mobile phone "swarms," governments will respond accordingly. Plath (2003) cites the case of India, where texting has been shut off at critical points to stem the spread of rumors and coordinated race riots during communalist uprisings. But an opposite structural constraint lies in the fact that governments also need the mobile phone network infrastructure for business and for their own communications; hence, Bolivia bombed the Pios Doce radio transmitter but not mobile phone base stations, the United States spared Iraq's cellular infrastructure, and the United Kingdom made it illegal to use cell phone jammers, devices that block mobile phone calls.

Three central arguments emerge from this paper. The first is that cell phone use is increasingly becoming an integral part of strategic CSO political campaigns. Second, the ubiquity of this global technology enhances the possibility of drawing in local participation, even from the poorer parts of the world, in both national and cross-border political activism. As a result, and third, there is need for better theorization of cell phone use in politics—perhaps from a spatial perspective.

Notes

1. Earlier versions of this chapter have appeared in Mudhai (2004, 87ff) and at <http://www.ssrc.org/programs/itic/publications/knowledge_report/memos/okoth.pdf>.
2. See also Cooper (2001).
3. Katz and Aakhus (2002, 315) include in structuration theories W. Orlikowski's "duality of technology" (like A. Giddens's "duality of structure"?), that technology shapes and is shaped by human action; M. S. Poole and G. DeSanctis's "adaptive structuration" theory that people appropriate advanced information systems into their work; and Silverstone and Haddon's "domestication" variant, emphasizing the integration of personal technology into everyday domestic life.
4. The mobile sector is open to competition in 66 percent of the countries, featuring between two and five operators. While fixed-line growth is poor (except in low-population Reunion Island, with 38 percent penetration, and Mauritius, with 26 percent), fixed wireless access has been adopted in different areas to serve remote, sparsely populated areas and meet roll-out obligations (Budde 2003a).
5. In mid-2003, Zambia mobile phone penetration reached 2 percent, compared to less than 1 percent for landline phones and less than 0.5 percent for the Internet. Kenya's two cellular operators shared a subscriber base of 1.9 million, 6.3 percent penetration (nearly five times the number of landline subscribers), by the end of 2003. Lesotho's mobile penetration passed 4 percent in 2002 while fixed line penetration remained at 1.57 percent, with an Internet penetration of about 1 percent. Angola's fixed line stagnated at 0.7 percent penetration, while the mobile sector grew by 70 percent to a penetration of 1.5 percent at the end of 2002. In Cameroon, with two cellular networks and plans to privatize Camtel, mobile penetration increased from 0.02 percent in 1999 to over 5 percent in mid-2003 while Internet penetration remained less than 1 percent; in the Democratic Republic of Congo, with fixed-line connection of less than 2000, mobile phone subscribers grew from 7,200 in 1996 to 600,000 with eight networks at the end of 2002. Botswana, with two cellular networks and one fixed operator, had 26 percent of its 1.6 million population as mobile phone subscribers, more than twice the fixed-line reach (at under 10 percent). Ivory Coast, with three mobile operators (and a landline monopoly until 2004) registered 885,000 subscribers by the end of 2002, more than double the 336,000 fixed-line subscribers, with Internet penetration of 0.54 percent. Senegal's cellular lines were about three times as common as fixed lines. South Africa had 14 million mobile subscribers, compared to 5 million fixed-line connections. Egypt, with two private operators with WAP and other services, had 5.1 million subscribers by mid-2003, compared to 1.5 million Internet users by the end of 2002 (Budde 2003b).
6. Author interview with Kajiado District information officer Jane Gicheru, May 2005.
7. "Umbrella people" are vendors of mobile phone services who carry out their "mobile" business stationed under umbrellas.
8. The mobile phone is the single technology with the greatest impact on development in developing countries; see "The Real Digital Divide" (*The Economist*. March 10, 2005).
9. Firoze Manji, quoting from press release "Africa Mobile Phone Users Rally for Women's Rights" (2004).
10. The message was, "Say no to poverty"; see <http://www.gcapsms.org/>. This was part of the Make Poverty History campaign of the Live 8 concerts around the world on July 2, 2005, when hundreds of thousands attending ten concerts around the world, as well as millions of web users, were urged to text petition using mobile phones; see <http://www.live8live.com/phone/>.
11. With a population of eleven million, the Filipino capital of Manila is among the ten worst-polluted cities in Asia, with automobile and gasoline engine emissions linked to 5,223 deaths in 1996 (Tan 2002).

12. Citizens were protesting attempts by U.S.-educated President Gonzalo Sanchez de Loza-da's five-billion-dollar project to export the country's natural gas reserves to California and Mexico through neighboring historical enemy, Chile, which annexed Bolivia's coast-line in an 1879 War of the Pacific.

13. The pay phone project by Grameen, one of Bangladesh's largest NGOs, plans to install 40,000 village phones by 2004 in a bid to serve 100 million rural inhabitants in the coun-try's 68,000 villages. One VP covers about 2,500 people in a particular village. Average usage is 1,600 calls a month—out of which 600 minutes are outgoing. Grameen Telecom (GT) provides the GSM 900 cellular mobile phones to the villagers, using digital wireless technology, and also acts as a sales agent for urban mobile phone subscribers. GT is a nonprofit company, holding 35 percent share of Grameen Phone Limited, the company awarded a nationwide license for GSM 900 cellular mobile phone services. Organiza-tional and infrastructural support is provided by Grameen Bank, a sister organization. See <http://www.grameen-info.org/grameen/gtelecom/index.html>.

14. The members are: Handicap International (France), Human Rights Watch (United States), Medico International (Germany), the Mines Advisory Group (United Kingdom), Physi-cians for Human Rights (United States) and the Vietnam Veterans of American Founda-tion (United States). See Beier (2003, 807 n. 33).

15. The convention's origin is widely seen to reside not in any state action or initiative, but in civil society. ICBL brings together more than thirteen hundred NGOs from over ninety countries and has succeeded in getting at least 141 states to ratify the Mine Ban Treaty (Beier 2003; ICBL 2003).

16. Major phone companies have launched multimedia phones for MMS. Jupiter research estimates that 40 percent of European mobile phones will be MMS enabled by 2007.

References

"Africa Mobile Phone Users Rally for Women's Rights." 2004. Press release; available online at <http://www.pambazuka.org/petition/pdfs/PressreleaseSMS.pdf>.

Akhter, F. "UNDP Human Development Report 2001: Shamelessly Siding with Multinational Corporations." FT Asia Intelligence Wire/*Bangkok Post*, via Lexis-Nexis; copy available online at <http://www.undp.org/hdr2001/clips/bangkokshame.pdf>, 21 July 2001.

Anderson, B. and K. Tracey. 2002. "Digital Living: The Impact (or Otherwise) of the Internet on Everyday British Life." Pp. 139–63 in *The Internet in Everyday Life*, ed. Barry Wellman and Caroline Haythornthwaite. Oxford: Blackwell.

Arquilla, John and David Ronfeldt, eds. 1997. *In Athena's Camp: Preparing for Conflict in the Information Age*. Santa Monica: Rand Corp.

Ashurst, M. 2001. "Africa's Ringing Revolution," *Newsweek*, 27 August.

BBC. "Mobiles Find Right Price for Farmers." BBC News Online; available at <http://news.bbc.co.uk/1/hi/technology/2290540.stm>, 6 December 2002.

Beier, J. M. 2003. "Emailed Applications Are Preferred: Ethical Practices in Mine Action and the Idea of Global Civil Society." *Third World Quarterly* 24, no. 5:795–808.

Budde, Paul. "Africa—Wireless and Satellite Communications." Web report; brief summary available at <http://www.budde.com.au/TOC/TOC1847.html>, 4 December. 2003

———. 2003b. "Africa Telecoms Report Briefs." Available online at <http://www.budde.com.au/Cat/Cat4.html>.

Cooper, G. 2001. "The Mutable Mobile: Social Theory in the Wireless World." Pp. 19-31 in *Wire-less World: Social and Interactional Aspects of the Mobile Age*, ed. B. Brown, N. Green, and R. Harper. London: Springer-Verlag.

Cooper, G. N. Green, M. G. Murtagh, and R. Harper. 2002. "Mobile Society? Technology, Dis-tance, and Presence." Pp. 286–301 in *Virtual Society? Technology, Cyberbole, Reality*, ed. Steve Woolgar. Oxford: Oxford University Press.

Dalpino, E. C. 2000. *Deferring Democracy: Promoting Openness in Authoritarian Regimes*, Washington, D.C.: Brookings Institution Press.

Gebauer, J. "A Theory of Task/Technology Fit for Mobile Applications to Support Organizational Processes." Seminar presentation, University of Illinois at Urbana-Champaign; available online at <http://www.tourism.uiuc.edu/Seminar/judith.ppt>. 10 March 2002.

Hermida, A. "Mobile Money Spinner for Women," BBC News Online; available at <http://news.bbc.co.uk/1/hi/technology/2254231.stm>. 8 October 2003.

ICBL 2003. "About the International Campaign to Ban Landmines"; available online at <http://www.icbl.org/info/about.html>.

"Internet Untethered: A Study of the Mobile Internet." *Economist*. October 13, 2001.

Katz, E. J. and M. Aakhus. 2002. *Perpetual Contact: Mobile Communication, Private Talk, Public Performance*. Cambridge: Cambridge University Press.

Margolis, M. and D. Resnick. 2000. *Politics as Usual: The Cyberspace "Revolution"* London: Sage.

Mudhai, F. O. 2003. "Methodological Issues in the Study of Digital Media and Perceptions of Civil Society in Urban Kenya and Zambia." SSRC's IT Civil Society Network Background Paper on Transnational Civil Society Organizations and IT; available online at <http://www.ssrc.org/programs/itic/publications/civsocandgov/okoth_fredrick_mudhai.pdf>.

Mudhai, F. O. 2004. "Challenges to the Hegemonic African State: Media and Civil Society in Kenya and Zambia" Ph.D. diss., Nottingham Trent University.

Myerson, G. 2001. *Heidegger, Habermas and the Mobile Phone*. Postmodern Encounters. Duxford, UK: Icon.

Obadare, E. 2004. "The Great GSM (Cell Phone) Boycott: Civil Society, Big Business and the State in Nigeria." Dark Roast Occasional Paper Series no. 18, Islandla Institute; available online at <http://www.isandla.org.za/dark_roast/DR18%20Obadare.pdf>.

Plath, H. E. "Re: Potential for Strategic Use of Cell Phones" (reaction to message from F. O. Mudhai). *itcivilsociety* (closed listerv); archived at <http://lists.ssrc.org/scripts/lyris.pl?enter=itcivilsociety>. 10 November 2003.

Rheingold, H. 2002. *Smart Mobs: The Next Social Revolution*. Cambridge, MA: Perseus.

Rushkoff, D. "SMS Activism—Don't Call Us, We'll Call You: Mobile-Enabled Politics Are Still Far From True Networked Solidarity." *The Feature*; available online at <http://www.the-feature.com/article?articleid=101664andref=7982525>. 14 July 2005.

Slawsby, A., A. M. Leibovitch, R. Giusto, K. Burden, D. Linsalata, and R. T. Llams. 2005. "Worldwide Mobile Phone 2005–2009 Forecast and Analysis." IDC no. 33290; available online at <http://www.idc.com/getdoc.jsp?containerId=33290>.

"Stakeholders Map Out Strategy for Freedom of Information Campaign in 2004." 2004. *Media Rights Monitor* 9, no. 1:5; available online at <http://mediarightsagenda.org/mrm2004/MRM%20Jan.%202004.pdf >.

Surman, M., and K. Reilly. 2003. "Appropriating the Internet for Social Change: Towards the Strategic Use of Networked Technologies by Transnational Civil Society Organizations," Knowledge Report Social Science Research Council; available online at <http://www.ssrc.org/programs/itic/civ_soc_report/>.

Tan, A. 2002, 9 July. "Cell Phones May Be Key to Cleaner Air in Philippines." *Christian Science Monitor*; available online at <http://www.csmonitor.com/2002/0719/p07s02-woap.htm>.

"The Real Digital Divide." *The Economist*. March 10, 2005.

This Day, "Another Look at Federal Roads." AllAfrica.Com, via Lexis-Nexis. 23 November 2003.

Ulrich, K. H. 2002. "Expanding the Trade Debate: The Role of Information in WTO and Civil Society Interaction," Pp. 175–99 in *Civil Society in the Information Age*, ed. Peter I. Hajnal. Aldershot, England: Ashgate.

White, D. 2003, 17 November. "How Africa Joined the New Wireless World." *Financial Times*.

CHAPTER 9

The Potential Role of Information Technology in International Remittance Transfers

SCOTT S. ROBINSON

Networking projects that aim to marry the potentials of information and communications technologies to ensure that innovative technology leads to community development involving civil society are well-intentioned, but tend to reflect polarized social hierarchies of rich versus poor. Organizational models of telecenters and cybercafés involve more than different funding and sustainability strategies in postcolonial societies. Here policy-making elites associate digital escapism with popular and widespread cybercafés and show a preference for mediagenic, government funded telecenters, whose added value is essentially training and demand creation. Official telecenters struggle because local buy-in is scarce, while telecenters anchored in the community, a distinct and rare breed, can survive only when a core of local champions provides staffing, continuity, and legitimacy. Government telecenters are often dumping grounds for large and lucrative hardware and software purchase contracts negotiated far from the village; maintenance is minimal and local teachers and health workers are often expected to administer the "digital cargo," dropped from above, without salary incentives. This pattern may be observed throughout Latin America, and overlooks how an alternative model, mom-and-pop cyber-cafés linked to microbanks, may serve as de facto training grounds for youth in remittance economies.

Elsewhere I have argued that the emergence of networking among indigenous organizations and amidst migrants' kin groups are notable exceptions to traditional cultural parameters and economic conditions that discriminate against extensive public community networking in Mexico and Latin America generally.[1] Cybercafés dot the central squares of every Latin American town, and appear increasingly in small villages.[2] Inside, young digital consumers chat, send e-mail and look at porn and sports websites while learning to use Internet tools. Learning linked to opportunities in the tight job markets is limited, largely for lack of incentives from state agencies and private sources. These cybercafés are today the reigning mode of digital inclusion, often disdained by elites who both distrust independent, local initiatives and profit from government projects distributing equipment to telecenters that compete unfairly with the small cybershops. The elites imagine that access to computers and the Internet may magically "improve" the benighted peasantry via some form of online illumination, while ignoring that fact that the poor share ample sources of social capital inside their remittance-generating kin-anchored diaspora networks. Information technology (IT) can be directed to enhance the leverage of the growing financial capital now flowing home from afar. How this can occur is a challenge for bottom-up organizing in the form of linking popular cybercafés to regional microbanks and migrants' organizations abroad.[3] This alliance can trump official telecenters' alleged training and "value-added," rendering government programs obsolete while empowering local organizations with technical competence and negotiating skills.

The growing global remittance economy and the migrant organizations abroad can provide the social capital for marrying these two proposals into a workable international alliance of microfinance institutions serving migrants and their communities while applying available technologies without a need for outside capital. In 2005, the United Nations predicts that more than two hundred million international migrants will send home via financial circuits around $235 billion; another $300 billion could be transferred informally.[4] It is estimated that approximately 10 percent of the global population is involved in the international migration and remittance economy, and the amount of funds moving in an informal fashion will continue to surpass that transferred via the banking system. What is certain, however, is that families in vast regions of many countries today are fed, housed, cured, and perhaps schooled thanks in large part to these remarkable remittance flows that complement subsistence incomes almost everywhere in the south.

The northern tier of Latin America and the Caribbean states offers a showcase example of this remittance economy at work. Today, the emerging Mesoamerica of remittances has transformed what was once a region that archeologists considered to have shared many cultural and technological traits in pre-Columbian times into a contemporary space, stretching from northern Mexico, across Guatemala, Honduras, and El Salvador to Nicaragua, whose rural and periurban communities now supplement in a similar fashion their meager incomes from remittances sent home by their sons and daughters in the United States and Canada. In 2005, this flow was likely to amount to more than $30 billion—much more than aid programs and private direct investment combined in all the countries in this socially polarized region. This situation also prevails in parts of Colombia, as well as in Ecuador and Peru. In the southern cone of the Western Hemisphere, Brazil, and to a lesser degree Argentina and Chile, contain significant migrant populations from neighboring Bolivia and Paraguay, as well as from Ecuador and Peru. As the MERCOSUR consolidates after the change of regime in Brazil and the steady recovery from the Argentine crash of 2001,[5] remittance flows stand to increase. In fact, it is not too much of a stretch to assert that Latin America today presents a regional scenario of what was considered in colonial times a dual economy: prosperous sections of cities and export-oriented ports plugged into the global financial system—what Saskia Sassen has called an emerging system of "Global Cities"[6]—now ringed by remittance-fed subsistence economies, urban and rural, with increasing access to microfinance, in addition to informal credit suppliers. Both segments of the dual economy are transnational; the burgeoning demand for cheap labor in the north and in the world city megalopolis pushes resources home to the small towns and urban slums the migrants leave to work, as well as in the "capital."

The relative anarchy or apparent disarray to be observed almost everywhere in the remittance sector operates in parallel with the formal, IT-driven global financial networks. This is the dominant paradigm that the market-oriented fundamentalism of our neoliberal era has produced. Whereas other regions in the world today have their specific profiles in relation to migration and remittance flows, I argue that a novel organizational model may be based on the fact that all countries share similar opportunities and constraints with respect to the potential of migrant groups—namely, their growing links to microfinance institutions and multiple possibilities for enhancing communication and lower remittance transfer costs that the emerging digital technologies now offer. This is not so much a hardware or software issue; rather it is an *org*-ware challenge the development agencies have yet to address.

What does this reconfiguration of remittance flows look like? It begins with offering more points of Internet access in the north with state of the art digital identification systems (e.g., "smart cards" and consular IDs) that allow registered migrant clients of microfinance institutions operating in their countries of origin in conjunction with credit unions in the United States and Canada, for example, to move their funds home while managing their account, and perhaps that of senior family members at home unlikely to become Internet users. So far, such a system has only been imagined, but its operation is just around the corner as migrants become better organized and tech savvy. A pilot program already exists whereby the World Council of Credit Unions (WOCCU)[7] has signed a working agreement with VIGO, a major money transfer operator, by which migrants approaching cooperating U.S. credit unions and VIGO money transfer franchisees are able to place their funds in family accounts in savings and loan cooperatives in Mexico and four Central American countries who are now collaborating with this project.[8] This means that migrants from El Salvador, Guatemala, Honduras, Mexico, and Nicaragua can take advantage of the lower remittance transfer costs on the market today while conveniently placing their funds in accounts in their home country credit union analogues, the savings and loan cooperatives. This is an innovative, vanguard project that began operating during 2003 with phenomenal growth in remittance transfers from month to month as word gets out within the migrant community in the countries involved. This is a prototype that could scale significantly in other regions and involves little development capital to expand as the results in 2005 indicate.

How could this pilot program expand IT services for migrants? The extant WOCCU–VIGO pilot program does not contemplate expanding points of access for migrants inside the United States, where, paradoxically, connectivity is limited to the public library system. Public libraries in North America have become sites for migrants to communicate via e-mail with their home communities. But these do not provide security or facilities for financial transfers; nor, generally, are the libraries culturally friendly places for undocumented Latinos. As well, the current pilot doesn't consider distributing generic software that would facilitate the integration of remittance transfer into the respective digital accounting systems of the participating microfinance institutions. Few migrants from Mexico and Central America leave home today with much Internet savvy, although this may be changing; nor they do presently consider this communication option as a priority, as subjective surveys suggest.[9] Thus, community telecenters or locally owned and operated cybercafés linked to microfinance institutions would be one alternative to expanding the level of connectivity and training in the minimal digital skills required to augment presently limited communication networks linking migrants and their families. These community telecenters or cybershops may have to exist on both ends of each diaspora network, in the north and in communities in the south. Smart-card readers at both sending and receiving points could dramatically reduce transaction costs. The savings in remittance transfer costs would more than offset the cost of creating these points of access, which could be designed as sustainable nonprofit organizations. The lack of easy-to-install and easy-to-use software for technologically limited microfinance institutions in Mexico and Central America, for example, is today a restraint on offering additional financial services for migrant clients and their families. The institutional analogues to the North American credit unions located in the Gulf States, Europe, Japan, and South Africa could also participate in kindred projects tailored to the needs of each migrant constituency.

What regulatory frameworks would need to be adjusted to facilitate such a development? There are many issues in expanding into a global system the microfinance institutions that currently serve or may serve migrant communities. One arena requiring a degree of political will on the part of national governments and their regulatory bodies involves relaxing and/or modifying regulations in the telecommunications and financial sectors so that microfinance institutions can accommodate remittance transfers via smart or stored-value cards in their menu of services to clients, while offering digital services to their clients, on or next to their premises, including local digital telephony (VoIP), while employing the emerging WiFi and WiMax technologies. In a word, the microfinance institutions should be allowed to operate commercial telecom services in the rural communities they serve, in conjunction with basic financial services. This is a natural fit, and one that the savings in communication costs plus lower remittance transfer fees can pay for the investments this proposal involves. In addition, local entrepreneurship and technical skills are mobilized.

What sectors will resist modifying the status quo in relation to this proposal? It is no secret the mainline banking industry looks upon the credit unions and their kin in the countries to the south as ugly ducklings of the financial community. As remittance flows grow in their strategic importance within each receiving country, and within their respective balance of payments calculus (thus contributing to social stability and family welfare without need for additional outlays in national budgets while elites are subsidized with cheaper dollars), the banks are profiting handsomely from the transfer commissions as well as exchange rate spreads and commissions. These powerful, private sector bodies see no need to pamper the struggling microfinance institutions that serve clients in communities where the commercial banks will probably not open a branch nor install an automatic teller machine, or ATM (with its attendant costs in terms of armored vehicle cash delivery, maintenance, etc.). Resistance from the banks to expanding remittance services for microbanks is expectable, as well as in each regulatory body governing telecommunications issues, where legacy players now control most if not all of the local and national markets while denying low cost service to presently un- or underserved rural areas. The prospect of microbanks competing with these players while offering VoIP telephony and Internet services may not be embraced enthusiastically by most of these telecom corporations. This is an arena where outside pressure is required.

How does this proposal relate to Internet governance? Encouraging economic democracy among the incipient migrant organizations that are and no doubt will increasingly participate in their home country political process is not an immediate outcome of migrating abroad, landing a job, legalizing one's status (where possible), sending money home to the family, and the like. Rather, the formation of hometown associations (HTAs) among migrants has become almost an obligatory process that underscores identity politics in the multicultural global cities where migrants now live and work, guarantees the provision of basic legal and sometimes social services for their membership, and increasingly leverages collective remittance flows for specific projects in the hometown or region. In Mexico and Central America, migrants today view their collective efforts in terms of acquiring the vote abroad, to date denied to most; and the argument has become simplified and summarized in the phrase "no taxation without representation." In this case, of course, the "taxation" refers to the voluntary remittance flows—individual and collective—that, in effect, substitute or nowadays often exceed public funds destined to their home communities and municipalities, a form of voluntary, supplementary taxation, if you will, that removes pressure on national elites to sacrifice their traditional rents folded into national budgets. A parallel microfinance system linked to the HTAs is beginning to provide essential capital for family welfare and the improvement of local infrastructure and basic services in the region. A robust microfinance system can evolve that offers investment opportunities for migrants that currently spend over 90 percent of their earnings on consumption.

On balance, fortifying stable and fiscally solid microfinance organizations while linking them to the growing number of economically and politically sophisticated HTAs can lead to a parallel remittance-transfer network that pays for its own growth and institutional consolidation. Cybercafés and community telecenters can provide the necessary local access to digital services. Only domestic regulatory hurdles and the always-complex process of organizing migrant groups serving undocumented workers may hinder the way this proposal becomes a reality over the next few years.

Notes

1. "Remittances, Microfinance and Community Informatics: Development and Governance Issues." In *Remittances, Microfinance And Development – Buiding The Links*, VOL. 1, Judith Shaw, ed., Brisbane, Australia: Foundation for Development Cooperation, 2005, pp. 75-83.
2. A 2003 survey of cybercafés in four Mexican states indicated that 80 percent of rural *cabeceras municipales* or county seats already had a cybercafé serving young clientele. This was and remains a digital asset ignored by the government's expensive official telecenter initiative; see <http://www.eMexico.gob.mx>.
3. This proposal was first presented at the Toronto Global Knowledge conference in 1997. A preliminary version appeared as "Rethinking Telecenters: Knowledge Demands, Marginal Markets, Microbanks and Remittance Flows," *OnTheInternet* 6: 2 (2000); available online at <http://www.isoc.org/oti/articles/0401/robinson.html>.
4. "La migración impulsa a la economía: Annan," *El Universal* (Mexico City), 6 October 2005. Francoise Bourgiugnon, World Bank chief economist, announced in the November 16, 2005, *Financial Times*, that "[m]igration can enrich all sides if interests are shared." A recently published World Bank survey indicates: total remittances worldwide, US$232 billion in 2005, of which US$167 billion went to developing countries. Migrants now number almost 200 million. India heads the list of remittance receivers, with US$21.7 billion, followed by China, with US$21.3 billion; México, with US$18.1 billion; and the Philippines, with US$11.6 billion. See, http://www.imf.org/external/pubs/ft/fandd/2005/12/basics.htm; also, "International Migration, Remittances and the Brain Drain," http://www.atdforum.org/breve.php3?id_breve=62 .
5. MERCOSUR (*Mercado Común del Sur*, or Southern Common Market) is a common market that allies Argentina, Brazil, Paraguay, and Uruguay in growing trade relations, with Chile now participating as well.
6. Saskia Sassen, *Cities in a World Economy*, 2d ed. Thousand Oaks, CA: Pine Forge, 2000.
7. See <http://www.woccu.org/prod_serv/irnet/>.
8. See the regionally-focused proposal to the Central American Bank of Economic Integration at <http://www.icamericas.net/modules/DownloadsPlus/uploads/Estudios_de_caso_y_Reportes/Remesas-Final_4-sep03.pdf >.
9. See Scott Robinson, "Cibercafés—Un activo social colectivo," in *Los Retos de la cultura en México*, ed. Lourdes Arizpe (Mexico, DF: CRIM-UNAM and Editorial Porrúa, 2004), 137–51.

CHAPTER **10**

Network Technology and Networked Organizations

EVAN HENSHAW-PLATH

The question of how civil society organizations can appropriate networked technology for social change needs to address both technical and the social and organizational transformations. The process of creating new patterns and models of use for technology lags long behind the introduction of a technology. After a decade of use, the Web is starting to come in to its own as organizations and forms of use arise that are native to the technology. This process of internalizing the use of the Web can have as profound effect on civil society organizations as e-mail had in the last two decades. Organizations that don't adapt will continue to exist, just as there are organizations that don't use e-mail today. But they will in part be marginalized by projects and organizations that are able to use the technology to be more efficient.

In this chapter, I explore three cases of how the Internet is used for innovative research and observation projects that lack the traditional organizational trappings of civil society. They arose and formed out of the network itself rather than as traditional organizations trying to use information and communication technologies (ICTs). The three projects profiled here are by no means the only ones that embody new networked social/organizational forums.

The projects that tend to use network technology most easily are those that arise out of communities that have been online longest, and those are centered around the technical communities. Groups like Indymedia, which are visible to and interact with nongovernmental organizations (NGOs) and the globalization movements, have adapted many of their communications and technology patterns from the free software technical community. Their projects are pushing observation and research via the Net in ways that weren't possible before, creating a new form of research based on a semiubiquitous end-to-end network.

Mini Case Studies for Internet Observation and Research

Groklaw.net is run by a volunteer paralegal and focuses on tracking the SCO Linux lawsuits. SCO (originally Santa Cruz Operations) is a longtime Unix software company converted to producing lawsuits centered around challenging the legality of GPL (general public license, or "copyleft") and demanding that large corporate users, developers, and distributors of Linux pay hefty licensing fees. The cases have been widely followed within the legal and technical community as they explore the legality and strength of the free software and open-source movements.

The Groklaw site is a series of articles and investigatory pieces related to this complex interplay between cutting-edge technology and law. Each posted piece of research attracts hundreds of comments from technical experts and lawyers who pick apart the information. The end product is not a single report, or anything that can be shown to a foundation, board of directors, or government committee. It is instead an evolving stream of dialog, ongoing collaborative research, and an exploration of the issues that would be impossible in a traditional research context. From a traditional research perspective, the question to ask is: Could people from that community compile articles pulled together to form the discussion to create a report? The raw material is there, but the inclination of the community is not directed toward creating reports. Many journalists, wanting to understand the complex issues, use the site to follow the story. In this way the project has an extensive impact beyond getting mentioned directly in the press. The person coordinating the site is unpaid, and the project covers costs from online donations.

Groklaw is in effect a networked information hub. Controlled by an individual, it is a space for collaboration and synthesis of information about a complex topic. It's the kind of research project that would have been expensive to conduct in the past, and the information produced would have been limited to a small group of people who would pay a hefty sum for the report directly or indirectly for publication in a narrowly distributed journal.

The Political State Report (PolState.com) is another research project similar to Groklaw. Started by "kos," a well-known political blogger from San Francisco, it's a collaborative attempt at tracking and understanding state (departmental or provincial) politics within the United States. The site is run and maintained by a couple hundred political news junkies who write about and are interested in their local state politics and most of whom have blogs of their own. Correspondents apply to get an account for publishing news about their state. They identify their political leanings (Republican, Democrat, Independent, Green, Libertarian) and provide links to their personal sites. The articles focus on upcoming or recently finished electoral races, endorsements, court cases, poll results, and referenda. Attached to each article is a discussion of the merits and political fallout of the news. Unlike at Groklaw, posting is open to anybody who has gone through the process to give their name, information, and sign up to be a local correspondent. Once through the initial vetting process, they have open access to publish news about their state. If there is abuse, it is caught before many end users notice by the network of correspondents who run the site.

The Political State Report isn't attempting to be a comprehensive update on the political situation in every state; rather, it's meant to create a space in which people can quickly get the direction and power flows of local politics in local perspectives. The idea is a move away from the vision of the world where everything can be known. Both Groklaw and the Political State Report are models of research in the form of "issue tracking," where the goal is to understand and follow a flow of information and issues rather than to capture reality in a comprehensive report. Issue tracking embraces understanding the world through many specific moments. The project couldn't exist if an organization tried to confirm or verify the quality of the contributors or their information. It would become stale, out of date, lacking vitality. Instead, reliability and "trust" are built from the ability to respond to and contest the accuracy of statements by members of the multitude rather than from an institutional form of control.

Wikipedia, the "open encyclopedia," is a large and participatory web-based research project that attempts to construct a free, collaboratively written encyclopedia using the Wiki technology platform, a content management system in which all webpages within the Wiki site can be edited by anybody. In Wiki, which means "quick" in Hawaiian, if you see something you want to change, click on the edit link, and you can edit the page through a Web form. Wiki-style programs allow publishing webpages in a markup simpler than traditional HTML (hypertext markup language). New pages can be created by simply stringing two words together with capital letters. That word then becomes a link to a new blank page. Most also support saving a version of the page after each edit, so if somebody deletes or tries to destroy a page, it can easily be replaced or fixed.

From this very simple technology, extensive websites can be built. Wikis are widely used within the technical and free software community, as well as in Indymedia, for internal organizing. Although the Cancun WTO and Geneva G8 and the United Nations World Summit on the Information Society protest mobilization websites used them, Wikis are almost unknown in civil society organizations—even tech-savvy ones.

The Wikipedia concept is to change the traditional notion of an encyclopedia from a closed repository of truth to an open collaborative project based on the contribution of users under a GPL license. As would be expected, it has more depth than a traditional encyclopedia in some areas, and weaker coverage in others. For example, in a traditional encyclopedia there would not be pages describing in detail hundreds of different programming algorithms, but Wikipedia's coverage of things like eighteenth-century military and political leaders is weaker than that in a traditional encyclopedia. The Wikipedia goal is to have something that can eventually replace a traditional encyclopedia for the Internet age. The traditional encyclopedia is encumbered by an organizational and technical format that is unable to address the needs of an ICT-saturated world.

The first response of many people to the Wikipedia concept is: "How can the information be verified?[1]" Anybody can put in false facts, or even make up a period of history that never existed. In practice, contributors abhor seeing factual errors. Nothing brings out responses and discussions in online communities like making a factually incorrect statement. People come out of the woodwork to correct errors because they like to demonstrate their knowledge and set the story straight. Given the right forms and incentives, a tremendous amount of reliable research can be conducted in this way.

The growth of Wikipedia has been very interesting. In 2003, its sustained traffic shot past that of Britannica.com. In terms of usage, the site has been become widely used as a reliable source of information, which leads us to question where reliability in information really lies. Within the traditional institution-based framework of knowledge and reputation, an encyclopedia written by an open group of self-selected volunteers who have no organizational or professional accountability would have no value. The site is published by a core group of eight hundred people.[2] It has a democratic decision-making process borrowed from open source and free software development projects that combines an informal model of working consensus with occasional sitewide voting on referenda, and rarely used intervention by the site's founder.[3] The project incorporated itself in the United States as Wikimedia, a registered nonprofit organization that legally owns the computers that host the site and that can receive tax-deductible donations and grants from foundations.[4] The content of the site is released under a free-use license, the GNU documentation license, and in an easy-to-use format ensuring that if the project collapsed anyone could easily start a parallel project. The Wikipedia project is coordinated virtually via mailing lists,[5] Internet relay chat,[6] and instant messaging,[7] using the same technology and similar organizational forms to those of the Indymedia network.

Wikipedia and other large Wiki-like projects succeed because they replace the old concept of a director with that of a community of gardeners. The WikiGardener is a person who tends to the information, keeping links together, adding cross-references, reorganizing pages, and generally making sure the overall project remains useful. Like the Indymedia concept of an editorial collective and open publishing, the WikiGardener comes in to clean up after the act of publishing and is not a gatekeeper who solicits or controls what information gets published. The gardeners of Wikipedia themselves coordinate their actions to manage and grow the project.[8] The practice of a gardener is different from that of a traditional researcher or project manager. The task is to foster a community and space for the free flow of contributions. An idea of the general direction and path for future project development is important, but only so long as it remains vague. Growing collaborative projects requires being flexible about the directions the projects take and the contributions that flow in. It is also critical to create a "buzz." If you can't be excited about a project and impart that enthusiasm to others, a collaborative bottom up research project will never take on a life of its own.

The Implications of Network Based Organizations

These network-based projects approach research from a perspective different from present work counterparts. Reports are sometimes produced by the projects, but are not the sole or final product. Research is the process of investigation, of debate, of discovering and creating links. The link is the fundamental concept that underpins the Web, and it can be a powerful force in transforming organizations. Traditional institutions are loath to provide outside links on their websites. The argument is that these links suggest an endorsement and that linking to another website or project says we have looked over this organization and their work. Indeed, linking does connote a bit of endorsement, but not as much as publishing someone's article in your newsletter. In this world, it denotes relevance and a sense for community, and groups that adopt it create websites with both incoming and outgoing links throughout their sites to take advantage of the Web as it was meant to be.

A common failure to understand and use this potential of the Internet is to install a forum system in order to encourage participation and discussion. The problem is that a disconnected and compartmentalized forum system ends up isolated and neglected. On news sites like Indymedia and Freerepublic, as well as research sites like The Political State and Groklaw, comments and discussion exist throughout, attached to everything. Original authors are taken off their pedestals in this "comment widely" model, which contrasts to the traditional academic conference where presentation of papers is followed by a short question-and-answer session.[9]

As with conferences, simply going to the other extreme and eliminating the speakers and direction doesn't work to foster effective collaboration. Communities, and especially research-driven communities, need people to act as points of direction, to shape and guide the growth of the conversation. A balance of power and of openness, of structure and fluidity, are critical to making a functional organization on the Internet as much as they are in face-to-face collaboration.

On Using Blogs

To take advantage of these features, civil society organizations trying to use the Internet effectively might consider giving their staff and members blogs—not as a place to chat about family and post pictures of their cats, but research blogs to chronicle their ideas, research, and work. In addition to sending around links, articles, files, and the like, posting them online opens up informal knowledge networks and provides an awareness of their community.

Blogs work for several reasons. They are informal. You can post something, link to something, muse about an issue, get feedback. If you make it clear it's a blog, you aren't held to the same standards as a press release or a full report. Spell-checking and grammar are important, but the standards are much lower than required for something official. Blogs can also be quick. Blogs are link-intensive: they build from the fundamental aspect of the Web, making links. A blog entry that is linked to other blogs and by other blogs, or an article that gets picked up and discussed by bloggers, will rank much higher on popular search engines like Google and have more staying power than one that appears with only the official organizational link and gets lost in the thousands of search results that aren't on the first page. Linkage and the attention it marks increases the impact of reports and other research beyond narrow publications. Finally, blogs, when done effectively, have a personal voice: they make people real, opening up and reducing formal barriers that prevent knowledge sharing and collaboration.

An effect of network-based communication is to shift emphasis from information producing to an "information synthesis culture."[10] Information synthesis only comes to be seen in disparities of power on the Internet. Some authors and websites become central focal points by their selective limiting and organizing of information; or strong personal voice attracts readers by providing synthesis. There may be hundreds of blogs with small groups of readers interested in the person or issue being discussed. In them, power comes to rest in a relatively limited number of sources who are compiling, organizing, and synthesizing information from across the network. By comparison to traditional repositories of power, networked power holders have a more limited monopoly, like barriers to new players. The balance of hubs and smaller points of connection create rich environments in which people register the intellectual space.

On Using Wikis

Wikis are also a remarkably effective tool for research and collaboration. They allow for easily constructed communal space. Like e-mail and blogs, their power lies in their informality and simplicity, and people can understand the essential concepts very quickly. Wikis encourage people to contribute to the project rather than maintaining a distance between information producer and consumer; but they also need nurturing, which is done by WikiGardeners.

It was initially assumed that Wikis would not be usable for political projects, and there have not been that many politically sensitive projects that have adopted the use of Wikis. In some cases, such as the independent media Wikis (like Indymedia.org), it has been necessary to implement a system where only people with user name and password can edit pages, but user names are widely distributed so as not to limit the essential accessibility of platform. With a little care for security, a Wiki can be a transformative tool. Tim Berners-Lee, the inventor of the Web, always advocated making pages as easy to edit and update as they are to read. The concept is not of a static reality, but a much more collaborative medium. Wikis are a meaningful step in the direction of making that collaboration real. They share the power to speak. For many professionalized civil society organizations and NGOs this devolution of power brings with it unwanted democracy, however.

The Democratic Implications of User/Network Driven Projects

The power of user-driven networked projects is directly dependent on their creators' ability to share control. The more participants see a site or project as theirs, the more participants will contribute. This diffusion of ownership has consequences, the most striking of which is demands for democracy. No visitor to the Ford Foundation or *New York Times* websites is going to get upset if they redesign their sites without consulting users. Yet no one would think of transforming an Indymedia site, Kuro5hin.org, dmoz.org, or Wikipedia without a consultation process.

The decision-making structure that arises with network-based projects and organizations is more emergent than created by design. Although aligned with many of the radically devolutionary principles of globalization, its decision-making format is distinct. It is neither direct democracy with everybody participating in a decision, nor representative democracy where decision makers are elected; nor is it really a one-person-one-vote referendum-style democracy. Instead, it's a consultative process known as "rough consensus and running code."

This concept was created by the free and open-source software communities. As David Clark of the Massachusetts Institute of Technology has put it, "We reject kings, presidents and voting. We believe in rough consensus and running code."[11] The principle is derived from what "works" when using networked technology, applied to shaping the future development of ICTs. It this view, the future of organizations and modes of production in globalization is best seen where the process has already happened within the technical community that created ICTs in the first place.

By comparison, most NGOs operate like corporations and governments, with top-down organizational structures where very little decision-making power is given to the people at the bottom of the organization's hierarchy, to say nothing of those outside the organization. When contrasted with projects that have successfully used or grown up around ICTs, it is easy to see why corporations, governments, and NGOs have been unable to adapt to really using this new technology. Wikis, blogs, and other simple ICTs such as instant messaging are not difficult or complex, but only become effective as social and organizational transformations, not technical ones. NGOs are a new kind of institution that has spread widely in the last decade. Their uses of ICTs is limited to the earliest technology, e-mail, which has been around since the 1970s. The Web, with graphics and multimedia, has been around since 1994, while we are just now, more than a decade later, beginning to learn how to use it.

Notes

1. Common objections to and critiques of Wikipedia may be found at <http://en2.Wikipedia.org/Wiki/Wikipedia:Why_Wikipedia_is_not_so_great>.
2. Wikipedians, the community of people who contribute to the Wikipedia project, can be found at <http://en2.Wikipedia.org/Wiki/Wikipedia%3Awikipedians>.
3. For power structures of the Wikipedia project, see <http://en2.Wikipedia.org/Wiki/Wikipedia:Power_structure>.
4. For the Wikimedia Foundation, which "owns" the Wikipedia project, see <http://en2.Wikipedia.org/Wiki/Wikimedia_Foundation>.
5. For Wikipedia mailing lists, see <http://en2.Wikipedia.org/Wiki/Wikipedia%3AMailing_lists>.
6. For Wikipedia Internet relay chat, see <http://en2.Wikipedia.org/Wiki/Wikipedia%3AIRC_channel>.
7. For Wikipedia instant messaging, see <http://en2.Wikipedia.org/Wiki/Wikipedia:Instant_Messaging_Wikipedians>.
8. For more information bout the Wikipedia project in general, see <http://en2.wikipedia.org/wiki/Wikipedia_About>.
9. The same is true of publishing on the Internet using portable document format (PDF) files. The format has its advantages: it allows easy publishing online of documents that were designed and intended for printing. The limitations are also very real. The PDF file is simultaneously part of the Web and separate. It exists in a box, cut off from a richly linked environment. The problem is in part technical: publishing software is configured to produce professional looking PDFs, while HTML export is substandard at best.
10. A concept introduced by Mark Surman & Katherine Reilly in *Appropriating the Internet for Social Change: Strategic Uses of Networked Technologies by Transnational Civil Society Organizations*, their unpublished report for the Information Technology and International Cooperation Project of the Social Science Research Council, November 2003. <http://www.ssrc.org/programs/itic/civ_soc_report/>.
11. A remark by David Clark at a 1992 meeting of the Internet Engineering Task Force and now informally known as the IETF Credo.

SECTION **III**
Formats

CHAPTER 11

Understanding the WSIS: An Institutional Analysis of the United Nations World Summit on the Information Society*

HANS KLEIN

The Cold War's end stimulated new interest in a longstanding United Nations institution: the world summit. World summits are one-time conferences organized by the UN to address global issues like environment, housing, or food. They involve thousands of policy makers working together over periods of years to develop consensual visions of principles and possible solutions to some of humankind's most challenging problems. Since the Earth Summit of 1992 and counting the World Summit on the Information Society (WSIS) of 2003/2005, the UN has hosted almost one summit per year for eleven years.

World summits are dogged by fundamental questions: What are they good for? Do they produce social and political change commensurate with

---

* Reprinted from Hans Klein, "Understanding WSIS: An Institutional Analysis of the UN World Summit on the Information Society," *Information Technology & International Development 1:34* (Summer 2004), pp. 3-14. Copyright 2005 by the Massachusetts Institute of Technology.

their enormous cost in money and policy makers' time? True, at least one world summit has yielded a major result: the 1992 Earth Summit produced the United Nations Framework Convention on Climate Change that led to national commitments to cut greenhouse gas emissions. Other summits, however, have not had such clear-cut results. The question remains, Is a world summit a vehicle for meaningful social and political change?

In what follows, I propose a conceptual framework for addressing this question, and I apply it to the WSIS. From that analysis, I conclude that summits can make a significant contribution to social change. Summits present *opportunities*, making valuable resources available for political advocacy. However, they are just one element needed for change; also needed are candidate policies that fit those opportunities and policy advocates with the influence to realize those opportunities. When all those elements come together, significant results can be achieved. Evidence of summits' power can be seen in the 2003 WSIS, which challenged the global Internet governance regime.

Conceptual Framework

In analyzing world summits, I begin by distinguishing between *form* and *content*. The *content* of any summit refers to the particular issues that were discussed at the summit and the particular results that were achieved there. The content of the 1992 Earth Summit consisted of the environmental issues and principles addressed; the content of the 1995 Women's Summit likewise included the specific policies for women discussed; and so on. In contrast, the *form* of world summits refers to the enduring organizational form employed for all of them, irrespective of their content. All summits employ a broadly similar form for participation, collective decision making, and implementation, and this form defines the "rules of the game"—which in turn defines opportunities for certain classes of political actors to achieve certain kinds of political outcomes.

Stated differently, a summit is an *institution*, a recurring social structure that constrains some actions and facilitates others, that presents an *opportunity structure*, a set of predictable causal mechanisms and political resources through which to pursue social and political change. To assess summits' utility as vehicles for change, I offer this analysis of the opportunity structures they present.

Two features of summits figure most prominently here: their characteristics as a policy forum and the mechanisms available to them for policy implementation. Summits' characteristics as forums help us understand what kinds of policies can be effectively advocated. Summits' repertoires of implementation mechanisms help us understand what kinds of policies, once adopted, can be translated into action. These two features help explain which visions of social change can be most meaningfully endorsed at a summit and then most effectively realized in practice.

Two additional, noninstitutional factors also figure in achieving change. The first is the existence of proposals that "fit" the opportunity structure. These are policies that can benefit from the mechanisms and resources a summit makes available. The particular resources presented by a summit will not be appropriate for all proposals, and those with good fit may advance the most. The second factor is advocacy, which provides the motive force to exploit opportunity; without advocacy opportunities can go wasted.

Thus, a summit is most likely to lead to real change when there exist (1) effective advocates of (2) policies that fit both (3) the characteristics of summits as forums and (4) their associated implementation mechanisms. It is this combination of advocacy, fit, and opportunity that produces change.

I apply this conceptual framework to the WSIS in an attempt to explain that summit's major outcomes. Held in Geneva in 2003, the WSIS served to articulate a collective vision about the benefits of information to society. It also produced some potentially important policies. Benefiting from a combination of opportunity, fit, and advocacy, two major policies advanced: (1) to review the global system for Internet governance, and (2) to provide funding for developing countries.

The World Summit Forum

Since 1992 the UN has hosted the following summits:

1992: Earth Summit (Conference on Environment and Development), Rio de Janeiro.

1993: Human Rights Summit (Conference on Human Rights), Vienna.

1994: Population Summit (International Conference on Population and Development), Cairo.

1995: Social Summit (World Summit For Social Development), Copenhagen.

1995: Women's Summit (Fourth World Conference on Women), Beijing.

1996: Habitat II (Conference on Human Settlements), Istanbul.

1996: World Food Summit, Rome

2001: World Summit against Racism (World Summit against Racism, Racial Discrimination, Xenophobia, and Other Related Intolerances), Durban.

2002: World Summit on Sustainable Development, Johannesburg.

2003/2005: World Summit on the Information Society (WSIS), Geneva/Tunis.

This list is not presented as definitive. There were summits held before 1992, and indeed many of the summits on this list built on previous events (e.g., the first Earth Summit of 1972 or the Habitat I summit of 1976.) Furthermore, not all summits are explicitly identified as such. Of the ten summits listed here, only four are explicitly titled "world summits." (For a larger list of "UN conferences," see the report by the Office of the Millennium Assembly [2001].)

Nonetheless, from this series we can discern the outlines of what could be called the world summit form. The form consists of a timeline of activities, a pattern of participation, and the summit products. The WSIS illustrates most features of this form (although it included some unique features as well).

Although a world summit lasts just a few days, the preparatory and follow-up processes occur over a period of years. Thus, the initial steps toward the 2003 WSIS began already in 1998, when the UN's International Telecommunications Union (ITU) proposed it within the UN system. In December 2001 the General Assembly formally authorized the summit, to be held in December 2003 (Phase I) and November 2005 (Phase II).

In any summit the most intense activity occurs in the preparatory phase. In the two years between the authorization of the WSIS in 2001 and the actual event in 2003, the ITU conducted two series of meetings: preparatory committee meetings ("prepcoms") and regional meetings. Prepcom I followed within six months of the General Assembly's 2001 Resolution, and Prepcoms II and III were held at additional six month intervals. All were held in Geneva. Regional meetings were held over a briefer period, but were distributed in locations around the world. Between Prepcoms I and II the ITU organized regional meetings for Africa, Asia, Europe/North America, and Latin America. These many meetings served to gather input from around the world and to prepare the documents that would be adopted in 2003.

The summit itself lasts just a few days. It is a ceremony of ratification in which heads of state make speeches and ratify the collective documents produced over the preceding two years. The first phase of the WSIS ran for three days in December 2003.

The final procedural step in the summit form is the follow-up conference, the so-called "summit-plus-five" event. Five years after the event there is a conference to assess the progress made toward implementing the summit plans. An assessment report is written and many of the participants from the original summit reassemble.

Throughout these stages in a summit there is broad and inclusive participation. With the UN grounded in the nation-state system, national governments are the main participants. Thousands of government officials participate in all stages, and the actual summit itself normally attracts most of the world's heads of state. Additional participants come from industry and from civil society (or nongovernmental organizations [NGOs]—the terms are used interchangeably here). Industry can play an important role in summits closely connected to industrial issues, like environment, food, or housing. NGOs often possess great expertise in issue areas and play important role in policy advocacy. Numerically, NGOs often outnumber other classes of summit participants.

The media is a fourth class of participant. With participation by heads of state, industry leaders, and NGOs, a world summit is a major media event. The 1992 Earth Summit attracted over seven thousand journalists alone, and they in turn provided intensive coverage in print, radio, and television (Grubb 1993). Although the WSIS attracted fewer media representatives, it still generated headlines around the world.

In addition to process and participation, the world summit form also defines product. In the abstract, a summit produces understanding and a collective vision. Concretely, most summits produce two documents: a statement of principles and a plan of action. A statement of principles articulates the normative framework for policy, often building on the UN charter and previous statements on rights. It might refer to earlier established rights, affirm their applicability to specific issue areas like development or women, and even propose their expansion to new areas. A plan of action translates principles into more specific actions. It might define high-level policy initiatives, set milestones for implementation, or call for funding of program areas. While certainly not a detailed statement of policy suitable for immediate implementation, these summit documents provide the broad outlines of comprehensive policy on the summit topic. (For the purposes of this study, I refer to the high-level principles and actions produced at summits as *policy*.)

While each summit embodies this form, each also departs from it in some ways. The WSIS adopted two significant innovations. First, the WSIS was a double summit, with the first meeting in Geneva in 2003 and the second in Tunis in 2005. This possibly offered opportunities for more pro-longed policy making. Second, the WSIS formalized the role of civil society to an unprecedented degree, creating an official "civil society bureau" that held formal meetings with the bureaus for governments and the private (business) sector. These two characteristics of the WSIS are discussed in greater detail below.

This, then is the world summit form. Two years of preparatory activity precede the event, the summit itself attracts thousands of participants (including heads of state), two documents are produced, and a follow-up conference occurs later. But does anything change as a result? The next section considers summits as a political institution offering an opportunity for policy change.

The Summit as Forum

The analysis here considers a summit as a means to make and implement policy. In this section I analyze a summit's means for policy making, and in the next section I will analyze its available mechanisms for implementation. Throughout the discussion I consider issues of policy fit.

A summit is first and foremost a *forum*, which is a means for policy making. A precondition for policy making is the existence of an appropriate forum, without which policy makers may be unable to meet to make collective decisions (Klein 1999). Fundamental characteristics of any forum are its jurisdiction, its participants, and its timing. A world summit embodies a unique set of these characteristics, making it better suited to address some issues than others.

A forum's *jurisdiction* can be of two types: *spatial* or *topical*. The *spatial* jurisdiction of a world summit extends—as the name implies—to the entire world. Participants come from all over the world, they collectively identify issues that are relevant at the global level, and they propose global policies. In light of the small number of global policy forums, this spatial jurisdiction renders a world summit a rare and potentially powerful institution. It provides one prerequisite (among others) for global change: a meeting place in which to discuss global issues and formulate global policy.

Topical jurisdiction refers to a summit's theme. A summit on the topic of environment can meaningfully address environmental issues, and summits on women, housing, or racism can meaningfully address topics on those other themes. Topical jurisdiction limits the kinds of policies a summit can produce but also increases its significance in its topic area.

Recognition of these jurisdictional characteristics allows us to identify issues that are a good fit for world summits. Issues that fit well are (1) in the topical area and (2) global in scope. Some issues that are typically global include functional systems (e.g., global climate, global environment, global economy); human rights (which apply to all humans on the globe); and global equity (which presupposes a global community within which some people suffer an injustice). For example, the issue of climate change was a good fit for the 1992 Earth Summit: climate fit the topic and is a global system.

A second characteristic of a forum is *participation*. Compared to other global forums, world summits are unusually open, both in the number and the diversity of participants. As described earlier, participants number in the thousands, and government, industry, and civil society all have access to the policy process. Wealthy countries and developing countries participate with formally equal status. At the WSIS the rules for participation broke new ground by granting civil society formal standing comparable to that of governments and industry. Such open access is more significant for less influential players, since there are few forums in which they can participate. Thus, summits present comparatively better opportunities for one class of political actors: politically weaker groups.

Summits, therefore, are often places where the rights of oppressed groups can be advanced. Proposals to acknowledge the rights of women, children, oppressed minorities, and the poor are a good fit. Likewise, proposals to transfer wealth from rich countries to poor may stand a better chance of being advanced at a summit than at other global forums (e.g., a G-8 meeting of the world's wealthiest nations). Given that summits are primarily intergovernmental meetings, weaker nations benefit the most. However, civil society also benefits by being given the opportunity to try to persuade policy makers.

Related to this are the rules for decision making. Summit decisions are made by nations on a one-country, one-vote basis. Thus, not only does a summit create an opportunity for global policy making, it employs an egalitarian procedure for deciding on those policies. Such rules favor weaker (and more numerous) nations.

A final characteristic of a summit as a forum is its *timing*. Unlike most policy-making forums that endure over time (e.g., a national legislature), a summit is a one-time event. It is active for about two years, and the main event lasts just a few days. A window of opportunity opens briefly in time and then closes again.

The innovation in WSIS broke potentially significant new ground in this characteristic. WSIS's two-phase approach kept the forum open for a much longer period of time, potentially allowing for an iterative process of policy-making and for more enduring political oversight of initial implementations. (At the time of this writing the second phase was just beginning, so the consequences of this temporal extension were not yet played out.)

Some policies fit this temporal characteristic. Policies that have lain dormant or that have been deadlocked for years may be resuscitated for a world summit. The summit may serve as a new forum in which to refight old battles. Or the timing of a world summit itself might be manipulated by the UN itself. Since it controls the timing of the events, the UN can launch a world summit when it wants. This can be particularly useful when the UN is challenging a rival institution, such as a neoliberal institution outside the UN system. As discussed below, the timing of the WSIS conferred advantage to the UN's ITU in its challenge to the Internet Corporation for Assigned Names and Numbers (ICANN) for authority over Internet identifiers. In general, issues in which the UN has an interest may be a good fit for a summit.

This temporal characteristic can also render a summit somewhat unpredictable. An issue in good political currency just at the time of the summit could receive disproportionate benefit, whereas issues temporarily in disfavor could miss an opportunity. An element of chance may affect whether policies fit or not.

In summary, institutional analysis reveals four features of summits' opportunity structure. Summits' *global jurisdiction*, *topical jurisdiction*, rules of *participation*, and *timing* all condition which policies fit the institution. Topical policies with a global dimension are a good fit to a world summit. Policies that favor players with little political influence are also a good fit (at least compared to other global forums). Policies that are in good currency at the time of a summit can benefit from the opportunity presented by a summit.

Implementation Mechanisms

So far the discussion has focused on words rather than deeds. As forums, world summits produce statements of principle and plans of action and, for the most part, they stop at that. Implementation happens later, if at all. In this section, I examine available mechanisms for translating summit plans into programs of action.

Review of previous world summits reveals both formal and informal implementation mechanisms. Most formal implementation mechanisms are UN or governmental organizations. Informal implementation mechanisms are political resources created by world summits that influence other policy processes. I consider each in turn.

Formal implementation mechanisms used by past summits include UN agencies, multilateral conventions, national governments, and funding programs. Of these four, UN agencies provide the closest parallel to conventional policy implementation, in which a national legislature makes policy and a national agency implements it.

UN agencies have frequently implemented summit policies. For instance, following Habitat II (the Conference on Human Settlements, held in Istanbul in 1996) the UN Centre on Human Settlements (UNHCS) launched a number of informational programs on housing. UNHCS actively collected and disseminated publications on best practices in housing and developed statistical and qualitative indicators to allow countries to assess their housing resources. A UNHCS website (www.BestPractices. org) made this information publicly available at no charge. Another example of UN implementation was the creation of the Commission on Human Rights. This commission provided a standing capability to pursue the policies endorsed at the 1993 Vienna Human Rights Summit.

Since the UN rarely has immediate jurisdiction over people or programs, the most effective mechanism for policy implementation is often national governments. This can take a variety of forms. At the highest level is a multilateral convention, in which national governments agree to a collective program of policy implementation. The Earth Summit provided the best known example of a multilateral convention: the Framework Convention on Climate Change. Although a nonbinding agreement, that convention set basic parameters to reduce greenhouse gas emissions. More important, it led to the Kyoto Protocol, which contained more formal mechanisms for enforcement. Rarely has a summit achieved such concrete implementation, however (and even the Kyoto Protocol later faltered after the United States withdrew its support).

National government implementation can also be realized by individual governments without a formal multilateral convention. Following the 1992 Earth Summit, as many as 150 countries created national-level commissions or coordinating mechanisms for sustainable development. The 1994 Population Summit in Cairo (UN International Conference on Population and Development) also led to country level implementations, as numerous countries repealed national laws against women (Cohen 1999). Policy statements at the global level were implemented in law by multiple national governments.

Finally, summit policies may, at least in theory, be implemented through funding programs. The UN can create and administer a fund. Nearly every summit has featured a debate between rich and poor countries about the need for financial support to realize summit goals. However, most summits have ended with dashed expectations. For example, at the 1995 Social Summit in Copenhagen (UN World Summit for Social Development) numerous countries called for debt relief as a means to promote development, but such policies were neither adopted nor implemented.

It must be noted that, in general, world summits do not have a strong track record of implementation. This is hardly surprising. First, it is almost always easier to promulgate policy than implement it; UN summit policies are not unique in this regard. Second, summits have addressed some of the most enduring and intractable problems of humanity (food, shelter, development). No one can expect a summit to easily achieve significant social change in such areas. Third, and perhaps most important, summits' statements of principle and plans of action attempt to be all-encompassing and as such are very general. Indeed, summits describe their product as "vision," not "policy." Their contribution is as much to define what the issues are as to propose solutions. A vision does not lend itself to concrete implementation and may be a precursor to further political debate.

Even without formal implementation, however, policy ideas may be translated into action. Much of a summit's impact may occur through *informal* mechanisms. Here the ideas developed in a summit achieve social change indirectly. Two such informal implementation mechanisms are discourse and legitimation.

Summits shape policy discourse. They define terms of debate in their issue areas, identifying problems and setting priorities that filter down to other policy arenas. Regardless of whether such ideas are supported or opposed, their codification in UN statements makes them more real. Existence of the terms can be a necessary prerequisite for achieving action.

Although this may sound abstract to the reader, the act of shaping discourse can have quite concrete effects. For example, the World Conference against Racism (2001 World Conference against Racism, Racial Discrimination, Xenophobia, and Other Related Intolerances) led to few identifiable policy implementations. However, it greatly raised the profile of debates over reparations for slavery. Extensive media coverage of this issue brought it to the attention of people and policy makers around the world, creating an environment where policies could be discussed. Another example was the 1995 Women's Summit in Beijing, which helped codify concepts like *honor crimes* and *conflict rape*. The summit helped make these terms nearly household worlds. By defining and diffusing a discourse about such crimes, it becomes possible for policy makers in other arenas to talk about them. Absent such a discourse, they might not even be discussed.

The media play an important role in diffusing discourse. As noted earlier, most summits attract considerable media attention, creating an opportunity to diffuse ideas to a global audience. Issues debated at a summit can spark further debate and possible policy action in other forums.

The second informal implementation mechanism is legitimation. Legitimation takes policy concepts one step further: not only are the concepts known, they are also validated. A UN summit carries great prestige, so the issues and ideas that it endorses are imbued with that prestige. Legitimated ideas are then more easily advocated and implemented in other policy arenas.

Legitimate policy derives from legitimate institutions, and summits' lengthy preparatory processes, open participation, and high-level political support give them considerable legitimacy. With so much input from so many groups, products of a summit are a strong statement of world consensus. That legitimacy is enhanced by the participation of heads of state, who bestow supreme political authority on the final products.

Policies that fit this institutional characteristic are those that need great legitimacy. An example of such a policy is the declaration of a right. As a political absolute, a right needs a solid foundation in legitimacy. Summits have repeatedly proven their value as forum for the affirmation of rights, such as the 1993 Human Rights Summit, which reaffirmed and strengthened the 1948 UN Universal Declaration of Human Rights. Subsequent summits have declared such rights as fertility rights (Population Summit), housing rights (Habitat II), and the rights of women (Women's Summit). Not all issues are successful in gaining legitimacy, however. For example, at the 1996 World Food Summit U.S. biotechnology firms were criticized for seeking endorsement of genetically engineered agricultural products. The genetically modified products would have benefited from the legitimation afforded by a summit, but they were unable to obtain it.

Endowed with such legitimacy, world summit policies may challenge powerful but less legitimate institutions. Even if another institution possesses funds, staff, and expertise, if it lacks legitimacy, then its policies might be susceptible to challenge. Thus, summits frequently criticize the global distribution of wealth and call for transfers from north to south. Or they may raise questions about policies emanating from neoliberal institutions that are justified by their alleged efficiency.

Sometimes formal and informal policies can work hand in hand. The practice of "naming and shaming" may achieve policy implementation through such indirect means. The definition of indicators (a formal implementation mechanism) allows observers to measure individual countries' standing in a policy area (e.g., housing). Then the legitimation of values (an informal mechanism) allows judgments to be attached to the measures (e.g., data on housing might be used to claim that citizens' "right to housing" is being violated). Countries found lagging in valued social characteristics can be subject to public criticism in an attempt embarrass policy elites into taking remedial action.

In summary, world summits can draw on a repertoire of policy implementation mechanisms. Formal mechanisms include UN administrative agencies, multilateral agreements, national governments, and funding mechanisms. Informal mechanisms include the shaping of discourse and legitimation. Proposed policies that fit these characteristics may be good candidates for achieving social and political change. Thus, world summits present an attractive opportunity to advance policies that can be implemented by a UN agency. Summits also present an opportunity to advance policies that need a solid foundation in legitimacy (e.g., rights) or that challenge powerful institutions. Finally, for advocates of conceptual innovations, summits provide a chance to diffuse new concepts in policy discourse. Concepts endorsed at a world summit may gain acceptance in policy debates in other arenas.

Understanding the WSIS

The preceding institutional analysis can now be applied to the outcomes of the 2003 Geneva phase of the WSIS. Although I will refer to them as "WSIS outcomes," the reader should bear in mind the summit is still ongoing at the time of this writing. The WSIS did generate policy change consistent with the preceding conceptual analysis—even though concrete social and political change remains in the future.

WSIS produced three classes of outcomes: significant policy action, significant policy inaction, and (a large set of) ambiguous outcomes. There were two significant policy actions, each embodied in an ad-hoc working group, the Group on Internet Governance and the Task Force on Financial Mechanisms. There was one significant policy inaction: information security. Despite the fact that terrorism—including cyberterrorism—was the most visible policy issue during the preparatory phase due to the 2001 terror attacks in the United States, the WSIS made no notable contribution in this area. Finally, there were countless ambiguous cases. From these last I discuss two: communication rights and free and open-source software.

In the table below I analyze these outcomes against the conceptual framework from above. The policies that resulted from WSIS exhibited good fit with the opportunity structure. This suggests that the world summit's provision of valuable political resources helped make these outcomes possible.

Analysis of WSIS Policies

Policy	Forum Characteristics				Implementation Mechanisms					
	Spatial Jurisdiction	Topical Jurisdiction	Legitimacy	Timing	UN Agency	Multilateral	National Government	Funding	Discourse	Legitimacy
I. Significant Outcomes	•	•	•	•	•	•				
Internet Governance	•	○		○						
Digital Solidarity Fund								•		
II. Significant Nonoutcomes										
Security	•	•		•		•				
III. Ambiguous Outcomes										
Free and Open Software	○	•	•	•			○			•
Communication Rights	•	•	•	○					•	•
Notes: • *excellent fit* ○ *some fit* [blank] *no fit*										

Internet Governance

The single most important outcome of the WSIS was a challenge to ICANN (Schenker 2003). Created in 1998 as a private, U.S.-based corporation under the sole political authority of the United States, ICANN constituted a nascent global governance regime for the Internet (Klein 2002a). It was unpopular because of its perceived violation of sovereignty through its control of the Internet's globally-shared core resources. Most Arab states, Brazil, China, and South Africa, in an implicit alliance with the ITU, successfully initiated a process to review and possibly change the ICANN regime (Peake 2004). The WSIS Plan of Action, included a recommendation that the Secretary General of the UN set up a working group to "investigate and make proposals for action, as appropriate, on the governance of Internet" (*Plan* 2003).

The advocates of this outcome benefited from the opportunity presented by WSIS. Nearly all the resources offered by the world summit proved relevant:

Jurisdiction. As a policy proposal for a global system (the Internet), the proposal to review Internet governance fit both the WSIS's global and topical jurisdiction. The WSIS provided an appropriate venue for the challenge to ICANN.

Participation. The governance initiative came from countries that normally would not play a leading role in Internet policy. However, the summit's rules for inclusive participation and equitable voting favored the challenging nations against wealthier countries.

Timing. The ITU was able to influence the timing of the WSIS, initiating it just when ICANN was being formed in 1998. ICANN was still new and vulnerable, so the timing supported the challenge.

Implementation. Although skeptics of the ITU were many, the agency was nonetheless qualified to implement policy in this area. Thus, an appropriate mechanism existed, increasing the likelihood that any policies adopted could be implemented.

Multilateral agreement. If needed, Internet governance could be implemented as a multilateral convention. (At the time of this writing, it was too early to know if this mechanism would be used.)

Legitimacy. This was a particularly valuable resource. ICANN suffered from a striking legitimacy deficit (Klein 2002b; 2004). In contrast, the challenge emanating from the WSIS could claim to express world consensus.

In summary, advocates of the review of Internet governance benefited from the political resources made available at the WSIS. Without the political resources made available by the WSIS, their challenge might have been impossible.

Digital Solidarity Fund

A second potentially significant outcome of the WSIS was the creation of a task force to consider a "digital solidarity fund." This would be a mechanism to address issues commonly known as the "digital divide" by transferring wealth from rich countries to poor. The same coalition mentioned above—the so-called Cancun Coalition (because they had blocked an earlier round of World Trade Organization negotiations in Cancun)—supported this proposal, although African countries played a leading role as well (Accuosto and Johnson 2004).

Again, the WSIS provided an opportunity, and advocates seized that opportunity. The summit resources most relevant here were:

Jurisdiction. Since the forum brought together rich and poor countries, it created an opportunity for global financial assistance. The summit topic was well-suited to justify a discussion of the digital divide in information technology. Thus, the a proposed global policy to address the digital divide was a good fit for the WSIS.

Participation. Poor countries could promote policies that addressed their needs.

Timing. The collapse of the ITU-based accounting rate and settlement system in 1997 eliminated an important mechanism for wealth transfer from rich to poor countries. The WSIS provided an opportunity for this dormant issue to be reconsidered.

Funding. This issue is a good candidate for a formal fund. Certainly, mechanisms existed for implementation. Proposals for wealth transfers are not uncommon at summits, but they often fail to win the support of the intended donor countries and so are not implemented. Although important, this outcome was probably not as significant as the Internet governance outcome.

Security

The lack of a security proposal at the WSIS would seem to present a puzzle. Computer viruses, denial of service attacks, and other destructive acts on and against computer networks were a widely recognized problem (Goodman, Hassebroek, and Klein 2003). Furthermore, unlike the previous two outcomes just mentioned, the United States was a strong advocate of greater information security. This policy area seemed a perfect fit for the WSIS:

Jurisdiction. Like Internet governance, global information security fit the WSIS's spatial and topical jurisdiction. The summit made available an appropriate forum for making such policy.

Timing. Global concern for security was at an unprecedented high. The coincidence of an issue in good currency and an appropriate forum presented an opportunity for a major policy initiative.

Multilateral agreement. This seemed to be an appropriate and available implementation mechanism. However, WSIS did not produce any significant outcome here. The reason is probably that the opportunity presented by the summit did not match the needs of this policy's main advocate, the United States. Just months before the WSIS, the United States was encouraging another country (Japan) to support information security initiatives in such forums as the G-8 and the Organization for Economic Cooperation and Development—restricted "clubs" of more powerful nations. A proposed policy on information security didn't really need the more open participation available at the WSIS. As a result, no major security outcomes were achieved.

Free and Open Software

Free and Open Source Software (FOSS) systems includes systems like Linux and various office software suites. FOSS is increasingly seen as an alternative to proprietary software sold by U.S. companies like Microsoft. Advocates of FOSS at the WSIS included civil society groups, major industrial firms (e.g., IBM), and countries other than the United States. Did FOSS advance at the WSIS? The nature of the FOSS makes that difficult to assess.

Jurisdiction. FOSS fits the WSIS's topical, but not its spatial, jurisdiction. FOSS is not a global system; rather, it is a global movement or market. Nonetheless, a global forum like WSIS was useful to reach the assembled policy community.

Legitimacy. This was very important, as FOSS had a great need for legitimacy. However, the legitimacy it needed was of a technical and market nature: ultimately the future of FOSS would be decided by users in the marketplace. Nonetheless, political endorsement of FOSS could help it win acceptance by governments and users around the world.

Timing. The timing was good: the WSIS occurred when interest in FOSS was attracting increased interest around the world.

Implementation. FOSS could benefit from some formal implementation mechanisms. The diffusion and adoption of FOSS probably benefited from the WSIS. Around the time of the WSIS, Brazil began considering switching officially to a FOSS standard, and the city of Munich officially adopted the Linux operating system just a few months after the WSIS (AP 2003; 2004). Whether they were influenced by FOSS's greater legitimacy following the WSIS is unknown, however.

Communication Rights

If the reader is familiar with the term *communication rights*, then advocates of this set of concepts shall have succeeded in shaping the policy discourse. Communication rights are comprised of a set of positive rights that go beyond the right to free speech. They include a right to access to media and education to be able to communicate to others and to the broader society. Some of the summit's resources were relevant to advocates of these rights:

Jurisdiction. As rights, these were appropriately treated in a global forum. Topically, they were also a good fit for the WSIS.

Legitimacy. This was very important. WSIS presented an excellent opportunity to legitimize this concept and bring it into the mainstream.

Timing. This proposal was of long standing, tracing its roots back to the UN's Educational, Scientific, and Cultural Organization debates of the 1980s. The WSIS presented an opportunity to reawaken this issue.

Discourse and Legitimacy. The WSIS was an opportunity to put this issue back on the communications policy agenda. Were the term to gain wider usage, the concept of *communication rights* might be more discussed and, ultimately, perhaps adopted. Communication rights were somewhat of a good fit for WSIS and were actively advocated. However, they encountered opposition from groups in the WSIS process, and were not explicitly included. The fact that there was a debate over communication rights at the WSIS did serve somewhat to disseminate this discourse.

Conclusion

Assessing outcomes in this way is not an exact science. But the conceptual framework above provides a general idea of what worked at the WSIS and why. The Internet governance initiative may not have been attributable exclusively to the WSIS, but it would have been difficult for developing countries to challenge ICANN without the legitimacy of the summit. That policy was nearly a perfect fit to the opportunity structure of a summit.

The conceptual framework presented here may be more useful for forward-thinking strategy formation than for backward-thinking historical explanation. When policy advocates successfully recognize the opportunity structure of a summit, they can select issues that best fit that structure and they can prioritize the resources that they will pursue. And although good strategy cannot guarantee success, it can reduce errors and contribute to success.

This analysis suggests that the two-part nature of the WSIS is a very important change in the summit form. With the extension of the summit in time, the forum's resources may be utilized for more time. Since summits proportionately benefit some classes of actors (weak parties) over others (influential parties,) the extension of the summit could facilitate more egalitarian global policy making.

Do summits make a difference? They can. They present an opportunity structure that, when combined with advocacy and well-fitting policy proposals, can lead to change. At minimum, summits offer an opportunity to define discourse, and it is in that realm of words that they have perhaps their greatest effect, consistent with the characterization of their products as "vision." But sometimes their effects are more concrete. Changing the governance of a global system—be it technical or environmental—is a major undertaking, but one for which anything less than a world summit could fall short.

References

Accuosto, Pablo, and Niki Johnson. 2004, June. "Financing the Information Society in the South: A Global Public Goods Perspective." Association for Progressive Communication; available online at <http://rights.apc.org/documents/financing.pdf>.

AP (Associated Press). 2003, 16 November. "Brazil Gives Nod to Open Source." *SiliconValley. com*; available online at <http://www.siliconvalley.com/mld/siliconvalley/news/editorial/8946662.htm>.

AP (Associated Press). 2004, 17 June. "Munich Approves Change-over to Linux." *SiliconValley. com*; available online at <http://www.siliconvalley.com/mld/siliconvalley/news/editorial/8946662.htm>.

<http://www.itu.int/dms_pub/itu-s/md/03/wsis/doc/S03-WSIS-DOC-0004!!MSW-E.doc>.

Cohen, Susan A. 1999. 'Cairo-Plus-Five' Review Is Finding Political Will Strong—But Funds Lacking. The Guttmacher Report. Declaration of Principles. 2003. World Summit on the Information Society, 12 December. Viewed at: http://www.itu. int/dms_pub/itu-s/md/03/wsis/doc/S03-WSIS-DOC-0004!!MSW-E.doc

Furrer, Marc. 2002, 1 July. "Opening address by State Secretary of Switzerland, Host Country, WSIS 2003." Available online at <http://www.itu.int/wsis/docs/pc1/statements_opening/furrer.doc>.

Goodman, Seymour, Pam Hassebroek, and Hans Klein. 2003. "Network Security: Protecting Our Critical Infrastructures." ITU Background Paper; available online at <http://www.itu.int/osg/spu/visions/networksecurity/paper3.html>.

Grubb, Michael. 1993. *"Earth Summit" Agreements: A Guide and Assessment.* London: Earthscan.

Klein, Hans. 1999. "Tocqueville in Cyberspace: Using the Internet for Citizen Associations." *Information Society* 15, no. 4:213–20.

———. 2002a. "ICANN and Internet Governance: Leveraging Technical Coordination to Make Global Public Policy." *Information Society* 18, no. 3:193–207.

———. 2002b, 8 August. "Creating the Illusion of Legitimacy." *Cyber-Federalist* no. 14; available online at <http://www.cpsr.org/internetdemocracy/cyber-fed/Number_14.html>.

———. 2004. "Working with the Resources at Hand: Constraints on Internet Institutional Design." *Continuum: Journal of Media and Cultural Studies* 9, no. 3:403–10.

Office of the Millennium Assembly. 2001, August. *Reference Document on the Participation of Civil Society in the UN Conferences and Special Sessions of the General Assembly During the 1900s,* version 1. Available online at <http://www.un.org/ga/president/55/speech/civilsociety1.htm>.

Peake, Adam. 2004, June. "Internet Governance and the World Summit on the Information Society (WSIS)." Association for Progressive Communication; available online at <http://rights.apc.org/documents/governance.pdf>.

Plan of Action. 2003, 12 December. World Summit on the Information Society; available online at <http://www.itu.int/dms_pub/itu-s/md/03/wsis/doc/S03-WSIS-DOC-0005!!MSW-E.doc>.

Schenker, Jennifer. 2003, 8 December. "UN Takeover of Internet? Some Are 'Not Amused.'" *International Herald Tribune.*

CHAPTER 12

The End of the Experiment: The Failure of Democracy in ICANN

JOHN PALFREY

Introduction

The Internet Corporation for Assigned Names and Numbers (ICANN) has failed with its experiment in novel forms of governance and representation of the global Internet user community.[1] Nevertheless, it will still warrant a footnote in the history books. Its inception in the late 1990s as the Internet morphed from a limited network of academics, technologists, civil servants, and other trailblazers into a widely used and incessantly discussed global phenomenon placed ICANN in an intriguing role. ICANN's mandate to coordinate a key aspect of the Internet's operations made it the first substantial Internet institution with a global reach. ICANN may also be worth chronicling as a *sui generis* institution that was at once obscure and a lightning rod for attention and criticism from government entities, legal scholars, and Internet users. These and other parties have struggled with the questions of who should govern the technical architecture of the Internet, and how to do so legitimately.[2] If its long-running reform process continues on its desultory path, or if time runs out on ICANN's multiple extensions of its Memorandum of Understanding (MoU) with the U.S. Department of Commerce, or if its most fierce critics involved in the World Summit for the Information Society (WSIS) process get their way, ICANN may well be remembered as a case study in organizational self-destruction.[3]

ICANN's ambitious experiment was to create its own legitimacy by harnessing the power of the Internet's potential for openness and representation. From the perspective of some stakeholders and onlookers, ICANN's central mission was to use the technologies, power, and attractiveness of the Internet to experiment in democratic governance on a global scale.[4] It sought to empower the Internet user community, including the private sector, to manage a system necessary for the stable operation of the Internet. Its novel, though ultimately flawed, structure has enabled a coalition of private-sector interest groups to manage the domain name system (DNS) with broad input from individual users and limited but growing input from nation-states.[5] However, ICANN has failed to attract and incorporate sufficient public involvement to serve as the blueprint for building legitimacy through the Internet. Those who sought to prove a point about the Internet and democracy through ICANN have misplaced their emphasis, because ICANN's narrow technical mandate has not lent itself to broad-based public involvement in the decision-making process.

Since its formation, ICANN has faced an uphill battle to establish the legitimacy of its authority. Its experimental decision-making structure grows out of its brief, unusual history and from the traditions of informal technical standards-setting bodies. Established by a few individuals, a few private standards bodies, several corporations, and the U.S. Department of Commerce, ICANN was founded in 1998 as a not-for-profit corporation based in California. It has sought to legitimate itself as an open and representative body, striving toward a bottom-up decision making process grounded in consensus and inclusion.[6] The corporation was charged with the seemingly limited role of technical coordination of the Internet for the benefit of the Internet community as a whole. To carry out this mandate, ICANN has involved hundreds of thousands of people around the world, much in the same manner as its predecessor organizations did.

ICANN has offered a wide range of ways in which members of the Internet user community may participate in the organization's decision-making process, but the extent to which ICANN paid attention to that user participation is much less clear. Throughout its history, users have had the ability to post public commentary about general or specific issues before the ICANN board. Users may attend or participate remotely in public meetings at which the board, staff, and other entities make decisions.

Also, users may serve on advisory committees and volunteer for a variety of tasks.

While thousands have sought to participate through these means, this extensive participation has affected few important decisions. The reason is that the structure ICANN adopted to fulfill its charter is so complex and obscure that too few people have been able to figure out how to contribute meaningfully. It is so complex, in fact, that there are few useful analogues.[7] From a legal perspective, ICANN is a corporation, governed by its own charter and bylaws, and the laws of the State of California. From a historical perspective, ICANN has attributes in common with a standards body: a volunteer-driven effort that joins corporate interests, academics, and interested people in their individual capacities from around the world. From a functional perspective, though, ICANN has elements of a government entity: an association of people joined by a compact to make decisions about a particular process or series of interests.[8] The election of 2000 (a global online election to choose five of its nineteen directors) strengthens the parallel between ICANN and a governmental form, particularly what political scientists call a "semidemocracy."

ICANN has elements of all three structural forms, but no single element dominates because this hybrid organizational form is a historical accident rather than the result of clear, principled planning from the outset. Would-be participants, and even academics with a lot of time on their hands, must work hard to understand the decision-making process. This complexity serves as a stumbling block to ICANN's goal of broad public participation. If it genuinely seeks to gain legitimacy of authority through openness, the public must know how to participate so they can be heard.

ICANN's 2000 election was its most ambitious in engaging the world's Internet users in a common, open, democratic process. Despite severely limited resources, the election enfranchised voters from every region of the world. More than 76,000 people registered to vote at the Internet polling booths set up by election.com. But the relative tactical success of this election is overshadowed by the overall failure of ICANN's experiment in at-large representation and participation. The story of formal representation through public elections of ICANN's board effectively drew to a close on December 15, 2002, as the elected directors' terms ended, and the bylaws changed to end the experiment. The shortcomings of this single experiment, which can be traced in large measure to a lack of widespread interest in the institution's highly technical mandate and a futile attempt to establish an unsustainable semidemocracy, should not stand for the proposition that Internet-based elections, activist movements, or global democratic institutions cannot or will not emerge. They suggest, however, that ICANN is not the organization to prove this point.

The outlook for ICANN's experiment in broad-based, global representation is dim.[9] Its leadership maintains that it is "encouraging other forms of at-large organizations to self-organize and create and encourage a body of individuals who could provide the user input and public interest input into the ICANN process."[10] Nonetheless, hope has been further lessened by the continued calls to review ICANN's structure and mission from members of the U.S. Congress, such as Senator Conrad Burns (R—Montana) and Congressman Edward Markey (D—Massachusetts), and leaders in nongovernmental organizations (NGOs), such as Zoë Baird, president of the Markle Foundation.[11] If ICANN is not changed radically, the tension between its efforts to make itself representative and its complex institutional structure will continue to create problems.

This chapter explores ICANN's struggle with legitimacy. Its experiment in legitimacy was actually two interrelated experiments: to use the Internet to create legitimacy through openness, and to create legitimacy through representation. The experiment in openness failed because openness requires clarity, but ICANN's hybrid organizational form has only obscured how decisions are made. When the experiment in openness failed, ICANN tried to salvage its legitimacy through representation in the election of 2000. This too failed because it made ICANN into a semidemocracy. To escape its current crisis of legitimacy, ICANN has to discard half measures and become either truly open, truly representative, or abandon such distractions and focus on succeeding in its narrow technical mandate.

This chapter argues that ICANN should relinquish responsibility for the experiment, because its highly technical mandate rendered it, as an institution, ill-suited to serve as the test bed for a new, user-driven model of decision making. As important as ICANN's mandate is, there are numerous technical aspects of the Internet that concern users more directly and substantially than the coordination of the DNS. The job of directing users to websites in response to the entry of search queries on the Web—run almost exclusively by private parties such as AltaVista, Google, Microsoft, Overture, and others—has greater immediate relevance today to users than the port allocation managed by ICANN. Similarly, the exercise of authority by state actors and those they regulate, such as internet service providers, to filter aspects of Internet traffic without warning or recourse has far greater impact on what a user of the Internet experiences and what resources he or she can access through the network. An institution that would be able to succeed in the experiment by enabling the user community meaningfully and directly to be involved in the decision-making process would likely have a mandate of greater accessibility and significance to the Internet user community than ICANN's narrow mandate to coordinate the DNS. We have yet to develop a compelling theory of governance of the technical architecture of the Internet.[12] We ought to consider ICANN's story in this broader context of Internet governance, considering the role not only of individuals but also of corporations and governments in the process of decision making regarding these issues of global and common importance.

I begin ICANN's story by briefly reviewing its history to illustrate how its founding principles and organizational structure conflict to drain legitimacy of authority. I then explain how a fundamental confusion about the meaning of "openness," combined with ICANN's convoluted decision-making structure, caused the experiment in openness to fail, because users could not reasonably believe that the board listened to their concerns. In the following section, I show how, in response to criticism generated by the failure of the experiment in openness, ICANN tried to achieve legitimacy through representation. This failed, however, because it made ICANN into a legitimacy-draining semidemocracy. In conclusion, I point to some of the implications of this short history for ICANN itself and for the study of how best to govern the technical architecture of the Internet.

ICANN's History, Structure, and Importance

The history of ICANN, and the principles on which it was founded, help explain the structure of the institution, the struggle over the issue of representation, and how its the problem of legitimacy came to be. Its founding principles are the seeds of its fundamental problem: if its legitimacy stemmed from the Internet user community and was rooted in its founding principles of openness and representation, then its history and structure set it up to fail on its own terms.

The story of ICANN's formation has been told, at least in part, by several scholars.[13] The most critical part of this story is that the founders—a mix of academics, government officials, corporate executives, and technologists—agreed upon a set of principles that have proven to be mutually exclusive. That is, the founders wanted a private sector corporation to operate in a manner that is "representative" of global interests and "open" in its management decision making. In striving for consensus, the founders set themselves up for failure by embarking on a mission that is impossible to achieve.

To a certain extent, the development of ICANN's structure has remained shrouded in secrecy. The means by which many of the initial board members and officers were chosen is particularly unclear. Prior to ICANN, the technical coordination of key aspects of the Internet's infrastructure was handled on an essentially ad-hoc basis by a number of individuals in loose-knit, consensus-driven standards bodies such as the Internet Engineering Task Force. ICANN's immediate predecessor, the Internet Assigned

Numbers Authority (IANA), consisted of Dr. Jon Postel of the University of Southern California and a limited administrative staff. After decades of management of the DNS, and as increasing numbers of people wanted access to the system and to the levers of control, the job became too large for these organizations. Disputes arose between these loose-knit organizations, the U.S. government, and private corporations such as Network Solutions, which had contracted to control the lucrative dot-com top-level domain.

The reliance on a single nation's grant of authority lies near the core of ICANN's legitimacy problems. Despite its global mandate, ICANN retains extremely close ties to only one nation, the United States.[14] ICANN emerged from a U.S. government initiative, in concert with members of the private sector and the technical Internet community, intending to resolve the brewing dispute over governance of the DNS. The United States briefly considered taking over the DNS, but instead produced two preliminary documents in 1998, known as the "Green Paper" and the "White Paper."[15] These papers set forth a series of policy prescriptions and principles to govern how the DNS would be managed. At the most fundamental level, the Green and White Papers established that the U.S. government would not actively manage the domain name system, but would rather empower the private sector to lead.[16]

In the wake of these policy pronouncements, representatives of the IANA negotiated an agreement with the U.S. Department of Commerce in November 1998. Based upon this agreement, ICANN came into being through the formation of a nonprofit corporate entity in California. Its charter and bylaws incorporated a series of principles that reflected the desires of the founders as well as those of the administration of President Bill Clinton.

Once formally established as a California corporation, ICANN's initial board and officers are believed to have been handpicked largely by the late Dr. Postel (who died abruptly in October 1998) through his authority at the IANA.[17] In theory, the board membership was chosen to be representative of a cross-section of geographic areas affected by the DNS. The initial board was made up of a number of highly respected members of the Internet community, including chairwoman Esther Dyson, an experienced U.S.-based entrepreneur, journalist, and longtime leader in the technology world. The formal role and governing principles of ICANN, as well as an explanation of the source of its authority, are set forth clearly in the MoU between the U.S. Department of Commerce and ICANN. The MoU delineates a role for ICANN that is largely confined to managing technical DNS functions, the numbering of Internet addresses, the coordination of port assignments, and assisting in the maintenance of the stability of the Internet. ICANN was established to work with the U.S. Department of Commerce to ensure that the "private sector has the capability and resources to assume the important responsibilities related to the technical management of the DNS."[18] The project listed the following among its goals: encouraging international participation; providing expertise and advice on the allocation of IP number blocks and coordinating the assignment of other Internet technical parameters as needed to maintain universal connectivity of the Internet; collaborating on written technical parameters for operation of the authoritative root; and, collaborating on a study and process to address operational requirements of the root name servers and the security of the root server system.

Most important for this inquiry, the MoU specifically set a goal for ICANN of achieving "representation" through process, as set forth in the following clause:

> 4. Representation. This Agreement promotes the technical management of the DNS in a manner that reflects the global and functional diversity of Internet users and their needs. This Agreement is intended to promote the design, development, and testing of mechanisms to solicit public input, both domestic and international, into a private-sector decision making process. These mechanisms will promote the flexibility needed to adapt to changes in the composition of the Internet user community and their needs.[19]

ICANN's founders acknowledged the global nature of the network, the global implications of the technical management that they were undertaking, and the need to take into account the needs and composition of the Internet user community. In so doing, they committed themselves to managing the organization so as to achieve representation of a constituency arguably unparalleled in its breadth. Its founders also established ICANN with a view toward testing new mechanisms for involving the public in a private-sector decision-making process. ICANN subsequently chartered a study on representation by the Berkman Center for Internet and Society at Harvard University Law School and frequently requested comment by others on the topic of representation.[20]

Despite—or perhaps because of—the articulation of this founding principle, much of the critique of ICANN to date has revolved around the problem of representation.[21] Representation has proven problematic because of the extremely high expectations (set by the governing principles) that the organization's leaders would represent such enormous and varied constituencies and the lack of precision about what "representation" means.[22] Critics of the ICANN have been vocal, expressing their views through websites, bulletin boards, listservs, and the news media. Some conclude that corporate interests have too much authority. Others think the process favors U.S. interests. But few have argued that representation should not be a governing principle of the organization. My argument is that if ICANN commits to holding itself out as representative of the Internet user community, it should then clarify and make good on its commitment.

In addition to seeking to represent the global community of Internet users, the founders of ICANN committed to an "open" manner of managing the DNS and making decisions. Like the variety of possible meanings of the term *representation*, a clash of several understandings of the meaning of the term *open* has also contributed to the hybrid nature of ICANN's structure. The notion of openness is often cited in the early writings about what makes cyberspace distinctive. Openness as a concept—as in *open source*, *open access*, or even *open law*—has taken on a nearly mythic status in cyberlaw writings. Longtime collaborators Lawrence Lessig of the Stanford University Law School and Charles Nesson of the Harvard University Law School have written and spoken about the importance of the "open society" in cyberspace and the many threats to that ideal.[23] The open society is held out as one manifestation of the great promise of the Internet as a digital commons in which empowerment of individuals, widespread sharing of ideas across cultural and other boundaries, and free expression are glorified. The idea of openness, with its many various connotations, has tremendous resonance and multiple special meanings to the activists of the Internet community.

Since the founding of ICANN, the officers and directors have continued to restate their commitment to representation and openness. One sentence from the organization's public website bundles the principles together: "It is ICANN's objective to operate as an open, transparent, and consensus-based body that is broadly representative of the diverse stakeholder communities of the global Internet."[24]

Nevertheless, scaling has proven hard for ICANN. As the scope of responsibility and number of constituents grows, so too does the difficulty of managing in a representative, open, and consensus-driven manner. Representation becomes more difficult as individuals grow further away from those who represent them, whether geographically or as a matter of sheer ratio. Whereas one representative used to have a constituency of one hundred, now she has a constituency of hundreds of millions (in the case of North America), or even billions of people (in the case of Asia). Similarly, openness—particularly in the sense of transparency—becomes harder with scale, as not all decisions can be made by a small group of directors and officers in front of the world at large.

ICANN's complex hybrid structure is the root of its problem with legitimacy. Rather than being chosen as the structure most able to manage the DNS, or to achieve the principles of openness and representation, ICANN's structure was a compromise in the worst sense of the word. The designers attempted to blend the best parts of a corporation, a standards body, and a government entity, but they ended up with a structure that does not carry the legitimacy of authority or effectiveness of any of its component parts.

ICANN is not purely a standards body, a corporation, or a government entity. It has elements of each, but none of these models suffices on its own to describe its current hybrid structure. This conclusion leaves open a vexing question, which has both positive and normative elements. What kind of institution is ICANN? What kind of institution should it be? Where does its legitimacy come from? The answers to these questions are not clear. It is important, though, to recognize that ICANN strives to operate by clear founding principles in a highly complex structure—the complexity of which makes fidelity to these principles all the more challenging. That complexity was also an opportunity to test the Internet's ability to enable a new, more democratic and empowering—though ultimately unsuccessful—form of decision making.

ICANN remains virtually unknown to the general public. A vast majority of the roughly six hundred million people who use the Internet to gather information, communicate via e-mail, or shop online appear to have little interest in the technical administration of the DNS. If many people who use the Internet neither know, nor much care, about what ICANN does, does it even need to legitimate its authority? Does it matter at all whether it lives up to its founding principles? Moreover, does it matter what sort of governance structure ICANN has? Given that its work is arcane and often remote from the lives of everyday people, many are tempted to answer "no."

Yet, in light of the its importance to the global economy and to the Internet, a better answer is "yes." ICANN's structure and management are important because its mission is important, and because ICANN presents an extraordinary opportunity to experiment with a new medium's power of institution building on a global scale. Few issues touch the lives of so many across such a broad geographical and functional spectrum, even indirectly, as ICANN's mandate does. While the world's societies are certainly divided into technology haves and have-nots, often along purely economic lines, the breadth of Internet usage and transactions across national boundaries continues to expand. This global reach highlights the potential importance of the ICANN experiment to the future of Internet governance. Some people care about ICANN's management because they fear expanding U.S. hegemony, the English language, or the power of multinational corporations. Others see its potential reach as an opportunity to energize Internet users across national borders into forging a global community and to test the Internet's ability to power global democratic institutions. That is, they think ICANN should serve as an experiment in strengthening participation in democratic institutions generally through innovative use of the Internet.[25] For them, ICANN is a test case for innovation in technology-powered democratic governance. Finally, those concerned with how we move forward in making technical governance decisions, particularly with the increased concern over abuse of the network, seek a new model for how to tackle such problems. For all of these reasons, ICANN and its experiments in representation matter.

The Failure of the Experiment in Legitimacy through Openness

The crisis of legitimacy that spurred the election of 2000 stems from ICANN's failure to garner legitimacy of authority through openness. The experiment in openness failed for two reasons: first, there was a fundamental confusion in what was meant by "openness," and second, ICANN's hybrid organizational form obscured the decision-making process so that even if it had wanted to ICANN could not listen to Internet user input.

At least three possible conceptions of what *openness* means have clashed in the development of ICANN.[26] First, activists have sought openness in the sense of an ability to participate in the decision-making process. Second, some conceive of openness as a variant of leading free-software guru Richard Stallman's nonproprietary model of the development of intellectual goods, in which the form of the final outcome is what matters most.[27] Openness, in this second sense, is about positive freedom to do whatever users want with the output of the process. Third, yet others have set forth an Eric Raymond–style production model, in which openness is a process by which a good end is achieved.[28]

In the first sense of openness, ICANN is meant to be managed so as to allow people to see what is going on, to be heard when they express their opinions, and to affect the decision-making process. Much of the criticism that ICANN has sustained to date has been proffered by those who believe that they were either excluded entirely from the process or afforded little meaningful voice in developing the its structure and system.

The second and third potential meanings of openness in the Internet lexicon—the Stallman-style and Raymond-style versions, for short—have been less prevalent in the discourse but certainly present. The Stallman-style version of openness, in which the output is meant to be free, as in nonproprietary, is hard to square with the nature of what ICANN is doing. In the sense that it seeks to allocate a series of necessarily proprietary resources, a nonproprietary series of outcomes is inherently difficult to achieve in ICANN's context. To maintain a stable system, ICANN can direct requests for Cocacola.com to only one address on the Internet. This conceptual difficulty is revealed in the reaction to the Free Software

Foundation's proposal, over Stallman's signature, to develop a "dot-gnu" top-level domain.[29] ICANN has not achieved openness in the sense of non-proprietary outcomes of the decision-making process.

In the Raymond-style conception of openness, the goal is to achieve the best outcome through a nonproprietary process. ICANN might be effectively defended in this sense of openness in that it has enabled many members of the user community to participate in the development of its process. Likewise, one might reasonably contend that the outcome of its work has been at least acceptable, and surely far better than it might have been. If the notion of openness is that the development of goods ought to involve as many users as possible to produce the highest-quality output possible—without prescribing precisely the manner in which the output is developed or prejudging its outcome—ICANN fares reasonably well.

The confusion lies in the fact that the its leadership seems to have taken the Raymond-style conception of openness, whereas the Internet user community and ICANN's critics have taken the activist sense of openness. ICANN's leadership was able to achieve a Raymond-style openness by including many people through its public message boards, but a systematic review of public input on a series of key issues suggests that users could not reasonably think that ICANN was open in the activist sense of the word.[30]

The review found that the tenor of public commentary regarding a proposal before the board did not correlate strongly to an outcome either for or against that proposal. In several instances, the board voted against the position adopted by the majority of users who commented. In contrast, other types of input to the board, such as the recommendation of a relevant supporting organization or of a hired technical reviewer, correlated more strongly to the board's ultimate decision. The Internet user community could not reliably expect that their input through these online forums would result in board consideration of their interests. These findings reaffirm the intuition of the critics who have questioned the extent to which ICANN has lived up to its principle of openness. Reform of the its decision-making structure should, at a minimum, clarify the channels for input from the user community to the decision makers and ensure that user expectations about the effect of their input are met.

Our review of the correlation between public input and board decisions is neither a complete study, nor a statement about whether the board reached a sound decision on any given matter. The board may in fact have reached the right decision to fulfill its narrow technical mission in every instance, which would constitute success in the Raymond-style conception of openness. Yet, even if ICANN made the right decision in every instance, it still loses its legitimacy of authority with every decision, because it based its legitimacy on openness and representation and has failed to live up to these principles, at least if we construe them strictly. Given the rhetoric of its founders and current leadership, ICANN must confront the frustration felt by the Internet community when they do not feel heard, despite assurances to the contrary.

The Failure of ICANN's Experiment in Representation

When it became apparent that its experiment in openness was failing, ICANN shifted its focus to representation in an attempt to salvage its legitimacy of authority. With the election of 2000, ICANN made a move toward becoming a more formally representative body. This approach failed spectacularly: instead of making ICANN into a representative government entity, it made it into a semidemocracy. Its current semidemocratic form not only fails to address the problem of legitimacy, but also brings along a host of its own problems.

This one-time election was one manifestation of the struggle among ICANN's participants to craft answers to the thorny questions regarding its legitimacy. The fact that there is a lack of clarity about the its structure and the source of its authority makes room for those with an agenda to impose it on the organization. The group that championed the at-large membership and elected directors was one of the most vocal groups of ICANN participants. Many members of this group are individual technologists or Internet users; some members also work for large corporations, NGOs, or other powerful entities.

The premise behind the election of 2000 was largely consistent with the overall goals and principles of ICANN, particularly with the goal of representation. Any person with Internet access who wished to become a member had the opportunity to do so during an open enrollment period by accessing the ICANN website and submitting a short form. Instructions were translated from English into Chinese, French, German, Korean, Japanese, Portuguese, and Spanish. ICANN then mailed a letter to the registrant's physical address to verify that each member existed as a discrete individual. The letters included personal identification numbers (PINs) that could be used prior to September 8, 2000, to activate membership and voting rights. Those who registered then had the right to vote in a global, online election to select members to the board of directors. Candidates could nominate themselves prior to an August 14, 2000, deadline. Once nominated, they needed to secure not only support from residents of two or more countries, but also the support of twenty individuals, or 2 percent of the at-large members in their geographic region (whichever was greater). In October 2000, five directors were elected from distinct geographic regions (Africa, Asia and Pacific, Europe, Latin America and the Caribbean, and North America). These five directors served on the nineteen-member board, with full and equal powers relative to other board members, until their terms ended on December 15, 2002. The at-large membership process was intended to make ICANN more representative by enabling any person who uses the Internet to have a formal voice in the management of ICANN. The election of 2000 used an online interface and an instant runoff vote, implementing Election.com technology.

The mechanics of registering voters, running the nomination and campaign period, as well as the actual election, went more or less smoothly, though some voters experienced frustrations in the process.[31] During the registration period, some would-be members experienced difficulties in accessing the ICANN server and using their mailed PINs. At the time of the voting, "'A few of the more than 76,000 at-large members discovered their online votes were not being accepted by the online voting booth,' said ICANN's Chief Policy Officer Andrew McLaughlin."[32] Contemporary reports suggested that about four hundred members may have been affected by this difficulty. But it is unclear whether any of these voters returned later to submit their ballot. These mechanical problems, which necessarily should be addressed in future Internet-based elections, do not appear so serious as to suggest that global online elections are unfeasible.

The at-large membership drive and election of 2000 were deemed a success by ICANN's staff and by some observers at the time of their completion. Of the 158,000 people who signed up for at-large membership online during the summer of 2000, 76,000 persons activated their membership and established voting rights. Of those eligible to vote, 34,035 cast valid ballots. Those voters represented a 45 percent turnout of those eligible and a 22 percent turnout of those who initiated the registration process. Of the world's estimated 375 million Internet users at the time, less than 0.01 percent voted in the ICANN election of 2000, with only 130 ballots cast from the continent of Africa.

On some level, the ICANN election of 2000 was historic. A *sui generis*, not-for-profit corporation held elections for five board members in which 76,000 people from most parts of the globe participated using Internet-based technology. ICANN's election of five of nineteen directors, with a goal of creating a representative organization, however, is unsettling when considered from the perspective of political theory. More specifically, the combination of its curious structure and its unconvincing attempts in representing the global Internet community has left ICANN in the awkward, unsustainable position of a semidemocracy. And this semidemocratic structure poses serious problems for the organization over the long term. Potential problems include capture by powerful interests, directors who do not represent the Internet community at large, a disengaged user community, and difficult transition periods. Finally, its semidemocratic structure has left ICANN without a solution to its problem of legitimacy.

In the wake of the election of 2000, ICANN's mixed board of directors—with five elected and fourteen nonelected directors—placed the organization into the nebulous zone occupied by semidemocracies, midway between the authoritarian and pluralistic models of governance. Even without the directly elected directors, ICANN's hybrid structure is semidemocratic. This authoritarian-pluralist model is characterized by a situation in which "the party or other governing group retains a monopoly on political power but is willing to grant a measure of political and cultural freedom at the individual, group, and regional levels."[33] One way to retell the story of ICANN's development is that the nonelected board members (and those chosen by the supporting organizations) continued to retain all political power. Although they temporarily acceded to the user community's demands for directly elected board members, they then removed those directors after only a single term.

The semidemocratic model fits ICANN particularly well, not just in light of the election of 2000, but also from the perspective of its corporate form. The board of directors retains absolute control over the decision-making process. It can grant the managers and other stakeholders, such as the supporting organizations, freedom to act. For example, the board delegates certain spending powers which allow the managers to independently authorize expenditures. Additionally, the staff and outside counsel can negotiate on behalf of the board with key partners and present agreements to the board for consideration, discussion, and subsequent approval. Supporting organizations are also empowered to make recommendations to the board. This suggests that parties other than the board and staff members are participating in the governance process.

One might think ICANN should be lauded for its move toward semidemocracy. Thus, those who believe that direct representation is the best structure for ICANN viewed the election as a first step in the right direction. The logical progression would be for it to gravitate from a fully appointed board to a fully elected board. The election of 2000 would be followed by a subsequent election to bring the next four elected members onto the board. After that experiment has proven itself a success, ICANN might move toward electing all its board members via the at-large membership. It could then capitalize on the success of its most recent elections to build greater legitimacy across the globe through a model of deliberation and inclusion. ICANN would thus be empowering the Internet user community to participate in the governance process. This incremental and hopeful view, however, is unconvincing in light of historical experiences with semidemocracies; it is also highly unlikely at this point that ICANN will, or should, move toward a purely democratic model.

From the other end of the spectrum, the harshest criticism of the election of 2000 posits that ICANN's move toward semidemocracy is nothing more than an instance of "placative politics." The ICANN board has sustained so much criticism that it sought a means of placating the user community. The most obvious means is to enable the user community to elect representatives to the board who, even when voting in a bloc, cannot effect change within the institution. The sole aim of such an election process is to placate the vocal critics—perhaps even landing some such critics in positions of nominal authority—with no intention of ceding any real power to the user community. Potentially, once the elected representatives behave poorly, or interest in electing powerless representatives wanes, the board can revert to its pure nonelected form. Even without fully reverting to a nonelected board, the placative approach might manage to squelch public interest in ICANN. In Roberto Unger's terms, placative politics involve "the adoption of rules and practices maintaining society at a relatively low level of political mobilization," with the goal of securing "property against populism."[34]

The political history of the second half of the twentieth century suggests that either model could be right.[35] Those who think in terms of U.S. and democratic triumphalism tend to think of semidemocracies as mere way stations between authoritarian or totalitarian regimes and the ultimate end state of representative democracies. History offers a few such transitions of various completeness, including but not limited to a number of Eastern European states and certain countries in South America in the late twentieth century.[36] Of these examples, Brazil and Chile may serve as the best examples of the gradual transition through semidemocracy toward an ultimately democratic regime.[37] South Africa over the past decade presents a particularly graphic example, though with a spin on the same notion of transition. In South Africa, the change took the form of a fairly abrupt movement from exclusion to inclusion of racial minorities, rather than a gradual transition from autocratic to democratic structures.[38,39] In contrast, examples from East Asia, such as Malaysia and Singapore, may lead to the conclusion that semidemocracy is a final or semipermanent stage rather than merely a phase in a long-term transition.

The effort to apply the political histories of modern nation-states to the study of ICANN is fraught with problems and is ultimately inconclusive. The difficulty of using case studies of this sort traces back to the fact that the parallel between ICANN and a nation-state is imperfect. ICANN is a new institution, and potentially a new kind of institution, filling a perplexing new void rather than replacing an old institution with a new one. Even if the parallels hold up under scrutiny, examples from political history present an unclear conclusion as to whether semidemocracies are way stations or end points. The period between the election of 2000 and the end of the elected directors' terms at the close of 2002, however, has seen a pullback away from the expansion of democratic decision making, not a continued push in the prodemocratic direction. ICANN itself is rapidly becoming an example of the perils of the semidemocratic structure.

Conclusion

The best way to manage the DNS, and the best way to prove that the Internet user community can be involved in the decision-making process on issues of global importance, are not one and the same. These two issues have been conflated in the debate over ICANN's legitimacy of authority. Its failure to create legitimacy through representation and openness means that its structure ought to be reformed to achieve its narrow technical mandate. Regardless of whether ICANN can endure as a technical body, the community as a whole is left with the continuing need to establish a compelling theory for the governance of the technical aspects of the global Internet.

Three key points emerge from this analysis of ICANN's experiment in governance structures. First, with a goal toward selecting the organizational structure most suited to its narrow mandate ICANN must move away from its semidemocratic phase, and continue to pursue substantial structural reform—more substantial than the marginal reforms proposed by the its leadership to date. Second, ICANN should clarify the way in which users can meaningfully involve themselves in the decision-making process to mitigate the risk of demoralization and to get the most out of the input offered by the Internet user community in a manner that is constructive rather than distracting. Such reform should make sure that individuals know the extent to which their participation through various channels will be considered by the decision maker. Third, we need to look past ICANN's troubled story and toward emerging issues of how to govern the technical architecture of the Internet in an increasingly networked world.

The last of these three points is the most important. The global Internet community still faces the hard questions that faced us in 1998, when ICANN came into being: Who "governs" the Internet and how? Can, and should, Internet users govern themselves? What is the role of traditional sovereigns and of powerful market players? If the private sector is still to lead, the private sector must learn to partner effectively with governments and civil society and to lead in a manner that guarantees meaningful public participation. Together, these parties should seek to develop new, open, and transparent governance models. Internet technologies still hold promise in terms of making new models possible and effective, though we ought to learn from the ways in which ICANN's use of methods such as simple bulletin boards, listservs, and the direct election of board members has come up short. The failure of ICANN to live up to its founding principles calls renewed attention to the need for experimentation in using the Internet to foster stronger democratic institutions. It needs to reboot, to establish a new set of principles for its operation, and to develop a structure from the ground up that enables it to carry out its narrow technical mandate. While it ought to be inclusive of the user community, ICANN should not be organized to prove a point about democracy on the Internet; as an organization that manages a technical function, and does not set standards or do much that interests or engages a broad swath of Internet users, ICANN is ill-suited to that end. Those who care about democracy and technology should shift their attention away from ICANN, which is almost certainly now beyond repair, and toward the many greener fields in cyberspace.

Notes

1. See David J. Farber, Peter G. Neumann, and Lauren Feinstein, "Overcoming ICANN: Forging Better Paths for the Internet" (March 18, 2002); available online at <http://www.pfir.org/statements/icann>; Dan Hunter, "ICANN and the Concept of Democratic Deficit," 36 Loy. L.A. L. Rev. 1149 (2003).
2. See Jonathan Weinberg, "ICANN and the Problem of Legitimacy," 50 Duke L.J. 187 (2000).
3. ICANN's woes are legion. Aside from collateral attacks by several governments and the perpetual dispute over representation, a distributed denial-of-service attack on October 21, 2002, in which seven of the thirteen DNS roots were cut off from the rest of the Internet, raised questions about ICANN's fitness to carry out its core mission (which has ordinarily not been a major source of controversy).
4. See Andrew L. Shapiro, *The Control Revolution: How the Internet Is Putting Individuals in Charge and Changing the World We Know* (New York: Public Affairs, 1999), 57–59; and Mark Poster, "CyberDemocracy"; available online at <http://www.humanities.uci.edu/mposter/writings/democ>.
5. See Kenneth N. Cukier, "Why the Internet Must Regulate Itself," *Financial Times*, 31 October 2003; available online at <http://www.cukier.com/writings/FToct03.html>.
6. ICANN Fact Sheet; available online at <http://www.icann.org/general/fact-sheet.html>.
7. See, however, Milton Mueller, *Ruling the Root: Internet Governance and the Taming of Cyberspace* (Cambridge, MA: MIT Press, 2002), 217–18.
8. See A. Michael Froomkin, "Wrong Turn in Cyberspace: Using ICANN to Route Around the APA and the Constitution," 50 Duke L.J. 17 (2000); Joe Sims and Cynthia L. Bauerly, "A Response to Professor Froomkin: Why ICANN Does Not Violate the APA or the Constitution," 6 J. Small and Emerging Bus. L. 65 (2002); A. Michael Froomkin, "Form and Substance in Cyberspace," 6 J. Small and Emerging Bus. L. 93 (2002); and Joe Sims and Cynthia L. Bauerly, "A Reply to Professor Froomkin's Form and Substance in Cyberspace," 6 J. Small and Emerging Bus. L. 125 (2002).
9. See A. Michael Froomkin, "Habermas @ discourse.net: Toward a Critical Theory of Cyberspace," 116 Harv. L. Rev. 749, 838–55 (2003).
10. Posting of M. Stuart Lynn, President and CEO of ICANN, to India Chennai, http://www.washingtonpost.com/wp-srv/technology/transcripts/archive_icann_062002.htm.
11. See Joanna Glasner, "Senators Weigh ICANN's Future," Wired.com (June 13, 2002), http://www.wired.com/news/business/0,1367,53159,00.html.

12. The definitive theory of control on the Internet is Professor Lawrence Lessig's description of architecture (or code), law, norms, and market in cyberspace. Lawrence Lessig, *Code and Other Laws of Cyberspace* (New York: Basic Books, 1999). See also Viktor Mayer-Schoenberger, "The Shape of Governance: Analyzing the World of Internet Regulation," 43 Va. J. Int'l L. 605 (2003); Steven R. Salbu, "Who Should Govern the Internet?: Monitoring and Supporting a New Frontier," 11 Harv. J.L. and Tech. 429, 454 (1998); Adam Thierer and Clyde Wayne Crews, Jr., eds., *Who Rules the Net? Internet Governance and Jurisdiction* (Washington, DC: Cato Institute, 2003).

13 The most thorough history of ICANN is probably Mueller's *Ruling the Root*. See also Weinberg; The Center for Democracy and Technology, Domain Name Management Policy: ICANN Formation, http://www.cdt.org/dns/icann/formation.shtml; ICANN, History of ICANN At Large, http://members.icann.org/history.html.

14. See "Memorandum of Understanding Between ICANN and the United States Department of Commerce" (Nov. 25, 1999), http://www.ntia.doc.gov/ntiahome/domainname/icann.htm.

15. National Telecommunications and information Administration, "A Proposal to Improve Technical Management of Internet Names and Addresses" (Jan. 30, 1998) [Green Paper], http://www.ntia.doc.gov/ntiahome/domainname/dnsdrft.htm.

16. National Telecommunications and Information Administration, "Management of Internet Names and Addresses" (June 5, 1998) [White Paper], http://www.ntia.doc.gov/ntiahome/domainname/6_5_98dns.htm.

17. Mueller, 1–10.

18. "ICANN't Believe What They're Doing," Nat'l J.'s Tech. Daily (Jun. 17, 1999), http://cyber.law.harvard.edu/pil-99/icannt.txt; see also Milton Mueller, "ICANN and Internet Governance: Sorting Through the Debris of "Self-Regulation,"" 1 Info. 497, 498 (Dec. 1999).

19. MoU 1998, arts. II.A–II.B.

20. MoU 1998, art. II.C.4.

21. Berkman Center. for Internet and Society at Harvard Law School, "Representation in Cyberspace Study," http://cyber.law.harvard.edu/rcs/.

22. See David R. Johnson and Susan P. Crawford, "Why Consensus Matters: The Theory Underlying ICANN's Mandate to Set Policy Standards for the Domain Name System," ICANN Watch (Aug. 23, 2000), at http://www.icannwatch.org/archive/why_consensus_matters.htm; David R. Johnson and Susan P. Crawford, "The Idea of ICANN," ICANN Watch (Feb. 12, 2001), at http://www.icannwatch.org/archive/the_idea_of_icann.htm.

23. Weinberg, 259–60.

24. Lawrence Lessig, "Reclaiming a Commons," Keynote Address at the Berkman Center's "Building a Digital Commons" (May 20, 1999), http://cyber.law.harvard.edu/events/lessigkeynote.pdf; see also Open Society Institute, www.soros.org/about.

25. Iregistrars.com: ICANN, http://www.iregistrars.com/icann.html.

26. Steven Hill, "ICANN: Secret Government of the Internet?: The Fight Over Who Will Control the Web," *In These Times* (May 15, 2000), http://www.inthesetimes.com/issue/24/12/hill2412.html.

27. I owe the concept of the three clashing senses of "openness" to conversations with Professor Jonathan Zittrain during the development of this paper. A more subtle view of meanings of openness in the context of standards setting may be found in Ken Krechmer, "The Principles of Open Standards," 50 Standards Engineering Nov./Dec. 1998, at 1–6.

28. See Richard Stallman, "Why "Free Software" Is Better than 'Open Source,'" *Free Software, Free Society: Selected Essays of Richard M Stallman* (Joshua Gag, ed. 2002) http://www.gnu.org/philosophy/free-software-for-freedom.html.

29. Eric S. Raymond, "The Cathedral and the Bazaar" (1999), http://www.catb.org/~esr/writings/cathedral-bazaar/cathedral-bazaar/.

30. Richard Stallman, "ICANN Yokohama Meeting Topic: Introduction of New Top-Level Domains Expression of Interest" (July 10, 2000), http://www.icann.org/yokohama/eoi12.htm.

31. This review, examining the majority of public commentary on ICANN's online forums, was conducted by the Berkman Center. For a web-based compilation of the data, see John Palfrey et al., "Public Participation in ICANN: A Preliminary Study," Berk-

man Center for Internet and Society at Harvard Law School, http://cyber.law.harvard. edu/icann/publicparticipation.

32. Carter Center for Election Monitoring, "Report on the Global, On-line, Direct Elections for Five Seats Representing At-Large Members on the Board of Directors of the Internet Corporation for Assigned Names and Numbers (ICANN)," http://www.markle.org/ News/Icann2_Report.Pdf.

33. James Evans, "ICANN Election Starts with Small Snag," *InfoWorld Daily News*, Oct. 2, 2000.

34. Muthiah Alagappa, "The Asian Spectrum," 6.1 J. Democracy 29, 33 (1995).

35. Roberto M. Unger, *Democracy Realized: The Progressive Alternatve* (London: Verso, 1998) 264.

36. Paul Brooker, *Non Democratic Regimes: Theory, Government and Politics* (New York: Palgrave Macmillan, 2000).

37. Richard Bellamy and Dario Castiglione, eds., *Constitutionalism in Transformation: European and Theoretical Perspectives* (Oxford, UK: Blackwell, 1996).

38. Andreas Schedler, "Concepts of Democratic Consolidation" (Apr. 19, 1997), http://136.142.158.105/LASA97/schedler.pdf. See also Unger; Elisabeth J. Wood, *Forging Democracy from Below: Insurgent Transitions in South Africa and El Salvador* (Cambridge, UK: Cambridge University Press, 2000).

39. Timothy D. Sisk, *Democratization in South Africa: The Elusive Social Contract* (Princeton, NJ: Princeton University Press, 1995); and Wood.

CHAPTER 13

Debating Communication Imbalances: From the MacBride Report to the WSIS

CLAUDIA PADOVANI

The WSIS in Historical Perspective

As Annabelle Sreberny reminds us, "Summits may be all about words, but the words have consequences" (2004, 201). In this chapter, I analyze the language used in the production of the World Summit on the Information Society (WSIS). To assess the potential consequences of this language, I look at the WSIS from the historical perspective of the proposal for a new world information and communication order (NWICO) in the 1970s. Which concepts from NWICO reappear in WSIS? How have some been transformed? What new concepts have emerged? My analysis demonstrates how the present need to redefine basic norms and institutions for the sectors of information technology, communication, and knowledge parallels the need that was perceived already in the late seventies. At the same time, it shows how the emerging discourse regarding multistakeholder approaches to governance is an evolution in conceptualizing the democratization of international relations.

World Politics and Communication: Historical
Precedents and Contemporary Transformations

Some of the authors who have written about the WSIS remind us of its legacy with the history of communication in the UN system. Marc Raboy recalls that:

> The WSIS is the third attempt by the United Nations system to deal globally with information and communication issues. In 1948 .... the Universal Declaration on Human Rights spelled out, for all, what the great revolutions of the 18th century had struggled to obtain for Europeans and Americans: that the capacity to seek, receive and impart information is a basic human right. In the 1970s . . . the non-aligned nations sparked a debate on a "new world information and communication order," drawing attention to such questions as the inequalities in north-south information flow, the cultural bias of technology and the lack of communication infrastructure in the so-called third world. 1948 was a moment of consensus, but the debates of the 1970s were fraught with conflict, as is well known. (2004a, 225)

Ulla Carlsson, in reviewing the role of the United Nations and the United Nations Educational, Scientific, and Cultural Organization (UNESCO) in the evolution of international agreements in the field of information and communication, reminds us that no less than forty-one international conventions and declarations were adopted between 1948 and 1980, which "focused on the legal status of various elements in mass communication and specify objects for regulation on a multilateral basis" (2003, 36).[1] In the mid-1970s, there were crucial debates around the proposal of a New World Information and Communication Order (NWICO). The underlying idea, in a time of decolonization and new international roles played by newly independent states, was that no real independence would have been possible unless real political, economic, and cultural autonomy for all states could be obtained. The proposal of a NWICO was discussed in several forums, particularly within the Non-Aligned Movement and the Group of 77, but also in the General Assembly of the UN and in UNESCO, raising harsh conflicts, mainly due to the Cold War climate of the time, which favored the opposing superpowers and shadowed the original motives and voices behind the proposal (Pasquali 2005). Such demands concerned a number of issues, which have been synthesized as the "four Ds": *democratization* (need for pluralism of sources of news and information), *decolonization* (struggle for independence from foreign structures and self-reliance), *demonopolization* (denouncing concentration of ownership in media industries), and *development* (Nordenstreng 1984). Actions were required to bring about changes in the international communication context in which states could "develop their cultural system in an autonomous way and with complete sovereign control of resources, fully and effectively participate as independent members of the international community" (Hamelink, cited in Carlsson 2003, 43).

Thus information and communication issues became both a tool and an end in the struggle for sovereignty through self-reliance. The idea of NWICO was refined through the work of the International Commission for the Study of Communication Problems, lead by Sean MacBride, and the report it produced, adopted by UNESCO at its General Conference in 1980, which can be considered the highest point in a debate that later became gradually marginalized.[2]

In the debates and documents around the MacBride Report, reference was often made to the need to democratize international relations: there was a clear awareness that a reordering of information and communication at the international level was crucial to bring about "radical changes in global power relationships" (Carlsson 2003, 42). Information and communication were recognized as closely linked to the overall structure of the international system. In a world that was undergoing profound changes, technological transformations (among which the speed and extension of transnational flows and infrastructures) required new regulations and rules.

This historical precedent to the WSIS is therefore meaningful in terms of the involvement of the international community in multilateral negotiations about information and communication, and because of the very issues that stimulated such debates: the potential of communication technologies in overcoming global inequalities and the recognized need for international agreements and regulation. There are thus strong parallels to the situation that lead to the idea of the WSIS at the start of the new millennium: inequalities and growing technological gaps, as well as the challenging need to reorder a world system in which multilateralism no longer seems to be a recognized principle, while institutional legitimacy is a contested matter (O'Brien et. al. 2000).

These are, in fact, aspects of contemporary global processes that affect practices of political conduct at all levels (Held et al. 2000; Rosenau 1999), as well as global "media- and techno-scapes" (Appadurai 1996). Changes on the global scene interfere with the separation between domestic and international political processes (Held 1999); we witness a shifting in the location of authority toward supra- and extranational forums, the emergence of a transnational civil society, and the reorientation of intellectual, political, and economic elites (Rosenau 1999). In this context, transformations in the role information technologies play in everyday life have stimulated comprehensive rethinking of societal development: an "infor-national paradigm" seems to be emerging while networks of power, wealth and communication spread around the globe (Castells 2000), strengthening the interplay between political processes and communication developments.

Moreover, as public institutions are forced to redefine their working rules, transnational corporations and business organizations are growingly influencing global processes, particularly in the communication and information sectors (Hamelink 2001; Hermann and McChesney 1997; Kleinwachter 2001) and are gradually being legitimized as interlocutors in international forums. At the same time, the "public space" is becoming transnational and its "inhabitants" are asking for institutional mechanisms and guarantees that allow them to participate meaningfully in developing not just norms and visions, but also concrete and effective governance structures (Nye and Donahue 2000; Padovani and Tuzzi 2004).

The more political issues—such as communication imbalances—become global in scope, the more global policies are needed, capable of giving voice to the different interests at stake. Current emphasis on generating a set of basic norms and institutions to govern the Internet and information technologies in general thus repeats an impulse already present in the seventies. At the same time, the emerging discourse about multi-stakeholder approaches to governance extends thinking about democracy in international relations.

These developments should thus be considered as the results of historical processes of interdependence now leading to "visions of global governance."

The governance concept is today generally accepted as a way to describe negotiation practices among public, private, and third-sector agents, creating complex networks of interdependence at different levels of authority. In order to appreciate the potential and challenges that go along with transformations in the global communication governance, it is important to assess continuity and fractures between how "infoscapes" have been in the past and are conceptualized today, in terms of who the main players were who set the stage, what the issues and factions were, if and how political discourse flowed beyond the restricted spaces of intergovernmental politics, and what the results of each process have been.

An Emerging Global Communications Movement

Looking at the WSIS from a historical perspective is also necessary because of profound transformations in the sociopolitical structure of world affairs. As a reaction to the opacity in the conduct of politics beyond the national level, new mobilizations from the grassroots have emerged. Reference to the "global civil society" is growing in literature (Kaldor 2003; Keane 2003), as well as in the political discourse. Criticism of unproblematic use of the term is also growing (Calabrese 2004; Kooiman 2003). The diffused use of the concept nevertheless suggests a diffused awareness that something new is happening in a transnational space that has greatly benefited from the spread of information and communication technologies (ICTs) and is now able to articulate its demands and actions through dynamics that connect the global context to local spaces.

The so-called no global/new global movement that became visible in Seattle in November 1999 has created its own spaces for reflection, through the World Social Forum, regional and local social forums, and through a number of countersummits that have been organized since on the occasions of high-level political gatherings (Pianta 2001). These processes have raised the interest of scholars who started to investigate the transnational dimension of mobilization and protest politics (Guidry, Kennedy, and Zald 2000; Hamel et al. 2001; Keck and Sikking 1998; Smith, Chatfield, and Pagnucco 1997).

ICTs and information sharing have become key resources for such mobilizations (Leòn, Burch and Tamayo 2003; Carroll and Hackett 2004; Keck and Sikkink 1999). Moreover, information and communication are more than instrumental tools for activist networking; they are fast becoming major issues to be discussed in themselves (Milan 2004; Muller 2004). The tension between an instrumental conception of information technologies and their effective impact in setting the context for more participatory political processes is still unresolved. Nevertheless, themes debated in civil society forums, increasingly include issues of media concentration, the need for pluralism and access to information, legal issues concerning individual freedoms and privacy, communication rights, and the application of ICTs.

It is therefore important, in reviewing the history of international communication debates, to recognize that reference to "the emergence of a global movement" on media and communication started in the early 1980s. Kaarle Nordenstreng recalls how, in 1983, a loose coalition of international organizations of journalists involved in the NWICO debates issued a document, "International Principles of Professional Ethics in Journalism," that stated, "'The journalist operates in the contemporary world within the framework of a movement towards new international relations in general, and a new information order in particular'" (1999, 241). The use of the term *movement* at that time was likely related to the nonaligned "movement" struggling for democratization of the international system. It could also have been occasioned by the experience of "new social movements" that had become relevant to Western societies in those years.

But the idea did not disappear subsequently. Some years later, Nordenstreng and Traber wrote a booklet, *Few Voices, Many Worlds: Towards a Media Reform Movement* (1992). By the early 1990s, NWICO was no longer on the international agenda:

> At present, the forum for debate over NWICO has been left to scholars and communication specialists. . . . What is needed is to bring the concerns of the MacBride Report to general attention, and encourage further debate and study by concerned individuals and non-governmental organizations (Nordenstreng and Traber 1992, 1).

The authors' call for an international mobilization was grounded on the evidence of a growing number of initiatives that aimed at fostering the debate outside institutional forums.[3] The "movement" was still very much restricted to specific sectors, like academia, some nongovernmental organizations, and a few media professional associations, and it was mainly focused on media-related issues; but the term was no longer used in close relation to the NWICO debate, which had been essentially characterized by the presence of state actors. There was an explicit awareness of the need to involve citizens' organizations.

At the end of the decade there had actually been developments in this direction. Vincent, Nordenstreng, and Traber wrote, in *Update to the MacBride Report*,

> What started, historically, with the proposed restructuring of the international information and communication order has grown into an alliance of grassroots organizations, women's groups, ecology networks, social activists, and committed academics. Some now call it a media reform movement; others emphasize media education, of which the mass media are an important part. There is a new NWICO in the making which sees itself as a network of networks based in civil society (1999, ix–x).

We can therefore trace an evolution in the use of the term *movement* that gradually brought the concept closer to today's reality.

Rooted in the debates of the 1970s and early 1980s, and subsequently developed in the course of initiatives such as the MacBride Roundtable, the proposal for a People's Communication Charter, and the Platform for Democratization of Communication, the sense of a movement has become stronger and more international. Indeed, the very WSIS process has enabled the movement to redefine its identity. One of its components, the campaign Communication Rights in the Information Society Campaign (CRIS), offered as a space where senior activists and scholars and younger interested individuals and organizations have created a virtual intergenerational bridge between NWICO and the WSIS.

Notably, however, the WSIS offered the opportunity for other mobilization experiences. Women's and indigenous peoples' movements have been able to make their visions about information issues heard. Furthermore, this happened in a dialogue with more recent mobilization experiences around digital rights and the governance of the Internet, as well as about youth presence in the ICT environment and the use of ICTs for an "Internet citoyen and solidaire." Attempts to map this articulated reality are being carried on, yet much remains to be done, as the landscape is continuously changing.[4] This complex phenomenon needs to be placed in a longer time perspective for a full appreciation of legacies and discontinuities, if we are to develop appropriate conceptual frameworks for conducting further research, capable of investigating social dynamics that are today characterized by a plural agenda, a multilevel *modus operandi,* and a transnational networking structure.

Information and Communication Landscapes

In May 2003 a high-level scientific colloquium was organized in Venice, "Information Society: Visions and Governance. WSIS and Beyond."[5] Two sessions were devoted to an investigation of the possible legacies between former debates on communication issues and the Geneva WSIS, and saw the participation of both scholars and protagonists of those debates,[6] among them Roberto Savio, honorary president of Inter Press Service, and Sean O'Siochru. Major changes that have occurred in the media and communication landscape globally were identified in terms of powerful actors, prevailing interests, and the extension and deepening of phenomena, including the debate itself.

These changes can be synthesized with reference to the deregulation of telecommunication markets and the privatization of television systems in many countries. A prevailing neoliberal logic has promoted and accompanied globalization processes. The outcome has been growing gaps between countries and the exclusion of communities and individuals (the so-called technoapartheid), alongside changes in the governance of global communication. Among contemporary features of the global "infoscape" are thus a deepening in cultural industries concentration and the shift of regulatory arenas on communication and information issues from UNESCO to the International Telecommunications Union (ITU), the World Bank, and the World Trade Organization (WTO). At the same time conceptual "dislocations" are also at play: "enabling environments" and "multistakeholder partnerships" are the new catchwords that replace formulas that were relevant in the past, such as "free flow of information."

This brief historical account alerts us to three key aspects of the debates over global communications: the structure and basic features of the international context, the actors involved, and their expectations, goals, and priorities.

The NWICO debate took place in a Cold War climate that witnessed profound changes in the structure of the international system through the emergence of new states, and the formation of a strong (though not always cohesive) coalition of Third World countries; a climate that profoundly affected the political confrontation in multilateral sites of debate, such as the UN and UNESCO, reducing issues and positions to the confrontation between the Eastern and Western worlds (Pasquali 2005). Today, neoliberal tendencies in communication governance have produced shifts in the venues where negotiations take place, and changes in the conduct of political negotiations: the ITU, with its focus on technological developments and its habit of cooperation with private entities but not with other social actors; the WTO, with its practice of "green room" negotiations; and "global business dialogues" are the new venues for deliberations where decision-making processes follow a path of "opaqueness."

States and governments were the predominant actors on the NWICO scene, alongside transnational corporations and Western media associations, which took some visible stands through initiatives such as the gathering held at Tailloires in 1981 to denounce the attempt to regulate global information (Nordenstreng 1999). Today we witness attempts to formally recognize the legitimacy of varied constituencies through "multistakeholder approaches"; yet the difficulty of the "old world of State diplomacy in facing the challenges of today's world" has become explicit.[7] States are caught up between the need for setting rules for a changing reality and their retreats from a rule-making role. Civil society organizations have become more active in advocacy activities at the national and international level, yet no defined mechanisms have been envisaged to set the norms and principles for their participation in institutional forums. Media and information conglomerates play an ever growing, generally "not visible" part, in influencing global governance, while a discourse on information and communication issues seems to be totally absent from those mass media that are thought to be promoters of a global public sphere.

Finally, though no ultimate definition of NWICO was developed in former debates, the basics were clear: the restructuring of the international media and information system was central to the possibility for all countries to develop their communication systems and strengthen their potential to become independent actors on the world scene. The democratization of the system, alongside the reduction of inequalities and the responsibility of media actors in fostering changes—expressing the voice of the "unheard"—were the major issues at that time. Today we witness two opposing models concerning information in society: the one promoted by governments, and supported by commercial interests, that sees "information society" as the catchword for a new world order based on the application of a single technologically driven model, in which information and knowledge are goods to be bought and sold on the consumers' market. On the other side is the idea of communication and information societies that should be open and inclusive, respectful of diversity and plurality, grounded in the belief that communication is a basic for all human organizations, and knowledge should be considered as a common good. Fostered by civic associations and advocacy groups, consistently with the growing discourse that "another world is possible," this position is considered to be evolving in the tradition of the NWICO (Nardi and Padovani 2004; O'Siochru 2004b).

Aware of these differences in context, let's now look at the "worlds of words" that are condensed in documents.[8]

Analyzing the "Worlds of Words": Documents and Voices

Conscious of the relevance of words and language in diplomacy and negotiations, and in order to assess continuity and change in debates, I selected and compared the language of three representative documents: the MacBride Report, the WSIS official declaration of Principles, and *Shaping Information Socities for Human Needs*, the "alternative" declaration adopted by the Civil Society Plenary. I focus first on the final section of the MacBride Report, in which the commission members synthesize their research on communication problems and add their proposals for attaining the NWICO. The proposals are arranged in "Recommendations and Conclusions" into five sections concerning the need for developing countries to build their own communication systems and news agencies; increasing national capacities and training in communications and information, and pursuing regional cooperative strategies; issues of cultural identity; content production and interregional exchange; and basic needs in terms of infrastructures and services.

Of particular interest is the section "Democratization of Communication," where explicit reference is made to individual and collective rights—specifically, the right to communicate, considered a cornerstone of a "new era of social rights." Media ownership concentration is mentioned as a major obstacle to the pluralization and diversification of communication systems. Emphasis is also placed on the design of effective legal and regulatory measures to foster democratization processes.[9]

The document is representative of the political climate of the time and of the specific language used in debates that involved Western and Eastern states—a cohesive group of nonaligned states, but also scholars, media industries, and professionals. It was the result of investigations conducted by communication experts, scholars, and policy makers and not the outcome of a diplomatic negotiation, but it was officially adopted by UNESCO (through Resolution 4/19, 1980). The text has therefore received official legitimization by the international community.

The second document I consider was legitimized as the output of a high-level political summit: the WSIS Official Declaration of Principles adopted in Geneva on December 12, 2003, and titled *Building the Information Society: A Global Challenge in the New Millennium*,[10] in which we read, "Representatives of the people of the world . . . declare common desire and commitment to build a people-centered, inclusive and development-oriented Information Society" and established basic principles toward that end, articulated into eleven points:

1. The role of government and all stakeholders in the promotion of ICTs for development
2. Information and communication infrastructures as foundation for an inclusive information society
3. Access to information and knowledge
4. Capacity building
5. Building confidence and security in the use of ICTs
6. Enabling environment
7. ICT applications: benefits in all aspects of life
8. Cultural diversity and identity, linguistic diversity and local content
9. Media
10. Ethical dimensions of the information society
11. International and regional cooperation

This document is the result of a diplomatic negotiation as reflected by its language. It also expresses the plurality of issues that make up the international agenda and mirrors today's official narrative and governments' priorities.

Equally legitimized by recognition as one of the official outputs of the Geneva Summit is the third document, *Shaping Information Societies for Human Needs*, the "alternative" declaration adopted by the Civil Society Plenary.[11] We consider the WSIS the first time in which nongovernmental realities, which have over the years grown in numbers and areas of interest, emerged to a visible stage, mobilizing for action, defining common priorities, and building a shared language.

The structure of the Civil Society declaration is quite different from the official one, as are the opening words:

> "We, women and man from different continents, cultural back-grounds, perspectives, experience and expertise, acting as members of different constituencies of an emerging global civil society . . . have been working for two years inside the process, devoting our efforts to shaping people-centred, inclusive and equitable concept of informa-tion and communication societies."

The preamble, "A Visionary Society," is followed by a list of "Principles and Challenges":

1. Social justice and people-centered sustainable development
2. Centrality of human rights
3. Culture, knowledge, and public domain (within which are found space themes such as linguistic diversity and the media)
4. Enabling environment (to parallel the official language, but referring to the ethical dimension, democratic and accountable governance)
5. Human development, education, and training
6. Information generation and knowledge development
7. Global governance of ICTs and communication

My analysis deals with two moments in history and three speaking voices, since one of the novelties of the WSIS process was the choice to have both governmental and nongovernmental actors formally involved. Referring to this triangle of voices, I address the following questions: What can we say about legacies and transformations, analyzing the language in communication debates? What are the issues at the core of each document and speaker? What are the "common" elements? Is it possible to identify conceptual links and elements of continuity? Are these to be found mainly in the relationship between the MacBride Report and the official declara-tion or in connections between the MacBride Report and the alternative Civil Society document?

The Colors of Language

In Figure 13.1 is a graphic representation of the interconnection among the selected documents.[12]

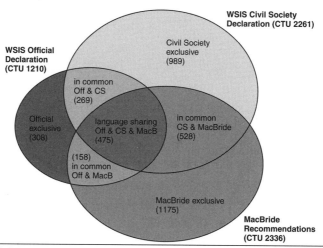

Figure 13.1 The colors of language. Interconnections among documents.

We have compared the vocabularies looking for exclusive use of language as well as for common elements, which has been done to test the following assumptions:

1. *Common elements between MacBride Report recommendations and the WSIS official declaration* could be explained as referring to intergovernmental processes.
2. *Common elements between MacBride Report recommendations and the WSIS Civil Society declaration* could be thought of as a legacy of the NWICO debate in the perspective of "communication societies" (O'Siochru 2004b), in the awareness that during the 1980s the debate had been marginalized to academic settings and grassroots groups (Lee 1995) while social mobilizations on related issues have grown.
3. *Common elements between the WSIS official declaration and the WSIS Civil Society declaration* could be thought of as new substantial elements with respect to former debates, due to changes in the world context, in technology, and in the conduct of policy. Common elements may also be explained by actors' participation in the same process over the eighteen months of the WSIS preparatory process to the Geneva phase.

Exclusive Language

In Figure 13.2, we consider the characteristic language of each speaker by analyzing textual units that are used only by one speaker and never by oth-

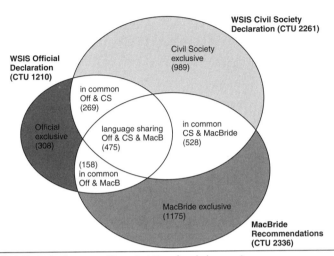

Figure 13.2 Exclusive language. Characteristics of each document.

ers, in order to identify which themes, issues and dimensions are central to each.

Numbers below indicate the number of times a Complex Textual Unit (CTU) occurs in the corpus with reference to how many times it is used by the speaker (total X/speaker Y):

The MacBride Report

News (23/23), journalists (32/28), professional (16/15), mass media (13/12), broadcasting (9/9), advertising (9/9), profession (8/8), new world (7/7), protection of journalists (7/7), dependence (6/6), self-reliance (6/6), disarmament (5/5), democratization (5/5), television (5/5), newspapers (5/5), transnational corporations (5/5), communication development (4/4), information flows (4/4), communication needs (4/4).

WSIS Official Declaration

Development of/building the information society (10/10), countries with economies in transition (4/4), ICT applications (4/4), connectivity (3/3), ICT infrastructure (3/3), productivity (3/3), Internet-related public policy issues (3/3).

WSIS Civil Society Alternative Declaration

Community media (9/9), free software (10/9), cultural and linguistic (10/9), indigenous people (10/9), transparency (6/6), transparent and accountable (3/3), communication societies (6/6), pluralistic (6/6), open access (8/7), conflict situations (6/6), knowledge societies (5/5), information and communications (5/5), knowledge and information (5/5), human knowledge

(5/5), women and men (5/5), to participate (7/6), freedom of expression (4/4), community driven (4/4), community informatics (4/4), unequal power (3/3), media workers (3/3), media freedom (3/3).

Shared and Specific Language

In Figure 13.3, we see that language can be shared by documents, but formulas can be highly specific to one speaker in relation to others (i.e., relatively more used by that actor). Therefore, together with the identification of common elements between texts, we also indicate which aspects are relatively more important for each speaker.

Numbers in brackets below indicate occurrence of CTUs in one document in relation to occurrence in another document 2. We indicate: (A) CTUs that are relatively more relevant to the first speaker (occurrence in doc 1 > doc 2); (B) CTUs that are relevant to the second speaker (occurrence in doc 1 < doc 2); (C) CTUs that are used in a similar way by both speakers (occurrence in doc 1 = doc 2).

MacBride Report/WSIS Official Declaration

(A) each country (7/2), independence (6/1), cultural identity (5/1), ethics (4/1), national development (4/1), all nations (4/1). (B) international and regional (2/4). (C) national and regional (2/2), international cooperation

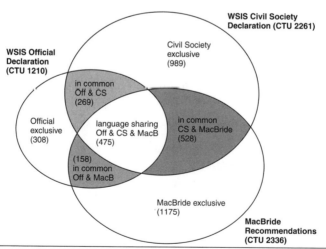

Figure 13.3 Specific language. Language shared by some documents.

(3/5), to create (3/1), to enable (1/3), to enhance (2/2), to increase (2/2), to serve (2/1), to evaluate (2/1), to assess (2/1).

MacBride Report/Wsis Civil Society Alternative Declaration

(A) journalists (28/4), journalism (6/2), mass media (11/2), exchange (8/1), infrastructures (6/1), researchers (5/1). (B) participatory (2/6), research (4/10), communities (2/22), independent (1/9), accountability (1/5). (C) communications (9/8), inequalities (6/5), control (4/7), power (3/4), capacities (4/3), means of communication (3/4), regulations (3/3).

WSIS Official Declaration / WSIS Civil Society Alternative Declaration

(A) information society (36/7), sustainable development (7/5), all stakeholders (10/2), private sector (6/3), special needs (5/1), enabling environment (3/2). (B) civil society (5/18), public domain (3/13), free software (1/9), indigenous peoples (1/9), cultural and linguistic (1/9), open access (1/7), intellectual property (2/5), to participate (1/6), regulation (1/5), international law (1/5), traditional media (1/5), global knowledge (1/5), public policy (1/4), people centered (1/4). (C) access to information (4/7), applications (3/4), digital divide (2/3), digital solidarity (3/2).

Overlappings

We also find CTUs that are common to all three documents, the assumption being that there exist few substantial issues that could be a hypothethical basis on which to ground the governance of communication problems.

We indicate the occurrence of each CTU in the documents in the following order: MacBride Report/WSIS official declaration/WSIS Civil Society declaration.

development (33/23/28)	democracy (1/1/5)
communication (60/2/9)	technologies (5/7/8)
information and communication (9/5/53)	knowledge (3/6/23)
research and development (4/2/1)	media (39/5/23)
national (28/5/5)	developing countries (26/6/7)
policies (8/3/7)	decision making (8/3/7)
must (10/3/39)	governments (2/4/10)
cooperation (12/8/7)	investment (3/5/1)
human rights (16/3/14)	responsibility (9/1/5)
diversity (5/2/6)	rights (5/3/15)
participation (8/2/11)	women (2/3/13)
	democratic (4/2/9)

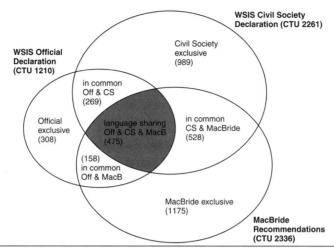

Figure 13.4 Overlapping language. Language shared by all documents.

Confronting Visions of Information and Communication in Society

Having compared the three documents and outlined similarities and differences in the use of language, we conclude by saying that, in spite of some shared language, each speaker expresses a quite different vision of communication in society.

Very few elements are common to all documents (see Figure 13.4). Only aspects related to development and technology seem to be equally relevant to all speakers. This demonstrates the general awareness of the need to overcome inequalities (divisions), which have actually become more evident over the past twenty-five years. The focus on technology, and a quite similar wording, also indicates that in spite of technological innovations that have intervened in the past decades, the language used to express the centrality and role of information technology in society has remained quite similar. This also confirms the ongoing challenge posed by technological innovation to the development of appropriate regulatory mechanisms. Within the global landscape of communication governance one crucial issue is what mechanisms and procedures can be promoted to favor the participatory dialogue that has been formally legitimized by the WSIS? Needless to say, the bigger challenge does not resides in procedures per se, but in a change of mentality that starts being perceived by public administrators as well as social actors (Mueller 2004; Padovani 2004a).

There are more elements in common between the MacBride recommendations and the WSIS Civil Society declaration than between MacBride and the official WSIS output. Issues of common interest are: human rights, freedoms, and a strong reference to the "public dimension" (public spaces, services, policies). Reference is also made to the institutional responsibility to develop legal frameworks through a decision-making process that should foster democratization processes. Yet, while democratization is expressed in a generic manner in the MacBride Report, consistently with the above-mentioned interest for "democratizing the international system"; democratic, open, and inclusive processes are crucial to the Civil Society document, which shows a more concrete approach to democratic processes, between as well as within societies.

Additional shared elements include the use of "power," references to "world peace," and two interesting evolutionary visions of human rights. The idea of a "right to communicate" appears in both documents, but is used three times in the MacBride reccomendations and once in the Civil Society declaration; while the formula "right to participate" is used three times in the WSIS Civil Society document and once in MacBride. This possibly reflects the different context in which visions were developed together with the contemporary recognition that it is only through inclusive decision-making that policies can be adopted which allow the democratic potential of communication to develop, thus fostering the right to communicate.

Few elements are shared by the official WSIS declaration and the Civil Society document, in particular the "access dimension" (access to information, universal, affordable, and equitable access) and the "development dimension" (promotion of development, levels of development, ICTs for development). Two specific sets of words, relating to the "digital divide" and to "sustainable development," reflect the evolution of concepts over the years. Sustainability has become an issue in the international agenda on the occasion of the UN Conference on Environment and Development, held in Rio de Janeiro in 1992, whereas in former times the focus would have been on self-reliant or endogenous development. Similarly, the so-called digital divide has been promoted as a central issue for the international community through the World Economic Forum in 2000: imbalances in information technologies have become "divides" mainly understood in a digital sense.

Few elements connect the MacBride recommendations with the WSIS official declaration—mainly the use of verbs, indicating commitments to be made (to create, to enable, to enhance), and reference to international organizations, cooperation, and community, maintaining a focus on the national dimension (national priorities, efforts, capacity) which appears stronger in the MacBride document. It therefore seems that the "official discourse" has definitely and profoundly changed.

Overall, each document expresses quite different visions. Highly relevant to the MacBride language is reference to mass media, broadcasting, the profession of journalists, news, and information flows. Strong focus is also on the concentration and monopolization of communication structures, which does not find equivalent in either of the two other documents. Exclusive to MacBride is reference to transnational corporations. This focus on the world media system and the role of media in development, which has actually been one of the major concerns in former debates, has been quite marginalized in the WSIS official discourse; raising criticism among civil society organizations as well as scholars (Carlsson 2003; Hamelink 2004; Raboy 2004a). In contemporary official narratives, problems raised by global media concentration are hardly mentioned, in spite of this being one of the most problematic developments on the world media scene. No conceptual articulation emerges from the WSIS declaration of the interrelation between traditional and new media, nor among public, commercial, and community media.

In the MacBride Report "communication" is widely referred to: means of communication, flows of communication, new communications, development communication. In spite of the focus on world information flows that characterized the NWICO debate, information and communication were conceived as two different things, both fundamental to social organizations and central to the broader international reality. The international arena is relevant to MacBride, but a strong focus is also placed on countries and national spaces. It may be interesting to note that in the report the word "state" is never used: the "national" dimension prevails. Furthermore, as anticipated above, democracy is conceived as a necessary horizon and is articulated in different ways—democratization, democratized, democratizing—but not in relation to actual decision-making processes.

Finally, we find "self-reliance" and "independence," which reflect the historical context in which the debate took place. Civil society is never mentioned, while sparse reference is made to organized social groups.

The basic idea in the official WSIS declaration is that of building the information society through technology and its applications, connectivity, technology transfer, and infrastructure development; the other strong focus being on economic growth, productivity, job creation, competitiveness, and investment. This reflects policy narratives around ICTs and communication that have developed since the early 1990s: the launch of the Global Information Infrastructure (GII) in 1994 and the European commitment to the "European information society" (Padovani and Nesti 2003). Language is consistent with contemporary global trends, "spurred by deregulation and privatization, concentration, and commercialization" (Carlsson 2003, 61). In the official discourse, a prevailing technologically oriented view of societal transformation goes along with a neoliberal approach, according to which institutional actors are essentially required to "foster enabling environments." The other peculiar element in the document is the exclusive and recurrent reference to security issues (cybersecurity, confidence and security, security of networks, global culture of cybersecurity) which has become central to the official WSIS language.

> As Padovani and Tuzzi have suggested, there is in the WSIS "two ways of conceiving security . . . on one side international security and stability (the international political dimension) and on the other side the need to enhance the confidence of consumers in the information society (the economic dimension). What seems to remain uncovered . . . is the individual dimension of a human right to personal security in an information environment that can be more and more un-safe for citizens, though safe enough for consumers" (2003, 31).

Several elements characterize the Civil Society declaration and its diversified language. The use of plurals is strong (societies, peoples, actors), and the emerging vision is very much "globally aware" (global civil society, global governance). Reference to communities is strong (community media, informatics, broadcasting), while information is always accompanied by communication and/or knowledge, thus stressing a broader conception of communicative flows, interplaying with culture and human knowledge. While communication is widely referred to in the MacBride document, a more substantial focus on "knowledge" seems to express the deepest concern of civil society organizations in the WSIS document. Democracy is also referred to by civil society organizations. In their view it goes along with accountability, transparency, and responsiveness of institutional powers and other actors who are called to commit themselves to shaping information societies capable of responding to human needs. The recurrent verb is *must* (must be ensured, must be promoted, must be protected), the focus being on the right to be guaranteed and not just on the action to be promoted. This articulation and the internal consistency of the document also show a growing awareness of the role to be played by nonstate actors in global communication governance. This participatory dimension becomes a crucial challenge, to be faced through the recognition of existing "unequal powers" and the need to "empower" citizens and communities.

Conclusion

The documents analyzed here are expressions of ages of turbulence and transformation. In the 1970s turbulence was the result of decolonization processes that challenged the structure of the (bipolar) world system, while at the dawn of the new millennium, turbulence is multidimensional (Held et al. 2000). Communication and information were, and still are, at the core of world turbulence: technological developments bring fast changes that imply political as well as cultural adaptations; the spread, adoption, and use of communication technologies, both by global and local actors, is challenging the traditional conduct of world affairs by state actors; inequalities in access to information and knowledge and in the capacity to meaningfully operate communication systems deepen other socioeconomic inequalities.

The focus of debates has shifted from mass media and information flows to new media and information technology, but we still find a plurality of visions concerning communication in society that will hardly be harmonized in the near future. Visions of the 1970s reflected the ideological confrontation between the two superpowers and the attempts of a "third voice" to be heard. Contemporary visions stem from the plurality of subjects that are "taking the floor" on the world scene. However, it should be stressed that a stronger linkage is found between "old" debates about democratization and development and the "new" visionary perspective developed by Civil Society groups at the WSIS than between any other set of documents.

In spite of the transformations that have been outlined, global turbulence has roots in the past: world divides are still major challenges to world peace; potentialities offered by new technologies must be properly channeled to produce positive effects; the basic issue remains the political will that is needed to face such challenges. Traditional actors in international politics do have a crucial role to play, not just in fostering "enabling environments" but in setting the normative context for strategies that should reflect such political will. Meanwhile the synergies created between local initiatives and international social mobilizations, thanks to creative uses of ICTs, have nurtured the seeds of a global movement on communication issues, which is now "challenging the old world of governments."

The WSIS has shown that politics from above and from below are experiencing new grounds around communication and information issues, but there is no one-size-fits-all solution. The challenge is a major one, and in order to address it appropriately it is crucial to develop mechanisms that will allow to combine different discourses into fruitful policy dialogues, capable of overcoming the "hybrid between new technologies and old organization forms" (Mueller 2004). A challenge for all stakeholders, looking at lessons from the past while entering the future.

Notes

I would like to thank my colleague and friend Arjuna Tuzzi, from the Department of Historical and Political Studies at the University of Padova, for the expert methodological support in conducting this investigation.

1. Several authors have been writing extensively and critically on this specific moment in history, which happened to intensively involve communication scholars in the course of the late 1970s and 1980s. For in-depth analysis, see the complete and updated reviews by Carlsson (2003); Golding and Harris (1997); Lee (2003); and Nordenstreng (1999).
2. See Traber, M., and K. Nordenstreng (1992). The MacBride Report has recently been republished, thanks to Andrew Calabrese, editor of the series Critical Media Studies at Rowman and Littlefield.
3. Examples include the research activities of the International Association for Media and Communication Research; the colloquia organized by the MacBride Roundtable; and the development activities in the field of communication carried out by the World Association for Christian Communication.
4. See the Center for International Media Action (CIMA) at <www.mediaactioncenter.org>. CIMA acts as a resource center for organizations and activists and has recently developed a directory of organizations that are active in advocacy initiatives on communication governance in the United States. See also the Convergence Center at Syracuse University, <http://dcc.syr.edu/index.htm>. The center supports research on and experimentation with media convergence and presents, among its latest projects, investigations on Citizen Activism in Communication and Information Policy.
5. Euricom Colloquium, Venice International University, San Servolo, 5–7 May 2003; scientific coordinator: Claudia Padovani.
6. Some scholars who participated are Andrew Calabrese (University of Colorado–Boulder); Ulla Carlsson (Nordicom); Cees Hamelink (University of Amsterdam); Micky Lee (University of Oregon); Bill McIver (State University of New York–Albany), and Marc Raboy (McGill University, Montreal).
7. This was expressed by the Civil Society sector at WSIS when, after the Third Preparatory Committee, they refused to continue contributing to the process and decided to autonomously elaborate their own document, the Civil Society declaration.
8. "WSIS as a World of Words" is the title of Padovani and Tuzzi (2004).
9. For a more in-depth qualitative analysis of this section of the MacBride Report, see Carlsson (2003), who envisions four underlying perspectives in the document: one about communication (and linkages among information, communication and media, and distinguishing institutions and organizations), one about development (concerning the role of information and communication media in development processes), one linked to the Third World approach (summarized by the aforementioned "four Ds"), and one about practicability (with a focus on levels of action). For critical evaluation of the text we also refer to a review proposed by Hamelink and Hancock (1999), in which they set the recommendations in context twenty years after the adoption of the report and evaluate their impact on international communication strategies.
10. Document WSIS-03/GENEVA/DOC/4-E; available at <www.itu.int/wsis>.
11. This is also available on the WSIS official website. A number of documents (eight) were mentioned at the closing ceremony in Geneva, which we have analyzed in order to identify the different "visions of the information society." But only the Civil Society declaration has been considered as an official output of the summit, alongside the governmental documents. We have written about the role of the civil society sector within WSIS and about the final documents adopted in Geneva; see Padovani and Tuzzi (2004, 2005).

12. Here is a short methodological explanation of the analysis, which has been a comparison among the vocabularies of each text, in terms of the amount of different Complex Textual Units (CTUs). By CTUs we mean not just words, but also multiple words or sequences referring to: an increase in the amount of information (they carry more information than simple word types); and a reduction in the ambiguity of simple wordtypes (which is due to their isolation from their context of usage). Overlapping among circles expresses joint use of CTUs, independent from their frequency in the text. The rest is "exclusive" language (that used only by a particular author). Frequency of CTUs has been considered in subsequent interpretation. Note that the three documents differ in dimension: MacBride and the Civil Society declaration are quite similar, while the official WSIS declaration is half the length of the others. This affects the relative weight of each CTUs occurrence.

References

Appadurai Arjun, 1996. *Modernity at Large: Cultural Dimensions of Globalizations*. Minneapolis: University of Minnesota Press.

Bailie Mashoed, and Winseck, Dwayne, eds. 1997. *Democratizing Communication? Comparative Perspectives on Information and Power*. Cresskill, NJ Hampton University Press.

Calabrese, Andrew, 2004. "The Promise for Civil Society: a Global Movement for Communication Rights" *Continuum: Journal of Media and Society* 18, no. 3:317-329.

Cammaerts, Bart and van Audenhove, Leo, 2003. *ICT-Usages of Transnational Social Movements in the Networked Society: To Organize, to Mediate, to Influence*. EU Project The European media and Technology in Everyday Life Network 2000-2003 EMTEL, final deliverable.

Cammaerts, Bart, van Audenhove, Leo, Frissen, Valerie, Engels Liz, Ponsioen, Arnout, 2002. *Transnational Civil Society in the Networked Society: On the Relationship between ICTs and the Rise of a Transnational Civil Society*. Study in the framework of TERRA 2000, International Institute of Infonomics.

Carlsson, Ulla, 2003. "The Rise and Fall of NWICO: From a Vision of International regulation to a Reality of Multilevel Governance." *Nordicom* 24, no. 2:31-68.

Carroll, William K. and Hackett, Robert, 2004. "Democratic Media Activism and Social Movements in Theory and Practice." Paper presented at Political Economy section of the IAMCR Conference, Porto Alegre, Brasil.

Castells, Manuel, 2000. *The Information Age*. Vol. 1 of *Economy, Society and Culture*. Oxford: Oxford University Press.

Diodato, Emidio, 2003. *Introduzione alla comunicazione politica internazionale*. Perugia: Guerra Edizioni.

Drake, William, 2004. "Defining ICT Global Governance." Memo prepared for the Social Science Research Council; available online at <www.ssrc.org/itic>.

Galtung, Joan, 1999. "State, Capital and Civil Society: A Problem of Communication." Pp. 3-22 in *Towards Equity in Global Communication: MacBride Update*, ed. Richard Vincent, Kaarle Nordenstreng, and Michael Traber. Cresskill, NJ: Hampton.

Global Civil Society Yearbooks. 2001, 2002, 2003. London: London School of Economics.

Golding, Peter and Harris, Philip, eds. 1997. *Beyond Cultural Imperialism: Globalization, Communication and the New International Order*. London: Sage.

Guidry, John A., Kennedy, Michael D., and Zald, Mayer N., eds. 2000. *Globalization and Social Movements: Culture, Power and the Transnational Public Sphere*. Ann Arbor: University of Michigan Press.

Hamel, Pierre, Lustigher-Thaler, Henri, Pieterse, Jan Nederveen, and Roseneil, Shasha, eds. 2001. *Globalization and Social Movements*. NY: Palgrave Macmillan.

Hamelink, Cees, 2001. "La *governance* della comunicazione globale." Pp. 143-179 in *Comunicazione Globale: Democrazia, sovranità, culture*, ed. C. Padovani. Torino: UTET Libreria.

———. 2004. "Did WSIS Achieve Anything at All?" *Gazette* 66, nos. 3–4:281-290.

Hancock, A. and Hamelink, C., 1999. "Many More Voices, Another World," In R. Vincent, K. Nordensterg, and M. Traber, eds. *Toward Equity in Global Communications*. MacBride Update. Cresskill, NJ: Hampton Press.

Held, David, 1999. *Democrazia e ordine globale. Dallo stato moderno al governo cosmopolitico*. Trieste: Asterios.

Held, David, McGrew, Anthony, Goldblatt, David, and Perraton, Jonathan, 1999. *Global Transformations: Politics, Economics and Culture*. Cambridge: Polity.

Herman, Edward and McChesney, Robert, 1997. *The Global Media: The New Missionaries of Global Capitalism*. London and Washington: Cassell.

Kaldor, Mary, 2003. *Global Civil Society: An Answer to War*. Cambridge: Polity.

Keck, Margaret and Sikkink, Kathrine, 1998. *Activists beyond Borders*. Ithaca, NY: Cornell University Press.

———. 1999. "Trans-national Advocacy Networks in the Movement Society," Pp. 217-237 in *The Social Movement Society: Contentious Politics for a New Century*, ed. David S. Meyer and Sidney Tarrow. Lanham, MD: Rowman and Littlefield.

Kleinwachter, Wolfgang, 2001. "Global Governance in the Information Age," Papers from the Centre for Internet Research, Aahrus, Denmark.

———. 2004. "Beyond ICANN vs. ITU. How WSIS Tries to Enter the Territory of Internet Governance." *Gazette* 66, nos. 3–4:233-252.

Kooiman, Jan, 2003. *Governing as Governance*. London: Sage.

Leòn, Osvaldo, Burch, Sally, and Tamayo, Eduardo, 2005. *Communication in Movement*. Quito, ALAI Publication.

MacBride Commission, 1980. *Many Voices, One World: Towards a New, More Just and More Efficient World Information and Communication Order*. Paris: UNESCO.

Mastrini, Guillermo and De Cgarras, Diego, 2004. "20 anos es nada: del NOMIC a la CMSI." Paper presented at the International Communication section of the IAMCR Conference, Porto Alegre, Brasil.

Nardi, Jason and Padovani, Claudia, eds. 2004. *Diritto a comunicare e accesso ai saperi. La nuova frontiera dei diritti nella società della conoscenza*. Brescia: Yema.

Nordenstreng, Kaarle,1984. "Defining the New International Information Order." In *World Communications: New York*, ed. George. Gerbner and Michael Siefert. London: Longman.

———. 1999. "The Context: The Great Media Debate." Pp. 235-268 in *Towards Equity in Global Communication: MacBride Update*, ed. R. Vincent, K. Nordenstreng, and M. Traber. Cresskill, NJ: Hampton.

Nye, Joseph, 2002. *Il paradosso del potere americano*. Bologna: Einaudi.

Nye, Joseph and Donahue, John, 2000. *Governance in a Globalizing World*. Washington, DC: Brookings Institution Press.

O'Brien, Robert, Goetz, Anne Marie, Scholte, Jan Aart, and Williams, Marc, 2000. *Contesting Global Governance*. Cambridge: Cambridge University Press.

O'Siochru, Sean, 2003a. "Democratizing Communication Globally: Building a Transnational Advocacy Campaign." In *Global Mediation? Democratizing Public Communication in the Era of Post-Capitalism*, ed. Robert Hackett and Yuezhi Zhao. Lanham, MD: Rowman & Littlefield.

———.2003b. "Global Governance of Information and Communication Technologies: Implications for Global Civil Society Networking," Report written for the Social Science Research Council; available online at <www.ssrc.org/itic>.

———. 2004a. "Civil Society Participation in the WSIS Process: Promises and Reality." *Continuum: Journal of Media and Society* 18, no. 3:330-344.

———. 2004b. "Will the Real WSIS Please Stand Up? The Historic Encounter of the 'Information Society' and the 'Communication Society.'" *Gazette* 66, nos. 3–4:203-224.

O'Siochru, Sean and Girard, Bruce, 2002. *Global Media Governance: A Beginner's Guide*. Lanham, MD: Rowman and Littlefield.

Padovani, Claudia, 2003. "Notes on Global Governance Analysis and Democracy. From Output (Strategies and Impact) to Outcome (Are More Participatory Political Processes Thinkable?). A Theoretical Approach (looking at WSIS)." Memo prepared for the Social Science Research Council; available online at <www.ssrc.org/itic>.

Padovani, Claudia, ed. 2004a. *Gazette*, special issue on the WSIS, "The World Summit on the Information Society: Setting the Communication Agenda for the 21st Century?" vols. 3-4.

———. 2004b, July. IAMCR newsletter.

Padovani, Claudia and Nesti, Giorgia, 2003. "La dimensione regionale nelle politiche dell'Unione Europea per la Società dell'Informazione." Pp. 215-232 in *Governo Locale e Spazio Europeo*, ed. P. Messina. Roma: Carocci.

Padovani, Claudia and Tuzzi, Arjuna, 2003, July. "Changing Modes of Participation and Communication in an International Political Environment: Looking at the World Summit on the Information Society as a Communicative Process." Paper presented in the Political Communication section of the International Political Science Association Congress, Durban.

———. 2004. "WSIS as a World of Words: What Can We Say about So Much Talking?" *Continuum: Journal of Media and Society* 18, no. 3:360-379.

———.2005. "International Political Communication and the Role of Civil Society: Words and Networks in the World Summit on the Information Society. Reflections on Governance, Participation and the Changing Scope of Political Action." Pp. 51-80 in *Towards a Sustainable Information Society*, ed. J. Servaes and N. Carpentier. Bristol: Intellect.

Pasquali, Antonio, 2005. "The South and the Imbalance in Communication" in *Global Media and Communication* 1, no. 3.

Raboy, Marc, 2002. *Global Media Policy in the New Millenium.* Luton, England: University of Luton Press.

———. 2004a. "The World Summit on the Information Society and its Legacy for Global Governance." *Gazette* 66, nos. 3–4:225-232.

———. 2004b. "WSIS as Political Space in Global Media Governance." *Continuum: Journal of Media and Society* 18, no. 3:345-359.

Raboy, Marc and Landry, Norman,. 2004. "La communication au coeur de la gouvernance globale. Enjeux et perspectives de la société civile au Sommet Mondial sur la Société de l'Information"; available online at <www.lrpc.umontreal.ca/smsirapport.pdf >.

Rosenau, James, 1990. *Turbulence in World Politics: Theory in Change and Continuity.* Princeton, NJ: Princeton University Press.

———. 1992. *Governance without Government: Order and Change in World Politics.* Cambridge: Cambridge University Press.

———. 1999. "Towards an Ontology for Global Governance." Pp. 287-301 in *Global Governance Theory*, ed. Martin Hewson and Timothy J. Sinclair. Albany: State University of New York Press.

Rosenau, James and Singh, J. P., eds. 2003. *Information Technology and Global Politics: The Changing Scope of Power and Governance.* Albany: State University of New York Press.

Smith, Jackie, Chatfield, Charles, and Pagnucco Ron, eds. 1997. *Transnational Social Movements and Global Politics: Solidarity beyond the State.* Syracuse, NY: Syracuse University Press.

Traber, Michael and Nordenstreng, Kaarle, 1992. *Few Voices, Many Worlds: Towards a Media Reform Movement.* London: World Association for Christian Communication.

CHAPTER 14

Trial and Error in Internet Governance: ICANN, the WSIS, and the Making of a Global Civil Society

AN INTERVIEW WITH MILTON MUELLER

GEERT LOVINK

In 2002 MIT Press published Milton Mueller's *Ruling the Root*, one of the first detailed investigations into Internet domain name policies. In it Mueller describes the history of the Internet address and name space and the root zone file and root name servers, without which the Internet would not be able to function. Ever since the birth of the Internet Corporation for Assigned Names and Numbers (ICANN) in 1998, the private company that oversees "name space," issues are becoming less technical and more political. Governments seek more influence in a world that is traditionally run by a select group of engineers and corporate managers. Mueller is a professor at the School of Information Studies, Syracuse University (Syracuse, New York) and director of the Convergence Center. He has widely published about regulatory issues in the global telecommunications industry. He is also the editor of, and a regular contributor to, the ICANNwatch website. Our interview took place via e-mail.

Geert Lovink: In *Ruling the Root* you mention the Internet's technical cadre's "allergy to democratic methods and public accountability." You mention that Internet pioneers, such as Jon Postel, refused to run for office in any electoral system. Those who ran the Internet in the early days were supposed to be selected with the consensus of the "community." Would you say that this mentality, being a mixture of male engineering and hippie culture, is lying at the heart of the ICANN controversies? Would a cultural genealogy help us to understand the current situation?

Milton Mueller: The "community consensus" idea of the early days of the Internet (1986–1996) was indeed part of a specific culture that developed among the (mostly male) engineers. Like all social groupings, that culture developed its own pecking order and ruling elite, but it also had communitarian, democratic, and liberal elements. *Democratic* in the sense in which the Magna Carta was democratic—peers demanding that their prerogatives not be impinged on by the king. *Liberal* in that they supported open systems and resisted the state. *Communitarian* in that there was a strong sense of collective identity and responsibility and because one of the key issues for them was whether you were inside or outside their community. Among these types of homogeneous cultures with shared norms, you can develop a rough community consensus.

You do need to understand this culture and history if you want to delve deeply into the politics of DNS [Domain Name System] and the Internet—not just ICANN. By that I mean, if you want to engage in Internet politics at the level of meeting and persuading individual people, then you need to know who are the anointed elders of this culture and what kind of norms exist among this community. But I would not say that this culture is any longer at the *heart* of the controversies. It was from 1995 to 1997, but gTLD-MoU [generic Top Level Domain – Memorandum of Understanding] and the creation of ICANN was basically the process by which this community came to terms with other political, social and business interests. "Community consensus" after that became a ridiculous and hypocritical notion.

As the theorists of institutional development have demonstrated, the process of forging new institutions is all about fighting over distributional effects—who is favored and who is disadvantaged when rules are defined and governance structures are erected. Of course there could be no consensus at that point. For example, any policy or rule that was favored by Network Solutions could not be agreed to by the IAB–IETF [Internet Architecture Board–Internet Engineering Task Force] elders, and any policy or rule favored by the trademark interests could not be agreed by the civil libertarians. So the invocation of this notion after 1998 shows that either the person is ignorant of what is going on or was trying to appropriate the legitimacy and the norms of the engineering community in a fundamentally dishonest way.

GL: Would it make sense to analyze ICANN (and its predecessors) as a test model for some sort of secretive "world government" that is run by self appointed experts? Could you explain why governments are seen as incapable of running the Internet? This all comes close to a conspiracy theory. I am not at all a fan of such reductionist easy-to-understand explanations. However, the discontent with "global governance" discourse is widespread and it seems that the international relations experts have little understanding of how the Internet is actually run. Where do you think theorization of Internet governance should start?

MM: ICANN is a test model for a global governance structure based on contract rather than territorial jurisdiction. That is an experiment worth having. The problem with ICANN is not that it is secretive. It is far less so than most international intergovernmental organizations. ICANN is in fact very political. It poses governance problems of the first order and directly involves states. It legislates rights, regulates an industry, allocates resources, and is trying to set de jure standards. So there must be political accountability. That means membership, elections, or something.

As for the "governments are incapable of running the Internet" part, the consensus is widespread because of direct experience and deeply engrained memories. Start with the OSI [Open Source Initiative] versus TCP/IP [Transmission Control Protocol/Internet Protocol] controversy of the 1980s. Then move to Yahoo vs. France, which regardless of which side you take indicates a jurisdictional problem that must, if taken to its logical conclusion, point either toward globalism or toward re-engineering the Internet to conform to territorial jurisdictions.

Now move to the present, as governments start to get aware of ICANN and more involved in it, what do they do? What is the first thing they ask for? Is it defending consumer rights, end-user civil liberties? Better representation for the public? No. All they are asking for is their own pound of flesh. Governments want special rights to country names in new TLDs. Intergovernmental organizations want special protection of their acronyms in the name space. Government law-enforcement agencies want untrammelled access to user data via Whois. In WSIS, they ask for making ICANN into an intergovernmental organization, so that states can control it, and presumably kick civil society out of all serious deliberations, as they do in WSIS.

This behavior is not an accident or an aberration. Governments participate in Internet governance to further their own power and pursue their own organizational aggrandizement. The emergence of countervailing power centers such as the tech community and ICANN is a good thing.

You'd be surprised at how much of the world is run by small interlocking communities of experts, and naive leftists would no doubt be thoroughly surprised at how poorly the world would work if that were not the case. For example, think of the importance of WiFi standards—those are set by IEEE [Institute of Electrical and Electronics Engineers] committees, which are nonpolitical and self-governing. Or think of how self-governing the academic community is or wants to be. Usually these kinds of systems work well and stay in the background until their operations create some kind of political problem demanding a more public resolution. This can happen in two ways: a public disaster that causes people to point fingers at responsible parties, or some kind of property rights conflict, which requires public and institutional solutions.

The real issue here is raised by your statement that "International relations experts have little understanding of how the Internet is actually run." True. The intimate relationship between technical knowledge and governance structures that Lawrence Lessig wrote about creates a space where technical experts assume political power, or policy requires deep knowledge of the technical system. Theorization should start by investigating the way complex, distributed technical systems respond to shape international rules and norms, and vice versa.

GL: In 2000, ICANN organized so-called membership-at-large elections to have members of the Internet community on its board. Soon after they were cancelled. How do you look back at this experiment?

MM: I do not consider it a failure. It was an experiment that succeeded. It clearly revealed the preferences of the wider public following Internet governance, and for that reason, it was killed. Everyone involved in ICANN up to that point knew how artificial the representational structure it created was, and how that structure distributed power to a very small, unrepresentative, insulated group. We knew all along—in every forum, from IFWP [International Forum on the White Paper (on management of Internet Addresses)] to the DNSO [Domain Name Supporting Organization] to the board selections—that ICANN was under the control of a small, self-selected clique dominated by Joe Sims. It was stunningly obvious to me, at least, that if there ever was a fair and open election conducted among the people involved that this clique would receive an overwhelmingly negative vote.

So the ruling party lost the election. That was perceived as a problem by ICANN management, and the solution was to eliminate elections. The fact that so many have accepted the ex-post construction of this, that the election was a "failure," shows how effective they have been in papering over the message that was sent. I recognize that when some people refer to the "failure" of the elections they are referring to mechanical problems, or more subtly and significantly, to the incursion of nationalistic competition that occurred in Europe and Asia. But again, I would argue that these phenomena were signs of success, not failure.

The mechanical problems occurred because more people registered to vote than ICANN was prepared for. The level of participation surprised even me. Think about the implications of that—a global electorate. Of course, election opponents could have claimed—more reasonably—that a small turnout was a symptom of failure too. If you look at the regional results for Africa, where something like thirty-five people appointed an ICANN board member, you get a sense of what a failed election might have looked like.

The election also revealed some issues regarding mass voter registration in China and Japan. But it was unclear whether this was due to attempted manipulation or to language problems that required Asian voters to go to English-language websites to be enfranchised. Either way, the mechanical and verification issues could be solved. At what price? That was the only real criticism that was ever made of elections. Could ICANN afford to do them? One could debate cost-benefit here, but that was not the debate we had.

As for nationalistic competition (e.g., ICANN membership races between Germany and France, or between China and Japan), here again the election simply revealed in a realistic way the ways in which voters define their preferences. In many parts of the world people still define their identity in national terms and would prefer a candidate from their "own" country. The same was true of any democratic experiment—in U.S. presidential elections, people are more likely to favor candidates from their own state. So what? One of the most intelligent things that Esther Dyson ever said about ICANN was her comment that the only solution to this was the development of the Internet-governance equivalent of political parties. This would have to occur over the long term, obviously.

GL: Confronted with Internet governance, many cyberactivists find themselves in a catch-22 situation. On the one hand they do not trust government bureaucrats to run the Internet, out of a justified fear that regulation through multilateral negotiations might lead to censorship and stifle innovation. On the other hand they criticize the corporate agendas of the engineering class that is anything but representative. What models should activists propose in the light of the World Summit on the Information Society? There seems to be no way back to a nation state 'federalist' solution. Should they buy into the global civil society solution?

MM: This is an excellent question and a big problem. It speaks to the lack of intellectual grounding and the absence of a solid institutional agenda that afflicts so many activists. Do we have alternative and better models for global governance? So much of what happened in the ICANN arena happened by default, because no one had a better proposal that significant groups had converged on and understood the implications of. But the problem goes well beyond Internet governance. In WSIS I see a danger that cyberactivism gets linked to an anticapitalist, antiglobalization movement, which I see as both reactionary and a certain dead end. We need to create new forms of democratic and liberal institutions at the global level, and tying that agenda to old-style protectionism, statism, and discredited neo-Marxist ideologies will take all the energy surrounding that project and flush it down the toilet.

The catch-22 you mention is not a minor issue; it is fundamental. Do not trust anyone who cannot explicitly address that problem and recognize the negatives of national governments and their international orgs, as well as the problems of the technical and business people. We have to set up structures at the international level that are governmental in nature, but we need creative ideas about how to distribute and balance power.

GL: One of the controversial issues is the power of the U.S. government over the Internet and the fact that, as you write, ICANN is a U.S. government contractor and a private company that operates under U.S. law. The fight over global governance, in part, is about a transfer of U.S. power, if I understand it well, which seems unlikely in this political climate. Is it true that the Pentagon can switch off entire countries, as it was rumored during the Kosovo conflict and Iraqi war, many people ask? On top of that there is the mistrust between country code top level domains (ccTLDs) and the ICANN staff, who have often been accused of bullying and obstruction in order to further their own aims. Will the U.S. government always, in the last instance, retain vital control over the Internet? Sorry, but like many U.S. Americans you look so terribly libertarian. You are suspicious of governments, except your own. Perhaps in the end you don't want to give away sovereignty over the Internet to a non-U.S. body.

MM: Not suspicious of the U.S. government? Me? *Ruling the Root* called the U.S. government residual control of the root a "ticking time bomb" and called for it to be dealt with. Given the U.S. government's movement toward distinctly unlibertarian attitudes on surveillance, security, and war since *Ruling the Root*'s publication I believe that even more strongly. With or without ICANN, under certain conditions the U.S. government and its allies would be able to switch off entire—marginalized—countries. I have already embarrassed certain members of NTIA [National Telecommunications and Information Administration] by publicly calling for the United States to give up its control (instead of privately grumbling about it, which is what most European authorities do), which of course has meant that I am exiled from certain key policy circles. The only thing holding me and certain other critics of ICANN back is that ICANN's current representational structure is so warped that we fear turning it loose completely. At least now, the residual U.S. government control provides some third party oversight, however pathetic. And to be honest, the deeper I have delved into this situation the more I have come to believe that the OECD [Organization for Economic Cooperation and Development] states, while perhaps ambivalent, are fully acquiescent in the U.S. government's current position. This is a kind of hypocrisy that any student of international relations is used to seeing: let the U.S. government take the lead, complain smugly to relevant constituencies about those darn Americans, while privately getting a few key concessions out of them and thanking your lucky stars that they have to take the responsibilities instead of you. It is also worth emphasizing strongly that simple jealousy of U.S. dominance is no substitute for a coherent policy regarding governance. The issue is the distribution of power, not nationality. An Internet governance system dominated by the E.U. or China or Brazil might make Europeans, Chinese, or Brazilians happier—or would it? But it would hardly be more just.

GL: Are you really suggesting that all anticorporate protesters want to return to an old school government control model? These movements are very diverse. I can assure you that you are making a caricature. People have moved on from the clichés you repeat here and look for "another world." Why don't you stress that?

MM: I know that the protesters are diverse. I know full well that most of them do not want, or would say they do not want, to return to old models. But that is a lot easier to say than it is to pull off. I am talking about a process that I have seen happen before—that I have witnessed firsthand in the 1970s. A mass movement forms, with wide appeal, based on a vague and inchoate sense of dissatisfaction with some aspect of society. The movement itself is diverse and non-ideological, but over time those with a well-defined ideology and a strong commitment take control of its direction, because only a coherent ideology provides the strategic guidance needed as things progress.

I said above I saw a danger; the danger is that instead of doing new thinking about global institutions and the relationship between market, government, and society we fall back into reasserting the old Left-Right dichotomy. I am not caricaturing any participants in current processes; I am just asserting that this could happen.

You can easily get a sense from your own language as to how it could happen. You characterize them as "anticorporate" protestors. What does it mean to be "anticorporate"? A corporation is a legal form of commercial organization that limits the directors' personal liability. You probably can't have an industrial economy, much less a postindustrial one, without that.

To be "for" or "against" corporations is meaningless because on any given communication-information policy issue, you can find various corporations on different sides. That idea that corporations per se are the problem isn't tenable; whatever those folks are protesting, it isn't "corporations."

Of course, I know what you mean: "anticorporate" is just a stand-in for a wide complex of cultural and political beliefs, involving sentiments of humanism, environmentalism, support for cultural diversity, and opposition to commercialism, vaguely democratic sentiments and, oftentimes, individual rights and freedoms. But a litany of "good things" is not enough to transform the world. A question I like to ask is, What does "democracy" mean at the global level? A global electorate? Avenues for civil society participation? Better representation within intergovernmental organizations? If you can't answer that question readily, there are lots of vested interests who will answer it for you.

Social movements create the instabilities and political opportunities that make change possible; but at critical junctures one must come forward with specific institutional structures, laws, and policies and develop support for them. That is where I see a danger. It is very easy for the agenda of anti–free trade protestors to be co-opted by simple protectionism—in fact, that is already happening. It is very easy for an emotional "anticorporatism" to be co-opted by simple state regulation or state socialism. Governments are still very powerful, and so are the special interests that thrive on protectionism. That will happen unless a new ideology with a more sophisticated institutional agenda is put forward. Good intentions are not enough. At the very least, I would hope that in the postcommunist, posttotalitarian world we can lay to rest the issue of market allocation and the price system and look for institutions and policies that improve things within that framework. And we need to recognize the important contributions that freedom of trade and investment has made in developing the telecommunications infrastructure.

GL: Your recent research project looks into media activism and how civil society groups can operate on a transnational level. What is your opinion about global civil society, the role of NGOs, and their alleged lack of accountability? Should there be a Greenpeace of cyberspace that can operate on a global level? So far no one can match the power of transnational corporations such as MCI/WorldCom, British Telecom, or Microsoft. Is the global NGO model the way to go? Will you eventually link this topic with issues of Internet governance?

MM: That research project (typically of me) took on a huge problem of the sort that takes at least five years to produce much of substance, yet this was done at a time when everyone aware of it (justifiably) wants instant results. I investigated the concept of media activism in order to destroy it and replace it with a new self-concept that tried to synthesize advocacy around all areas of communications and information technology policy. Like the concept of "environmentalism," such a movement should be able to encompass all the technical subareas such as privacy, IPR [Intellectual Property Rights], freedom of information, telecom infrastructure regulation and policy as well as the traditional mass media issues. Of course, the smarter "media" activists were already doing that or moving in that direction, but labels are important.

My opinion is that the concept of "global civil society" is probably the best point of departure we have right now for motivating transnational collective action. I particularly like the formulation of John Keane (http://www.wmin.ac.uk/csd/Staff/jk.htm). The alternatives to civil society seem to be religion (e.g., Islamic fundamentalism) anticapitalism (which at this stage of the game probably belongs in the religion category), or some kind of racism. To me, the issue is less one of substantive policy positions (which only have meaning in a specific institutional context) than it is one of institution-building at the international level.

I am unimpressed with the complaints about the "lack of accountability" of NGOs and civil society representatives. Of course it is entirely true—but also entirely unavoidable at this stage. Institutions are what create accountability, and if the global institutional environment does not provide any means for formal representation of nongovernmental and noncorporate interests, then of course the ones that assert themselves into the process are "formally" not accountable. We are dealing with a form of entrepreneurial politics at the transnational level, where those who have the intelligence, persistence, and resources to participate are the ones who get to define the agenda. The fact that such activity can emerge out of the interstices of the system is a good thing. Longer term, there will be more accountability. Of course, I link analysis of transnational collective action in communication-information to the problem of Internet governance, as well as WSIS, and other arenas. Internet governance is particularly interesting because of the institutional innovation it attempted, although the policy issues it poses are somewhat obscure.

GL: So you are saying, "Act now, democratize later." Sounds a bit like global land grabbing to me, in the hope that a *good* elite and not the bad boys will be in charge. Who are the potentially interesting antagonists in this saga? Not the Internet society, I suppose.

MM: You say, "Act now, democratize later," and it sounds bad. But let me respond by asking, if you don't act, how can you ever democratize? And are you saying that no one should act until and unless they are sure that their agenda and their organizations are perfectly representative? Seems like a recipe for paralysis.

GL: How do you look at WSIS? Some see this event as a desperate attempt by ITU [International Telecommunication Union] circles to regain ground they lost in the nineties. However, there are not many indications for that. Others see it as a painful demonstration of the global inability to address the real issues and a useless, politically correct digital divide circus. I have the impression that, for instance, activists do not quite know what to make of it. Of course, there is the neoliberal agenda around intellectual property rights but apart from that the 'information society' is still in search for topics and controversies. This is not the time for UN conferences. Would you agree?

MM: In the research project you mention above I will attempt to situate WSIS in historical context, relating it to the UNESCO New World Information and Communications Order of the 1970s. My initial view of it was almost exactly as you describe above: a politically correct digital divide circus, similar to the Digital Opportunity Task Force, where fine noises would be made and nothing would happen. I still believe that nothing concrete will come of it, but as an institutional development process I am finding it more interesting. I think the small tactical opening that was given to civil society has been important, and that the civil society activity associated with WSIS has already stolen the show. WSIS thus provides a fertile field for an emergent communication-information movement to come into contact and in an initial confrontation with traditional IGOs, develop a stronger sense of where to go next.

GL: Ever since WSIS I in Geneva, December 2003, your interest in the processual aspect of such a world summit must have grown. Has it?

MM: (I am not sure what the word *processual* means, but I will try to answer your question anyway.) It is true that I have become more deeply engaged in the WSIS civil society process, and especially the Internet governance caucus of WSIS civil society. This happened because Internet governance moved to the center of the WSIS stage after the 2003 summit. I and others felt that the WSIS-CS Internet governance caucus was too much of a small clique and too timid in developing policy positions. Early on, it tended to be dominated by people who wanted to shield ICANN from WSIS. So with my colleagues Hans Klein, John Mathiason, Derrick Cogburn, and Marc Holitscher, the Internet Governance Project was formed (www.internetgovernance.org). Its purpose was and is to provide policy analysis capacity to WSIS civil society on Internet governance issues.

Many civil society actors who became involved in the first phase of WSIS have had a great deal of trouble relating to the key issues of the second phase, especially Internet governance. In the first phase, civil society dealt with very broad social norms around such issues as "digital divide," gender, communication rights, and so on. Internet governance, on the other hand, is a very specific institutional and political struggle that requires knowledge of how policy issues are related to technical systems.

One of the most interesting issues in the second phase was the process used by the Internet governance caucus to recommend names to the UN secretary general regarding who would represent civil society on the Working Group on Internet Governance (WGIG). In this case, civil society's organic structures (caucuses and working groups) interacted with the official UN structure not just in a consultative or advocacy role. It had to produce a real decision—a list of recommended names—and of course that decision was highly political, as the composition of the WGIG would affect its output. Many people wanted to be on the WGIG and not all of them could be, so competition for nominations was keen.

The process illustrated both the strengths and the weaknesses of civil society engagement with international institutions. On the strong side, the leaders of the internet governance caucus developed and cultivated a very close relationship with Markus Kummer, the Swiss diplomat who served as the secretariat of the WGIG. In return, Kummer didn't do anything with input from other civil society entities and privileged the recommendations of the Internet governance caucus. To everyone's amazement, virtually all of the names forwarded by the caucus were placed on the Working Group (many of us had assumed that only a few names would be selected from any list we developed). Most important, the people selected by the caucus have proved to be among the most informed and productive performers on the working group. I am referring to people like Karen Banks, Carlos Afonso, Wolfgang Kleinwachter, William Drake, Avri Doria, and Raul Echeberria, to name a few of the most active ones. They also have done a fairly good job of consulting with other members of civil society in formulating positions. An active dialogue has been maintained on the caucus list regarding policy positions. The Internet Governance Project has contributed significantly to the advancement of that dialogue, but so has the expertise of the other parties.

As a weakness, the process revealed WSIS civil society's lack of institutional capacity; by which I mean its inability to develop and follow an objective process, and its reliance on close-knit groups of friends rather than objective procedures to make decisions. The cocoordinators of the Internet governance caucus failed to define a nomination procedure until the last minute, and ultimately the process they used was so improvised and arbitrary that hard feelings and conflict were created. Indeed, they might have failed to come up with a procedure altogether had not their hand been forced by actions taken by ICANN's Noncommercial Users Constituency (NCUC). NCUC, which has a structure of elected officers, instituted its own process of nominating civil society people to the

WGIG. Because of the existence of a charter and formally nominated and legitimated officers, this process went very smoothly. This seems to have prompted the caucus leaders to institute, finally, a selection/nomination procedure. But the procedure the caucus proposed was vague, rushed, and required improvisation during the crucial end game. Some parties, notably the free software groups, felt they had not been treated fairly. The Latin American caucus split over the selection process, too, although this may have happened regardless of the procedure used.

The point here is in some sense an obvious one, but one that many civil society actors still seem unwilling to face and accept: civil society engagement in policy making processes of global governance requires that consequential decisions be made by "civil society" as a collectivity. Unless there are procedures and rules for organizing "civil society," it will be incapable of responding to those requirements without huge upheavals and struggles among itself. But once it "bureaucratizes" itself by creating those structures, is it still "civil society"?

GL: Do you still feel that you have a deeply U.S.-American viewpoint on Internet governance, or is it politically not correct to ask about one's own cultural bias? Obviously it is hard for everyone to jump over one's own shadow.

MM: Of course, my radically liberal approach to free expression and other civil liberties, my antistatism and antimilitarism, and my belief in economic freedom is deeply rooted in Anglo-American political traditions, going back to Locke and Jefferson. But I have been exposed to non-American perspectives for many, many years. From 1989, I lived in Hong Kong and China and studied the policy environments there. I know about Maoism and have observed firsthand the effects of British colonialism on economics and policy. I've done international comparative studies of telecommunications policies since the early 1990s. I confess a visceral dislike of ponderous, clubby European notions of corporatism and "coregulation," but also feel increasingly alienated from the position of the U.S. government and U.S. business interests, who have abandoned the ideals the country claims to have been founded on. And I've recognized for years the difficulty many Americans have viewing Internet issues from a standpoint that transcends their own national perspective, because it is just a pale reflection of the same trouble they have in foreign policy. But hey, ordinary Europeans are probably as nationalistic as ordinary Americans. Most Geneva-based international organizations are Eurocentric in outlook. Asians are more nationalistic than Europeans and Americans.

GL: Lately you have traveled a lot, I noticed. Did this provide you with a broader perspective on WSIS, the role of the Internet? Could we, for instance, say that what counts, in the end, is a truly global and diverse involvement up to the point of productive friction and not "governance" per se?

MM: The amount of international travel I did was normal for the past ten years. The only difference is the Geneva-centric pattern, caused by WGIG/WSIS.

GL: The Internet governance debate seems not to have transcended beyond stereotypes like "Californian neoliberal corporates defending the medium of the free West against power-hungry Chinese communist party censors and crusty UN bureaucrats." How could we move on from these clichés?

MM: Don't forget: there *are* censors, inside and outside China, who would like to control the Internet. And the UN bureaucracy *is* annoying and plodding. That being said, these observations have very little relevance to the Internet governance debate, because the UN is in no position to control anything.

One good result of the WGIG [Working Group on Internet Governance] process is that the involved international community has already moved beyond those clichés. No one is proposing that the UN control the Internet. There is growing consensus that control of the DNS root needs to be internationalized. It's hypocritical to talk about how terrible governments are when one government, the most powerful one in the world by any measure, holds unilateral power over one aspect of the Internet. Also, people have learned that just because ICANN is private does not means that it is a "free market, liberal" solution. ICANN is a regulatory agency with centralized control of key aspects of the Internet. And the work of NCUC [Noncommercial Users Constituency] on privacy and the Whois database is beginning to make it clearer and clearer that it is the U.S. government and U.S.-based IPR interests that want to exploit their control of current Internet governance arrangements for surveillance and regulation. So the "government control" rhetoric can be and is being turned against them.

We will debate these clichés again, however, during the next stage, when or if the WGIG proposes something useful and WSIS adopts it. The debate will move into a broader public and people who want to prevent change will raise those old arguments again. That renewed debate is why it is important that the WGIG propose something more substantive than the creation of some poorly-defined new discussion forum. Creating a new bureaucracy will be hard to sell to a broader public; it will look like just expanding the UN bureaucracy to cater to a bunch of would-be regulators. There is already an alphabet soup of UN agencies with authority over different parts of the Internet and communications, and the solution is to create another one?

GL: Recently, as a part of the Internet Governance Project, you have launched the surprising idea that ICANN and ITU should compete with each other. You wrote, "People in the U.S. Internet community love to beat up on the ITU, and I am not a big fan of it as an organization myself. The fact remains, however, that a lot of countries, especially developing ones, see it as a more legitimate forum for policy making and administration. So if ICANN and ITU represent two radically different governance regimes, why not let them compete with each other?" So instead of dialogue and compromise, which are vital parts of the dominant "multistakeholder" approach, you suggest the opposite: competition. Would this go through a tender system, for instance?

MM: Actually, ICANN–ITU "competition" would constitute an important form of compromise. What you have now is a "winner take all" power struggle between the intergovernmental system of ITU and the private sector–led system of ICANN. We'd like to see that destructive power struggle end. A workable international regime might resolve this conflict by permitting both to coexist and giving the key actors a choice among the two. One might be able to retain the best of both worlds.

Anyway, we need to talk about the whole proposal, not just the ITU–ICANN competition idea. We proposed reinstating democratic elections for ICANN's board. To our surprise, we learned that many official representatives of civil society in the Internet governance caucus were unwilling to support that. But I think our proposal stiffened their spine a bit and we are now seeing support consolidate. We also proposed reforms in ICANN's constituency structure and the abolition of the Governmental Advisory Committee.

Regarding your reference to "multistakeholderism," I am starting to hate the word. As a catch word it serves as a Rorschach blob—everyone can see whatever they want in it. The word papers over the really difficult questions about institutional arrangements, power, and rights. The point is not "stakeholders" representation per se. The point is individual rights and democratic procedure. Sometimes—many times, in fact—those bigger causes are advanced by permitting civil society to participate more fully in institutions that were once restricted to governments. But let's not fetishize those simple advances. Let's use them to institutionalize greater advances in global governance that facilitate freedom.

Some of the leaders of civil society in the WGIG would like for the final outcome of WGIG to be the creation of a new international organization that will serve as a "multistakeholder forum." My colleagues in the Internet Governance Project, in contrast, are advocating an international framework convention as the best next step. This would require governments to negotiate a set of globally agreed principles and norms regarding the governance of the Internet. This would turn the momentum of

WSIS/WGIG into a lasting, influential process of institutional change at the international level.

Both ideas have strengths and weaknesses. A new discussion forum would facilitate continued participation by civil society groups, but might become irrelevant unless it has real power, which probably isn't possible due to rivalries with existing international organizations and their constituencies. A framework convention might be too government-centric, (although the process can be designed to include civil society) and some have argued that the parties are not ready for that level of negotiation.

For Further Research

Milton Mueller's homepage: <http://istweb.syr.edu/~mueller/>.
Martin Mueller's global civil society research page: <http://dcc.syr.edu/ford/tnca.htm>.
ICANNWatch: <www.icannwatch.org>.

Glossary of Acronyms

BBC	British Broadcasting Corporation
BBS	bulletin board system
ccTLD	country code Top Level Domain
CNN	Cable News Network
CNRG	Computer Network Research Group
CREDO	Centre for Research Education and Development
CRIS	Communication Rights in the Information Society Campaign
CSO	civil society organization
CTU	Common Text Unit
DNS	Domain Name System
EU	European Union
FEMNET	African Women's Development and Communication Network
FIS	Front islamique de salut
FLOSS	Free-as-in-Libre/Open Source Software
FOSS	Free and Open Source Software
FWA	fixed wireless access
G8	Group of 8 (Canada, France, Germany, Italy, Japan, Russia, US, UK)
GDL	GNU Documentation License
GNU	GNU's Not Unix
GPL	General Public License or "copyleft"
GPRS	General Packet Radio Service
GSM	Global System for Mobile Communications
gTLD-MoU	generic Top Level Domain—Memorandum of Understanding

HTA	Hometown Associations
HTML	HyperText Markup Language
IAB-IETF	Internet Architecture Board - Internet Engineering Task Force
ICANN	Internet Corporation for Assigned Names and Numbers
ICBL	International Campaign to Ban Landmines
ICT	Information and communication technologies
IDRC	International Development Research Centre
IEEE	Institute of Electrical and Electronics Engineers
IETF	Internet Engineering Task Force
IFWP	International Forum on the White Paper (on management of Internet Addresses)
IMCs	Independent Media Center
IPR	Intellectual Property Rights
IRC	Internet Relay Chat
ITU	International Telecommunication Union
LJO	Laskar Jihad Online
MCT	Mobile Communication Technologies
MERCOSUR	A common market of Brazil, Uruguay, Argentina, and Paraguay
MMS	multimedia messaging service
MPEG	Moving Picture Experts Group (designator for graphics files)
MUD	Multi-User Dungeon
NCUC	Noncommercial Users Constituency
NGO	Nongovernmental Organization
NIIO	New International Information Order
NTIA	National Telecommunications and Information Administration
NWICO	New World Information and Communication Order
OECD	Organization for Economic Cooperation and Development
OSI	Open Source Initiative
P2P	Person to Person
PAMR	Public Access Mobile Radio
PDF	Portable Document Format
PGA	People's Global Action
RSS	Really Simple Syndication
SCO	Santa Cruz Operations
SMS	Short Message Service
TCP/IP	Transmission Control Protocol/Internet Protocol

UN	United Nations WSIS World Summit on the Information Society IANA Internet Assigned Numbers Authority
UNESCO	United Nations Education, Scientific and Culture Organization
UNCHS UN	Centre on Human Settlements
VoIP	Voice over Internet Protocol
WAP	Wireless Access Protocol
WELL	Whole Earth 'Lectronic Link
WGIG	Working Group on Internet Governance
WiFi	Wireless Local Area Network
WiMax	Worldwide Interoperability for Microwave Access
WIPO	World Intellectual Property Organization
WOCCU	World Council of Credit Unions
WSIS-CS	World Summit of the Information Society-Civil Society [caucus]
WTO	World Trade Organization

Editors

JON W. ANDERSON is professor and chair of Anthropology at the Catholic University of America. He is codirector of the Arab Information Project with Michael C. Hudson at Georgetown University's Center for Contemporary Arab Studies, where he created the first course in North America on new media and information technologies in the Middle East. He served as editor-in-chief of the *Middle East Studies Association Bulletin*, as chair of the Electronic Publication Committee of the Middle East Studies Association and the Advisory Group on Electronic Communication of the American Anthropological Association, and is founding editor of *Working Papers on New Media & Information Technology in the Middle East* (http://nmit.georgetown.edu). His research has ranged from tribal culture and Islamic cosmology to new media in Islamic cyberspace and information technology in Arab countries, where he has conducted research in Jordan, Egypt, Syria, Jordan, Saudi Arabia, and Qatar. Recent publications include "Vers une théorie technopractique de l'Internet dans le monde arabe," (*Maghreb-Machrek*, 2004), *New Media in the Muslim World: The Emerging Public Sphere* (co-edited with Dale Eickelman, 1999; second edition 2003), *Arabizing the Internet* (1998), "The Internet in the Middle East" (*Middle East Executive Reports*, December 1997), "Globalizing Politics and Religion in the Muslim World" (*Journal of Electronic Publishing*, September 1996).

JODI DEAN teaches political theory at Hobart and William Smith Colleges. Her books include *Solidarity of Strangers* (U of Cal Press, 1996), *Aliens in America* (Cornell UP, 1998—chosen as one of the *Village Voice*'s Best Books of the Year), *Publicity's Secret: How Technoculture Capitalizes on Democracy* (Cornell UP 2002), and *Zizek's Politics* (New York: Routledge, 2006). She serves on the editorial board of the journals *Theory and Event* and *Constellations* and has edited symposia on new technologies for the journals *Constellations* and *Signs* as well as the books *Feminism and the New Democracy* (Sage 1997) and *Cultural Studies and Political Theory* (Cornell UP 2000). With Paul A. Passavant, she edited *Empire's New Clothes: Reading Hardt and Negri* (Routledge 2004).

GEERT LOVINK (NL/AUS), is a media theorist and activist, Internet critic and author of *Dark Fiber* (2002), *Uncanny Networks* (2002) and *My First Recession* (2003). He worked on various media projects in Eastern Europe and India. He is a member of the Adilkno collective, authors of *Cracking the Movement* and *The Media Archive* and co-founder of Internet projects such as The Digital City, Nettime, Fibreculture and Incommunicado. He is co-organizer of the tactical media festivals' Next Five Minutes. Recent conferences he coinitiated dealt with the history of web design, critique of ICT for development, urban screens, net porn, and creative industries research. Since 2004 he has been director of the Institute of Network Cultures at Amsterdam Polytechnic (HvA) and associate professor at the Media & Culture Department, University of Amsterdam. In 2005-2006, he was a fellow at the Berlin Institute for Advanced Study where he finished a third volume of his ongoing research into critical Internet culture to be published by Routledge New York. His blog address is www.networkcultures.org/geert.

Contributors

Evan Henshaw-Plath is the lead engineer for Odeo, a San Francisco-based Internet company specializing in podcasting and participatory radio production and distribution tools. He is a principle organizer and technical lead in the free software inspired community and participatory media movement, Indymedia. His work has included co-organizing Indymedia centers in Latin America, the United States, Europe, and South Asia.

Lina Khatib is lecturer in world cinema and library coordinator at Royal Holloway, University of London, where she teaches media theory, non-Western cinema, and international television. Her research fields include media representations of Middle Eastern politics, Middle Eastern cinema, and postcolonial theory. Her recent publications include "The Politics of Space," *Visual Communication* (vol. 3, n. 1, February 2004); "Communicating Islamic Fundamentalism as Global Citizenship, *Journal of Communication Inquiry* (vol. 7, n. 4, October 2003, and, "The Orient and its Others: Women as Tools of Nationalism in Political Egyptian Cinema" in *Women and Media in the Middle East,* Naomi Sakr, ed. (London: I.B. Tauris 2004). She is finishing a book on contemporary Hollywood and Arab cinemas and beginning another, *Imagi-Nations*, on Lebanese national identity as constructed in Lebanese films representing the civil war in that country.

Jamie King is a lecturer, essayist, and information activist living in East London. He is information politics editor at the London technology and culture journal *Mute* and editor of the industry journal *n3*, dedicated to the analysis of the Domain Name System in business practice. He writes a weekly column for Channel 4 News and teaches the masters programme in Digital Media at Ravensbourne College. He recently completed the novel

Dead Americans, his second attempt to write a novel entirely online and in full public view. He is also at work developing Pretext, a project providing a new approach to publishing literary fiction, www.pretext.org.

Hans Klein is associate professor in the School of Public Policy at the Georgia Institute of Technology. His research focuses on public interest dimensions of communication policy. He has published articles on Internet governance, Internet and democracy, social movements, U.S. technology policy, and community media. Klein directs Georgia Tech's Internet and Public Policy Project (IP3) and formerly chaired the board of Computer Professionals for Social Responsibility.

Merlyna Lim is a PhD candidate in technology and society studies, University of Twente, Enschede–the Netherlands. Her research revolves around the mutual shaping of ICTs and society. In the last few years, Lim has authored six journal articles, five invited book chapters, and more than twenty invited conference papers. Lim is a member of the research network organized by the Social Science Research Council program on Information Technology and International Cooperation.

Noortje Marres recently completed her dissertation at the University of Amsterdam, entitled *No Issue, No Public: Democratic deficits after the displacement of politics.* As of May 2005, she will work as a post-doctoral researcher at the University of Amsterdam's Department of Philosophy. Recently she co-organized the workshops-series *The Social Life of Issues,* together with Richard Rogers, and she was one of the editors of *Next Five Minutes 4, Festival on Tactical Media,* which took place in Amsterdam, 2003. Marres is a member of the research network organized by the Social Science Research Council program on Information Technology and International Cooperation.

Okoth Fred Mudhai is a journalism lecturer in the Communication, Media and Culture subject group of the Coventry School of Art and Design, Coventry University, where he is affiliated with the Centre for Media, Arts and Performance Research Group. His publications include "The Internet: Triumphs and Trials for Kenyan Journalism," in *Beyond Boundaries: Cyberspace in Africa,* Melinda B. Robins & Robert L. Hilliard, eds. (Heinemann, 2002), and "Researching the Impact of ICTs as Change Catalysts in Africa," *Ecquid Novi* 25 (2004). He wrote his PhD on the use of the World Wide Web, e-mail, and mobile phones by urban political civil society organizations in Kenya and Zambia, at Nottingham Trent University.

He previously worked as a journalist based in Kenya and also contributed to publications in South Africa and Britain.

Milton Mueller is a professor at Syracuse University School of Information Studies, where he directs the school's graduate program in telecommunications and network management. Mueller received a PhD from the University of Pennsylvania, Annenberg School, in 1989. He codirects the Convergence Center and is cofounder of the Internet Governance Project, a consortium of university scholars working on international Internet policy issues. He is author of *Ruling the Root: Internet Governance and the Taming of Cyberspace* (MIT Press, 2002) and *Universal Service: Competition, Interconnection and Monopoly in the Making of the American Telephone System* (MIT Press, 1997). He is one of the founding members of ICANN's Noncommercial Users Constituency (NCUC) within the Generic Names Supporting Organization and was elected to chair or represent NCUC on ICANN's GNSO Council various times.

Claudia Padovani is researcher in political science and international relations with the Department of Historical and Political Studies at the University of Padova, Italy. She teaches international communication and institutions and governance of communication, while conducting research in global and European governance of the information and knowledge society. She is particularly interested in the role of civil society organizations and transnational social movements as "stakeholders" in global decision-making processes. From this perspective she has followed closely the WSIS process and written extensively on the experience. She is a member of the International Association for Media and Communication Research (IAMCR) and of the international campaign Communication Rights in the Information Society (CRIS).

John Palfrey is executive director of the Berkman Center for Internet & Society at Harvard Law School and a lecturer on law at Harvard Law School. A version of this paper was published in *Harvard Journal of Law & Technology*, vol 17, n. 2, Spring, 2004. A much earlier version of this paper was submitted in partial fulfillment of the requirements for the JD degree at Harvard Law School.

Drazen Pantic, a native of Belgrade, is the founder of OpenNet, the Internet department of Radio B92 in Belgrade, and Serbia's first Internet service provider (est. 1995). For the use of new media technologies to counter political repression in the former Yugoslavia, Pantic was rewarded by the Pioneer Award of Electronic Frontier Foundation in 1999. He has established numerous public Internet access centers, including the cultural center CyberRex and is cofounder and program director of the Center for Advanced Media in Prague (C@MP), established in 1998 by the Open Society Institute. He has taught, lectured and published widely on use of the Internet to support independent media and free expression. Pantic is a member of the steering committee of the Information Technology and International Cooperation program of the Social Science Research Council. See also http://open4all.info/.

Scott S. Robinson, PhD, Cornell 1979, is a social anthropologist, documentary film and video producer, cofounder of NACLA in 1966, a signer Declaration of Barbados for the Liberation of Indians, and since 1983 professor in the Anthropology Department of the Universidad Metropolitana, México, D.F. He has been an activist in campaigns against the Summer Institute of Linguistics, lobbyist for participatory and transparent hydropower dam involuntary location projects, and since 1994 committed to research and action on the social benefits of the global digital technologies' rollout. Recent publications include: "Rethinking Telecenters: Microbanks and Remittance Flows - Reflections from Mexico," in *Shaping The Network Society - The New Role Of Civil Society In Cyberspace*, D. Schuler & P. Day, eds., (The MIT Press, 2004), "Cybercafés and national elites: constraints on community networking in Latin America," in *Community Practice In The Network Society*, D. Schuler & P. Day, eds. (Routledge, 2004); *"El Reto Inmediato: Reconfigurar el Programa E-Mexico,"* in *El Reto de México ante La Cumbre Mundial de la Sociedad de la Información*, B. Solís, ed. (Fundación Konrad Adenauer, México, 2003); and "Reflexiones sobre la Inclusión Digital," *Revista Nueva Sociedad*, nr. 195 Caracas, 2005.

Ned Rossiter is a senior lecturer in media studies (digital media) at the Centre for Media Research, University of Ulster, Northern Ireland, and adjunct research fellow at the Centre for Cultural Research, University of Western Sydney. Rossiter is coeditor of *Politics of a Digital Present: An Inventory of Australian Net Culture, Criticism and Theory* (Melbourne: Fibreculture Publications, 2001) and *Refashioning Pop Music in Asia: Cosmopolitan Flows, Political Tempos and Aesthetic Industries* (London: RoutledgeCurzon, 2004). He is also a cofacilitator of fibreculture, a network of critical Internet research and culture in Australasia <www.fibreculture.org>.

Clay Shirkey writes about social and cultural effects of internet technologies. He teaches at New York University's interactive telecommunications program, and works as a consultant on the design of large, decentralized networks. See also clay@shirky.com.

Index